BOULEVARD PARK
& TAYLOR AVENUE DOCK
on the
Old Bellingham Waterfront

by

Brian L. Griffin

Brian Griffin Dec. 2007

Knox Cellars Publishing Company, 2007

Dedication

THIS HISTORY OF BOULEVARD PARK is dedicated to Robert Moles, Senior. Bob Moles was an outstanding community leader, highly respected for a lifetime of good works in Bellingham and Whatcom County. He was a long-time member of the Rotary Club of Bellingham, a past president of that organization, and had been chairman of the Community Service Committee that initiated the club's commitment to Boulevard Park as a project. His determined leadership over a period of years was a major reason that Boulevard Park was successfully built.

Before Bob's death in 2006 he asked me to write the history of Rotary's role in the creation of Boulevard Park and entrusted me with the research file that he had accumulated. His file consisted of copies of the *Tattler*, the weekly newsletter of the Rotary Club of Bellingham, and copies of the club's Board of Directors meetings that contained mention of the Boulevard Park project. I think Bob was intending to write this history himself. I feel privileged to have done it for him.

Brian L. Griffin

Robert Moles

Contents

Photos and Illustrations

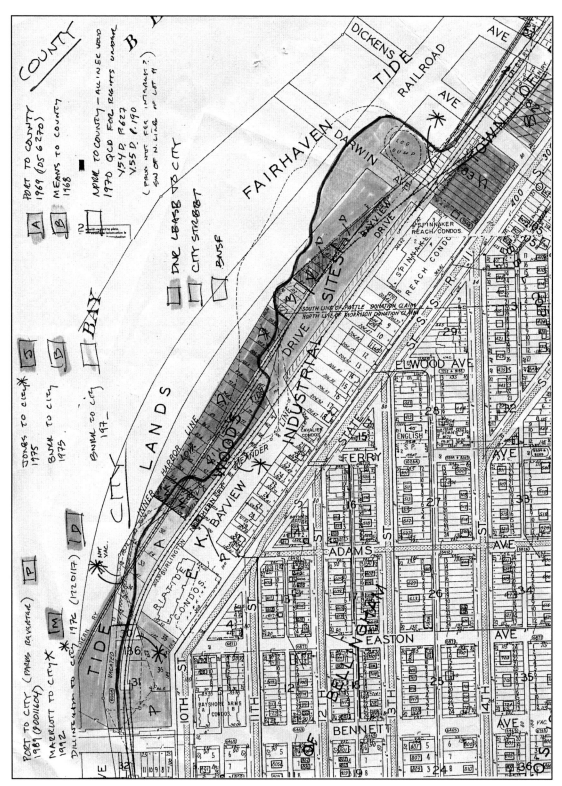

Tim Wahl's response to my first telling him of my project was to send me a color-coded map marked with the names of the former owners and the date of sale or transfer to the city of the various properties which were combined to become Boulevard Park.

Acknowledgements

RESEARCHING AND WRITING about history is surely not a lonely activity. In my wanderings between the Washington State Archives, the municipal library and the Whatcom Museum, I have made some valued new acquaintances and enjoyed time spent with some old friends met again in our common interest in community history. I have learned a bit about the remarkably thorough records kept by the Chicago Title Insurance Company, a private for-profit organization, and been stunned and gratified by their willingness to help a researcher like me simply as a public service. It has been a pleasing social experience, one that I shall remember with great pleasure.

I am grateful for the competent and eager assistance given me by James Copher of the Washington State Regional Archive at Western Washington University (WWU), and to Ruth Steele who so capably assisted in my use of the resources of the WWU Center for Pacific Northwest Studies. Both of these entities are housed in the very impressive Goltz-Murray Archives at the south edge of the University campus. While working there I was also helped by a volunteer historian, Candy Wellman, who pointed me to the historically rewarding practice of reading old lawsuits. The records that reside in that building are indeed amazing. My experiences with our varied sources of archival information leaves me with the warm feeling that a civilization that takes such care of its historical records is indeed stable and sound. There is hope for the future when I consider how well we are caring for the past.

In a class by himself is the remarkable archivist at the Whatcom Museum of History & Art, Jeffrey Jewell. Jeff must know more about the History of Bellingham and Whatcom County than anyone who lives today or has ever lived in Whatcom County. He is the veritable font of knowledge and he is eager to share what he knows, and to dig out information for the researcher. To Jeff I owe a great debt of gratitude for his enthusiastic assistance. He is a historian's historian.

Gordon Tweit, that ageless icon of Fairhaven, was most generous with his knowledge of the park area. His amazing personal museum in the basement of the Fairhaven Pharmacy held many treasures and understandings that have helped me immensely. Thank you Gordie.

In some ways Tim Wahl is responsible for my writing this book. His response to my first telling him of my project was to send me a color-coded map of the various properties which were combined to become Boulevard Park, marked with the names of the former owners and the date of sale or transfer to the city. It sparked my interest in going beyond just the Boulevard Park years, and back to the beginnings in the 1850s.

Further along in the process, Tim kindly read the final book draft for historical accuracy. He pointed out several areas where my sources, prior historians, were simply wrong. His warnings sent me back to the Archives for several days of digging in the books of Whatcom County Deeds. The buy and sell transactions of the Pattle and Morrison Donation Land Claims and the early history of the dock at Taylor Avenue are hopefully presented accurately thanks to his vigilance, knowledge and help.

Researching a history really cannot be done only by one's self. The process requires repeated requests for help and information from an ever-growing group of people. I have had the pleasure of interviewing many people, and have enjoyed hearing their stories of people and days long gone. In this category I include Pat McEvoy, Ken Hertz, Byron Elmendorf, Joel Douglas, Tim Douglas, Bob Reid, Leslie Bryson, Jay Bornstein, Frank Imhoff, Bill Geyer, Martin Kuljis, and Gay Dubyk.

Writing is also a collaborative process. I have asked Ken Hertz, Tim Wahl and Jeff Jewell to read my manuscript for historical errors, and I have returned to my good friend Beverly Johanson for her third effort at guiding me editorially and for the application of her considerable skills at cleaning up my grammar and punctuation gaffes.

This was also my third collaboration with that computer graphics, book design whiz Kate Weisel in designing, formatting and putting together what I have written in a readable printable fashion. Working with Kate has been a delight as usual.

A final acknowledgement should be made to the long-suffering patience of my wife Marya, and a cast of friends who have had to listen to my tales of discovery in the fields of history. Being an enthusiastic sort it was difficult for me to resist sharing what I learned as I progressed through the research.

Thanks to each and every one of you.

Preface

THIS BOOK BEGAN as the story of how Boulevard Park was conceived, promoted and finally constructed. Its inspiration was the request by a critically ill Robert Moles that the story be written and that the seminal role of the Rotary Club of Bellingham be recorded. At the time of Bob's illness and subsequent death twenty six years had passed since the park was dedicated in June of 1980. The Rotary Club's initiation of the park campaign had begun seven years before that in 1973. Community memory is short and already many of the people who were involved at the beginning of the Boulevard Park effort are gone. Moles, a long-time funeral director, understood, perhaps better than most, how quickly the generations pass and that the true story of how a community achieves its goals is too often lost in that passage. It was his desire, and mine, to keep the story of Boulevard Park's creation from becoming lost.

Researching and writing history is an intriguing process. At some point during the effort the history muses seem to take you by the hand to lead you down pathways that you had never anticipated. As I worked through archives and records I began to realize that each part of Boulevard Park was built upon preceding foundation events in history which made the current reality possible. It soon dawned on me that to truly appreciate today's park it would be necessary to understand all that went before.

In resignation, I decided to expand this book about Boulevard Park to include the story of all of the waterfront that it spans and the southside neighborhood that rises above it. To accomplish that I will take the reader back to the very beginning when the first men of European descent settled on the shores of Bellingham Bay. I will attempt to tell the entire story of that long strip of Bellingham's shoreline that was to become Boulevard Park or to be spanned by the park. I think you will be as delighted as I have been by the many surprising and forgotten activities that have occurred on this storied piece of land along the water. I hope that you will enjoy a new understanding of the history of the communities on Bellingham Bay.

I found the writing of this book to be an extremely personal endeavor. I have lived just a few blocks from this strip of land for my entire life. I have watched it, played on it, enjoyed it for as long as I can remember; and I often found myself writing in the first person. I finally decided to write the book in a personal voice. My goal is to bring you into the story through my recollections and experience, and share with you my fascination and joy of discovery while researching the story.

In this, my first effort to write about history, I have learned that the historian's true challenge is to find truth. The discovery of facts does not necessarily bring the researcher to the true story of what happened. Facts, such as the date of a purchase, or a photo proving the existence of a building, are the bones of history. Adding the human stories of why something was purchased, built, or demolished is to put the living flesh on the bones and to achieve meaningful history.

You will find that occasionally I have interpreted the known facts of time and place and added my guess at the human story. In every such case I have signaled my interpretation of fact with a qualifying statement such as, "I have presumed" or "it is my guess that". I hope that the reader will evaluate my presumptions and perhaps provide some of his (or her) own.

The book is divided into chapters featuring particular areas of the park. The stories I have found in the history of each area frequently cause me to tell a story that leads far away from the waterfront. I take you with me as I follow those stories wherever they lead, but eventually we come back to the main story line—that narrow strip of waterfront land spanned by Boulevard Park. Finally, at the end of the book, I return to the park itself, discussing the gas works site, art in the park, and the history of the railroads that crossed the park site.

So come with me on an examination of what has happened along our southside waterfront that has culminated in our community treasure, Boulevard Park.

The story begins in the year 1853 with the arrival of William Pattle to stake his donation land claim, and ends one hundred and fifty four years later in the year 2006 with the completion of the southern-most extension of Boulevard Park, the small outlook park at the entrance to the Taylor Avenue dock.

The first chapters discuss the early development period of the waterfront in broad general terms and lead the reader directly into the story of how Boulevard Park came to be. Later chapters break the long strip of waterfront into sections and probe deeply into the history of each section. I have attempted to relate the history of each section, revealing not only its development and industrial history, but also the stories of the people whose personalities and accomplishments have added so much to the fabric of their community.

Each of these later chapters begins with a graphic display of that section of the waterfront being discussed in the chapter. These sectional pieces are taken from the larger map appearing on the next two pages. This excellent map provided by the City of Bellingham planning office shows buildings existing at the time of this writing and will allow the reader to easily associate the historic areas being discussed with the shadow image of a building that exists today.

The book contains many photographs, some of them digital pictures taken of the huge pages of old Sanborn maps in the collection of the Center for Pacific Northwest Studies at the Washington State Regional Archives and at Whatcom Museum of

History and Art. These unique maps, relics of a long-abandoned service to the fire insurance industry, show in great detail the location, construction and use of old buildings, so often long ago dismantled or destroyed.

I have included in an appendix information about the Sanborn Map Company and their unique service in the sure knowledge that most readers have neither heard of a Sanborn map, nor know the interesting history of the company that made them.

I have used a great many photographs to illustrate the waterfront story in order to show what used to be and to impress the reader with how quickly and inexorably change occurs. Bellingham is blessed with a remarkable photographic record thanks to an unbroken succession of fine photographers who have made this area their home. Photographers like Eric Hegg, James Sandison, Darius Kinsey, and Jack Carver, along with collectors and preservers like Galen Biery and Gordon Tweit have carved their niches in history with their important work.

That these priceless photographs and the written records have been preserved, cataloged and made available for public use is one of the glories of our society. The photographic record of the Northwest region is capably archived by the Whatcom Museum of History and Art, the Center for Pacific Northwest Studies at Western Washington University housed in the Washington State Regional Archives at WWU, and at the Bellingham Public Library. The friendly and willing assistance of the good people at these institutions made research a joyful and warm experience.

Sitting atop all of the history of this storied waterfront is Boulevard Park itself. The park is one of the true jewels in Bellingham's excellent park system. It has brought the community back to its waterfront and preserved the public views from the boulevard that runs above it—the two goals that its advocates had set for it at the beginning in 1973. It is the result of many years of public concern and effort and is a classic example of involved citizen volunteers working with enlightened County and City governments to achieve a great civic advance.

I hope this history of the park and the waterfront that it spans will illuminate our past and honor those people who went before us to tame a wilderness, build a city, and finally come together to create a great park. It is the story of a public/private partnership in which caring citizens and organizations worked with their government to achieve a community treasure.

Finally, I hope that the book will instruct and encourage those who would work for their community's welfare in the future.

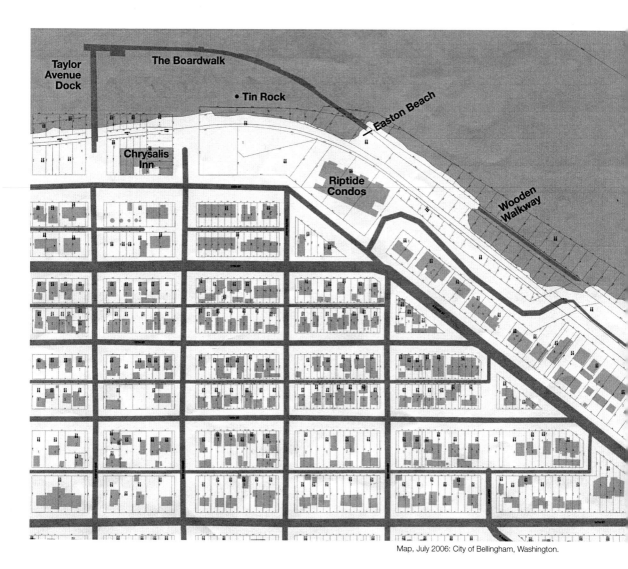

Map, July 2006: City of Bellingham, Washington.

The map sections shown here are taken from current (2006) maps provided by the City of Bellingham Planning Department.

The map depicts the entire sweep and depth of Boulevard Park from the Overlook Park south of Taylor Avenue Dock to the "Burlington Northern" lots which end where the Boulevard and South State Street reconnect. The map accurately depicts in grey buildings that existed in 2006.

The City map is annotated with location descriptions to aid the reader. Slightly enlarged sections of this map will be used in certain chapters to illustrate the location and configuration of the chapter's subject. Dark outlines will show specific lots that are being discussed.

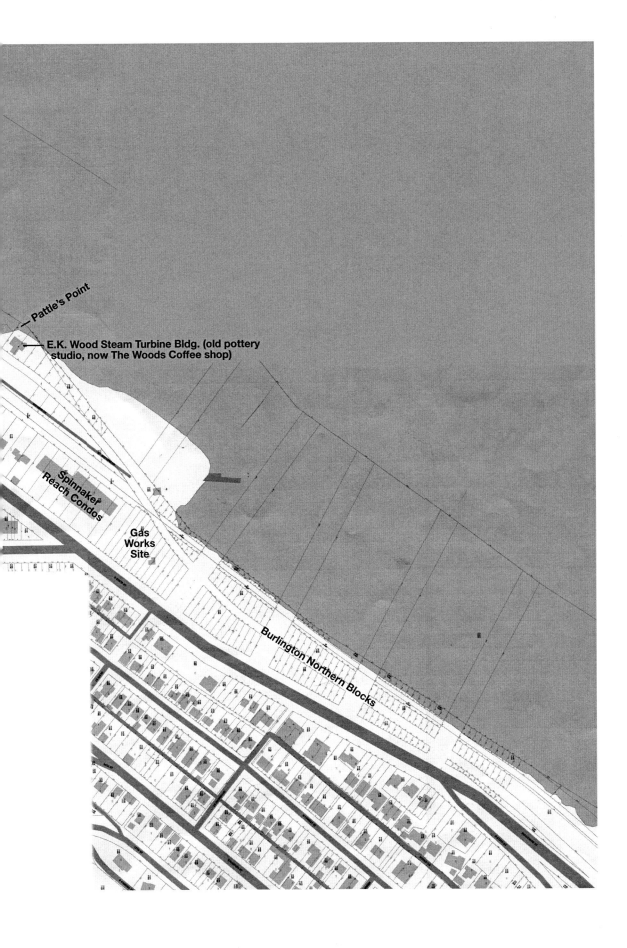

Pattle's Point

E.K. Wood Steam Turbine Bldg. (old pottery studio, now The Woods Coffee shop)

Spinnaker Reach Condos

Gas Works Site

Burlington Northern Blocks

Historical Time Line

1852	Roeder and Peabody land at Whatcom Falls
1853	Pattle, Morrison and Thomas lease coal rights to F. Rogers Loomis
1853	William Pattle files Donation Land Claim
1853	Morrison and Thomas file Donation Land Claims
1853	Dirty Dan Harris arrives and moves in with Thomas
1853	Edward and Teresa Eldridge join Roeder Mill
1854	Thomas dies of tuberculosis
1856	Pattle sells half of his land to McLea
1858	Charles Richards builds first brick building in Whatcom
1860	McLea and Pattle sell entire claim to Simson
1861	Morrison sells his Donation Land Claim to Seth Doty
1861	Union Coal Company formed by C.A. Richards
1861	Union Wharf built
1866	Morrison Donation Land Claim receives USA patent deed
1866	Erastus Bartlett buys half of Morrison claim
1868	Unionville destroyed by forest fire
1870	Pattle Donation Land Claim receives USA patent deed
1871	Erastus Bartlett buys second half of Morrison claim
1871	Bellingham Hotel is built
1880	14th Street School is built
1883	Eldridge and Bartlett plat town of Bellingham
1883	Bellingham Bay & British Columbia Railroad begins
1887	E.B. Hill Co. builds dock at Taylor Avenue
1888	Bartlett buys Morrison's final acre at Sheriff's sale
1889	Nelson Bennett comes to town, forms Fairhaven Land Company
1889	Nelson Bennett & C.X. Larrabee buy Fairhaven
1889	The Fairhaven Boom begins
1889	Fairhaven & Southern Railroad begins
1889	W.H. Welbon builds mill
1889	C.W. Waldron starts the Bank of Fairhaven
1890	Fairhaven Land Co. buys Bellingham
1890	Fairhaven Land Co. buys half of Eldridge & Bartlett Mill
1890	Fairhaven & Northern Railroad begins
1890	Thomas Monahan builds Monahan Building on 11th Street

1890	Bellingham Bay Gas Co. completes plant
1890	Bellingham Land Co. incorporated
1890	Eldridge & Bartlett sell Bellingham and 2000 acres to Bellingham Bay Land Co. for one million dollars
1891	Waldron Building completed with three floors
1891	Bellingham Bay & Eastern R.R. formed
1892	F&S R.R. building Chuckanut route to Burlington
1892	Gamwell House completed
1894	Waldron Building extended to four floors, fire razes upper floors
1896	Antone Glenovich arrives from Croatia
1897	Fairhaven Canning Co. opens at foot of Taylor Avenue
1898	Franco-American North Pacific Cannery built, foot of Harris
1898	Aberdeen Canning Co. built, foot of Harris
1898	Reid Boiler Works begins operations in Fairhaven, foot of Harris
1898	Pacific Sheet Metal Works builds brick Can Factory & Warehouse
1899	George J. Hohl Company operating Feed & Seed store in Waldron Building
1900	E.K. Wood buys Bellingham Mill Co. from Eldridge and Bartlett and Fairhaven Land Co.
1900	George J. Hohl elected mayor of Fairhaven
1900	Pacific Sheet Metal builds three warehouses over water
1901	Fairhaven Canning Company sells to Pacific Packing & Navigation Company
1902	Pacific Packing & Nav. sold to Deming, becomes Sehome Canning Co.
1902	Great Northern R.R. buys Fairhaven & Southern
1902	Murchison Mill built at foot of Douglas
1902	Erastus Bartlett dies
1903	Fairhaven & Whatcom consolidate as Bellingham
1903	Northern Pacific R.R. buys Bellingham Bay & Eastern
1903	Murchison Mill burns, conflagration includes Hill Welbon Wharf
1904	Reid Boiler Works burns, foot of Harris. Rebuilds on site
1904	Aberdeen Canning Company sells to Welsh, becomes Bellingham Canning Company
1907	George J. Hohl builds Flour Mill, foot of Taylor
1907	P.A.F. buys Pacific Sheet Metal's four buildings, operating them as Bellingham Warehouse Company

1911	George J. Hohl now manages Whatcom Flour & Feed on Roeder Avenue & F Street
1911	Dan Campbell builds warehouse, foot of Bennett
1912	Reid Boiler Works builds on Tenth St.
1914	14th Street School replaced; Lowell School is built on the site
1917	Flour Mill at Taylor Avenue goes out of business
1919	*Vigilant*, last of the lumber schooners, is launched
1922	George J. Hohl now managing Bellingham Feed & Seed, Railroad Avenue
1923	George J. Hohl opens Hohl Feed & Seed at present location, Railroad Avenue
1925	E.K. Wood Lumber Mill burns and is closed forever
1926	California Petroleum buys Flour Mill site
1928	California Petroleum sells to the Texas Company
1928	Texaco builds finger pier with office beside Taylor Dock and begins marine service
1932	Charles McEvoy becomes Texaco consignee
1934	George J. Hohl dies, age 71
1935	George P. Jeffers buys Lummi Bay Packing Company, renames it Beach Packing Co.
1935	Bornstein Seafoods opens at Campbell's Warehouse
1938	Gilmore Oil builds at Taylor Avenue
1940	Standard Oil buys Gilmore Oil
1945	Southside Boat Haven destroyed in storm
1945	*Vigilant* burns in Bahia Blanco, Argentina
1946	Jeffers sells Beach Packing Company & moves to Bellingham
1946	E.K. Wood Industrial Sites plat filed
1949	Bellingham Tug and Barge sold to Foss
1953	Patrick McEvoy joins McEvoy Oil
1956	Can Factory Warehouses sold to George P. Jeffers
1956	Gas works ceases operations
1962	Texaco abandons operations on the dock
1963	Bornstein's buys Campbell Warehouse
1963	David Thomas suggests a park north of gas works
1965	S.B.A. forecloses on Jeffers
1965	Port of Bellingham gets Can Factory property
1967	Rogan Jones buys gas works site
1967	Rogan Jones proposes tower condominium
1968	Pacific American Fisheries closes, Port buys land

1968	Ken Hertz, Whatcom County Parks buys Pattle Point
1968	Ken Hertz, Whatcom County Parks gets Northern Pacific R.R. right-of-way
1969	Ken Hertz, Whatcom County Parks gets Easton Beach
1969	South Hill Neighborhood Association suggests park
1969	Dillingham Corp. buys Foss Tug & Barge
1970	Northern Pacific, Great Northern, Burlington Line merge to become Burlington Northern
1970	Zuanich, McBeath petition for street vacations on Boulevard
1971	Bruce Row & Western students park plan
1973	YWCA Eco-Action protests development on Boulevard
1974	General Petroleum, now Mobil Oil, ceases operation at Taylor Avenue
1974	Haggen Brothers buy Mobil Oil site
1974	Rotary Club of Bellingham takes on Park Project
1975	Bellingham City Council commits to Boulevard Park
1975	Gas works site purchased
1975	Burlington Northern land blocks purchased
1976	Joel Douglas leases Taylor Avenue Dock
1976	Dillingham land purchased
1978	Bellingham passes Park Bond Issue, $350,000 for Boulevard
1979	J.I.J. Construction wins construction bid
1979	Consignee McEvoy Oil buys out Texaco
1980	Park construction completed, Park dedicated
1980	Milwaukee-St. Paul R.R. ceases operations on Railroad Avenue
1988	City buys Douglas leasehold interest
1988	Taylor Avenue Partnership options Haggen parcel
1988	Hotson Plan commissioned
1989	Option given to City
1990	Vandals torch trestle walk, walkway rebuilt
1990	City buys Haggen land
1996	McEvoy Oil Company sells property to Ken Imus
1996	Old Pattle/Union Coal Mine discovered and sealed
1997	Chrysalis Hotel constructed
2005	The concrete "Boardwalk" completed
2006	Overlook Park completed

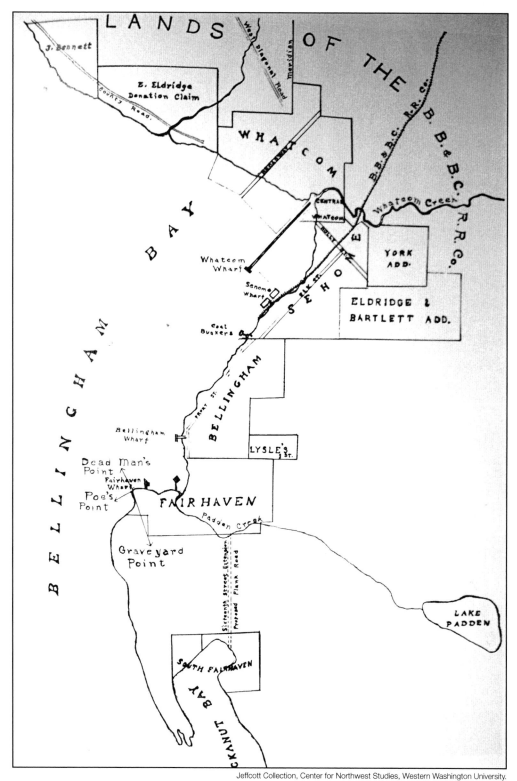

Early map (possibly 1884) showing the boundaries of the four pioneer towns that grew on the shores of Bellingham Bay.

Chapter 1

The
Industrial Waterfront

THE WATERFRONTS of Whatcom, Sehome, (old) Bellingham, and Fairhaven—the four small pioneer towns that grew to life along Bellingham Bay— were places of robust industry and commerce. In those hard scrabble early days there was little time nor room for public entertainment or community recreation on a water-front lined with docks, lumber mills and coal loading facilities, and eventually shipyards and salmon canneries. Their hardworking residents were busy wresting a spare living by mining coal and producing lumber from the dense forest that covered the land to the very edge of the sea. The thought of building parks and preserving public access to the waters of the bay was lost in the urgent need to build an economy and a way of survival in the midst of a wilderness.

These fledgling communities relied on the salt water for transportation. For many years there would be no roads, nor railroads, only ships to bring the necessities of civilized life from the outside and to ship out the lumber and coal that were the well-spring of their primitive economies. Timber pilings and large sawn planks were cheap and plentiful. Pile driving was easier and cheaper than clearing land and paring down the bluffs. For an economy dependent on water transport it made sense to build your business on piles and docks protruding from the shoreline below the bluffs. It was logical and inevitable that the waterfront be reserved for industry.

Lumber mills, shingle mills, coal bunkers, canneries, even a flour mill, soon lined the shoreline of Bellingham Bay.

The railroads which came to the bay in the 1880s completed the physical separation of residents from their waterfront. Miles and miles of beaches were bisected by the trestles built upon piles driven into the sea bottom. Many beaches were covered entirely by the coarse rock of roadbed ballast. Shoreside bluffs and rock faces were blasted down to provide rock and fill for the adjoining roadbed. Folks were too busy and too eager for economic opportunity to object to the loss of water access and property owners along the shore were eager to have rail service to their land and industries. Eventually the beaches and water access were all gone.

The Valued View

Generations of Bellingham Bay residents experienced almost no ready access to the water but their affection for a view of the Bay became firmly rooted. The finest residential districts were always sited on locations with a "view" meaning a view of the bay and the islands beyond. The first families of Whatcom built their homes on Eldridge Avenue on the bluff overlooking the bay. The grand mansions of Sehome were on the hill above State Street with a view of the water. Fairhaven's best homes built by Gamwell, Wardner, Bateman and others were invariably high on the South Hill with a grand view of the Bay and islands. When Whatcom and Fairhaven consolidated to become Bellingham in 1903, in-fill between the cities began. The most valuable lots were always those with a view. Eventually the Larrabee family developed Edgemoor and its attraction was of course the "views."

For those who could not afford a "view" lot there was still the pleasure of going for a drive and enjoying the view from the "Boulevard," that stretch of road from Sehome to Fairhaven that skirted the bay and offered an almost unbroken drive with excellent vistas of water and islands.

In the 1950s Bellingham began to grow in population. Its population had seemed fixed at around 30,000 souls for decades but slow growth began with the advent of the Mobil Refinery at Cherry Point. An improving economy brought investment in many forms. The platting and sale of the old E. K. Wood Lumber mill site in the late 1940s had allowed for development of land along State Street that had for years been only vacant land occupied by grazing cows. Suddenly what was formerly unused lumber mill land along the view corridor saw the construction of what are now the Riptide Condominiums and Spinnaker Reach Condominiums. People began to worry that the valued "public" views from the Boulevard might someday disappear altogether.

Others began to think about the lack of public access to the water, deeming it a failure in public planning for a city with 17.5 miles of salt water frontage to have virtually no way for the public to put their collective feet into the water.

As early as June of 1963 public concern was expressed when David Thomas, an artist and faculty member at what was then Western Washington State College, wrote to the Parks Advisory Board asking them to look into the possibility of acquiring three blocks along the Boulevard in the vicinity of the old gas works for an outlook park. The City Engineer at the time estimated the land cost would be $328,000. The City did not act.

Thomas did not give up. The February 5, 1969 minutes of the Parks Advisory Board contain a letter from the South Hill Neighborhood Association.

"As officers of the South Hill Neighborhood Association we know that there is widespread support in our area for the formation of a park on the bay side of the Boulevard that would preserve the fine view of the bay for the public.

"We are aware that widespread support for such a park is also present throughout many other areas of Bellingham. Certainly this would be one of the most popular projects which you might undertake," David L. Thomas. President.

There is no record that any action was taken by the Parks Board.

The Students' Park

In 1971, Bruce Row, a senior student from Western's Technology Dept., along with several other students created a proposal for a "bayside park". The students built an eight-foot-long model, assembled a photo essay, and displayed both wherever they could find an audience around town.

They presented their scheme to the Planning Commission on Feb. 10, 1972, and to the Parks Advisory Board on May 8 of that year. An article appeared in *The Bellingham Herald* the next day.

Their proposed Bayside Park encompassed 35 acres and was over a mile in length stretching from the old Bloedel Donovan Cargo Mill site at the foot of Cornwall Avenue to the Uniflite site in Fairhaven south of Taylor Avenue dock.

None of these citizen initiatives apparently carried enough weight or momentum to push a conservative city government into action. In fact, there was a counter belief among some of the more conservative business interests in town that, "The waterfront needs to be reserved for industry." Many community leaders were closer in age and philosophy to an earlier industrial time when the economy did rely on waterfront industry. Their positions were an extreme contrast with those in positions of leadership today who recognize the very real value of the waterfront providing a mixed use of light industry, residential, recreational, business and education opportunities—a mix of activity leading to a superior quality of life. Today the gentrification of the waterfront is seen as an economic and cultural positive.

Residential builders had long ignored the land seaward of the Boulevard. There were a number of reasons. Perhaps it was too close to the smoking and noisy industries of an earlier time, or the land was in the ownership of industrial interests and was simply not available. Much of the land was rather narrow and steep and did not appear to be economic to build on; some of it was on a grade substantially below the road level and that did not seem to be ideal for building either. The railroad ran along the entire waterfront presenting noise and vibration problems. For whatever reason, the views from the Boulevard were unimpeded for many years. The public developed a sense of ownership and appreciation for the outlook and perhaps a false sense of security that the views would always be there for their enjoyment.

Threat of Development

It then came as a shock to the community, in 1973, when a rumor began to circulate that the precious "Boulevard view" might be threatened by several new apartment buildings to be built along the narrow strip of land north of the old gas works site. Already the views south of the gas works had been compromised by the construction of Spinnaker Reach in 1973 and the Riptide Condominiums in 1972. Those developments gave impetus to the rumors of further view loss to come.

Bellingham's citizens had good reason to be concerned about losing their views.

Lafayette Rogan Jones.

Forward thinking business people were awakening to the opportunities to be found along the Boulevard corridor. As early as 1967, application had been made for a specific use permit to build a nine-unit, nine-story apartment tower on the gas works site. The applicant was Lafayette Rogan Jones, one of Bellingham's most visionary and respected citizens. Jones was a pioneering radio and television businessman and a person of great prestige and influence in the City. He and his wife Catherine were the owners of the area's first and largest radio station, KVOS. He had been the first to see the terrific potential of television in the Northwest corner of Washington close to the huge consumer market existing in and around Vancouver, British Columbia.

In a stroke of genius Jones had decided to establish his television transmitter on the top of Mount Constitution on Orcas Island and from there, broadcast his signal on a line-of-sight basis into the Vancouver, B.C., area at a time when Canadians hungered for the broader programing of U.S. television. It was a brilliant concept, ultimately worth millions of dollars to him.

Rogan Jones was an extremely creative man. His former employees fondly tell the story of his daily after-lunch naps in a specially equipped nap room. During his nap times he would take with him a pad of paper and a pencil. Apparently in the relaxing calm, either as he was falling asleep or as he was waking, his unique mind would unfailingly produce an idea or two and Jones would write them down before they slipped away. The late Lee Facto, one of his key lieutenants, told me that Jones almost always came out of his nap time with an idea. Most of them were impractical and promptly discarded by his staff, but every once in a while he would emerge with a brilliant idea which would lead the corporation off in a new direction.

One of Jones' inspirations was to build, on the old gas works site that he had purchased, the aforementioned tall tower with but one living unit on each floor. A slender distinctive view tower. Once again, Jones was a man ahead of his time. After considerable community debate the planning commission and City Council denied his request. Given the present furor over building condominium towers in Fairhaven and Downtown Bellingham in the present year 2007, one can easily imagine the public response in the early '70s to the thought of a narrow nine-story residential tower to be built on the view sensitive Boulevard. This dream was never to be. Five years later Jones died and the still unused gas works site passed to his estate and his widow Catherine Jones.

The Burlington Northern Lease

The next alarm was sounded in 1969 when a group of Bellingham businessmen secured a forty year lease to the three-block-long narrow strip of land north of the gas works owned by Burlington Northern railroad. Their lease gave them control of the land between State Street and the Burlington Northern track down at water level. In 1970 they petitioned the city to vacate the street right-of-ways which bisect the property every 300 feet. They intended to build apartment buildings along most of the length of the property.

For many years the Fairhaven Lions Club had maintained this strip as a community project. They cleared the brush and trimmed trees keeping the view sites open. They even provided some parking spots and picnic benches. In addition they had originally painted and now maintained the large "Welcome To Bellingham" sign on the concrete wall where South State Street and the Boulevard meet. The Lions abandoned their efforts when they learned of the developers' lease.

Each of the leased blocks was three hundred feet long and they were flanked by five 80-foot street right-of-ways. If the City had vacated the five right-of-ways, the developers' property would have stretched 1220 feet along the view corridor. Members of the group included Peter Zuanich, Malcolm "Dutch" McBeath, and possibly George Livesey Jr., their attorney.

Their vacation request stirred a hornet's nest of public concern. The potential loss of Boulevard views alarmed many in the community and aroused the citizenry as no similar issue had previously done. Citizen concern over this issue proved to be the ignition point for the community drive to build Boulevard Park. The street vacation petition was denied in the face of public opposition and on the basis of a state law dealing with vacations of public right-of-ways leading to water.

The would-be developers were not deterred for long. By 1973 a new rumor surfaced. They were contemplating construction on the narrow strip once again. This time without the street vacations. The erstwhile developers were well connected and respected local business people. Pete Zuanich was a long-time Port Commissioner, a leader in the Puget Sound salmon fishing industry and of Bellingham's Croatian community. Malcom "Dutch" McBeath was the co-owner of McBeath Glass Co., a member of the Rotary Club of Bellingham, and a significant business leader.

Both Zuanich and McBeath were stalwart leaders of the Bellingham Junior Chamber of Commerce (JC), a hyper-active group of young businessmen who for years had accomplished wonders in the realm of community service. The famous JC Christmas ship, the World's Tallest Christmas Tree erected on Railroad Avenue, and the paper drives which funded many of their community projects were all hallmarks of the Junior Chamber. Zuanich and McBeath were two of the JC's acknowledged leaders. George Livesey Jr. was a prominent second generation attorney, the legal council for the Port of Bellingham, and a partner in a prestigious law firm which included senior partner Burton Kingsbury.

YWCA Eco-Action to the Rescue

The obvious threat to the public view alarmed a group of women who called themselves YWCA Eco-Action. Its members included Ann Rose, Phyllis Jones, Joanne Cross, Carol Batdorf, Delight Green, Penny Berg, Elsie Heinrick, Sharon Schayes, Phyllis Graven, and others—all capable, intelligent and determined women—a formidable collection of crusaders who would leave their mark on Bellingham in many ways over many years.

YWCA Eco-Action swung into action by launching a petition drive asking the City to downzone the property along the Boulevard to "Residential Low Density

One". This zoning designation would have rendered the property unsuitable for multiple housing, effectively killing the developer's plans. Seven hundred thirty-one people signed the petition. It was presented to the Land Use Commission and debated in a lengthy public session.

The petitioners expressed fear "that development would create a barrier or wall between the heavily traveled arterial and the view of the bay. While they recognized the property owner or lessor's right to make a profit from their land, they felt that this was a situation where "the peoples' rights" far outweighed any property rights.

Burt Kingsbury, attorney for the potential developers, remarked in prescient fashion, "It seems to me what these people want is for this to be a park." He went on to say that his clients would be happy to negotiate a fair deal with the City for purchase of the property lease to be used for a park.

The Land Use Commission turned down the zoning request on April 13, 1973.

The Eco-Action group had been defeated, but as fate would have it, their defeat was only temporary. Their impassioned campaign to protect the community's views had called attention to the issue. Other organizations were taking an interest.

Chapter 2

Rotary Steps In

At a 1973 Community Service Committee meeting of the Rotary Club of Bellingham, Chairman Bob Moles led a discussion of potential projects that his venerable club might undertake.

The Rotary Club of Bellingham, chartered in 1916 (the first Rotary Club in the county) and steeped in a history of service to its community, was seeking a new project to continue that role of service. Its members had for generations been leaders and persons of influence on Bellingham Bay. The club had enjoyed a solid record of achievement throughout its history. Now they searched for another way to serve.

The Tattler, the club newsletter of July 30, 1973, reads, "Chairman, Bob Moles, reports that the committee is setting plans for a survey to identify likely projects for the club to sponsor. Suggestions to date include: kidney machine, Big Brother Club, beautification of city entrances, city dock, mental health project, benches throughout city, Boys' Club bus, neighborhood house, and a Rotary park. Most promising projects appear to be the beautification and Rotary park ideas, children's recreation equipment at the new mental health center, and benches in a variety of locations throughout the community."

Moles recalled that at one of their meetings someone had mentioned the threat to the views along the Boulevard posed by rumored construction plans on the west side of the Boulevard. The committee determined to examine ways to preserve those views.

At the club's Board of Directors meeting of October 11, 1973, the minutes show, "Bob Moles, Community Service Committee Chairman, attended the Board meeting. Bob Moles also presented a proposal for small parks along the waterfront for the community to enjoy the views. The idea was discussed and it was decided to have the

Community Service Committee do more investigating and that it would be a good subject for the upcoming fireside."

Each year in those days the Rotary Club held a series of "fireside" meetings hosted in members' homes. The purpose was fellowship and the opportunity to discuss a topic pertinent to the club or its plans. The membership was divided up and assigned to a member's home, perhaps fifteen members to a home. *The Tattler* of November 12, 1973, contains this item. "Mark your calendars for 7:30 next Tuesday night, November 13th. One possibility is a commitment to a long-term project such as a Rotary Park."

While The Rotary Club was searching for a project, YWCA Eco-Action group was still hard at work. In the hopes of getting guidance in working with the City of Bellingham on the views issue, they had contacted me asking that I help them understand how best to move the City to action. I had recently initiated and accomplished the public/private effort which resulted in construction of the Bellingham Parkade. The women of Eco-Action hoped that I could advise them on lobbying the city, raising money, condemning property, and all the other actions that might have to be taken to preserve those Boulevard views. My meeting with Eco-Action convinced me of the urgency of the threats to the views along the waterfront.

Rotary Fireside Meeting

I determined to enthusiastically support a park plan at the Rotary Club of Bellingham fireside meeting to be held at my home several weeks hence. At that meeting I made a strong appeal for Rotary involvement proposing that Rotary option all of the land along the Boulevard north of Spinnaker Reach Condos beginning at the old gas works site and ending at Wharf Street. Further, I proposed that those options be offered to the City, with strong Rotary persuasion encouraging the City to purchase the land and develop it into a municipal park.

The dozen or so Rotarians present at my home that evening voted unanimously to recommend that action to the larger club as the Rotary project of the year. Apparently other Rotarians at other homes came to the same conclusion. When all the fireside reports were compiled by the club, the project of choice was indeed "building a park along the Boulevard." The weekly *Tattler* report was guarded. "Bob Moles, Community Service Chairman, reported a generally favorable reaction to enhancing the view along the Boulevard." The Rotary Board met the very day that the *Tattler* had been published, December 3, 1973. Its minutes were more emphatic, "The Board met to discuss the finding of the Firesides that were held with regard to the Community Service Committee suggestion of the possibility of a small park proposal on the Boulevard. The Board authorized the committee to look further into the possibilities and property available."

Passing The Torch

Delight Green, a YWCA member, recalls attending a meeting at the Bellingham Yacht Club shortly thereafter, where the Eco-Action women passed the view-saving torch to a committee of Rotarians. She recalls sitting beside the southwest corner window of the dining room with a group of interested Rotarians discussing the Rotary Club's taking on the project. Probably present at that meeting would have been Bob Moles, and Donald L. "Jim" Fickel, the eventual project chairman to be appointed by Rotary.

Dr. D.L. Fickel, D.D.S., led Rotary's effort to establish the park.

Fickel, a local dentist, was to chair the project for the entire seven years that it took to build the park. He was so committed to the project, and it occupied so much of his time and attention, that his children recall calling the project *Daddy's Park*.

Green also recalled that the City's Planning Director, Eunice Wolf, was very much in favor of a park project but she was restricted by the administration's reluctance to become involved. In the beginning the park idea did not have the blessing of Bellingham's Mayor Reginald Williams. Ms. Wolf remained determined to be helpful to Eco-Action despite the Mayor's lack of enthusiasm and would send them information in unsigned messages written on blank paper in order to hide her identity.

The Mayor had been opposed to public involvement at the park site for some time. Ken Hertz related that when he was Whatcom County Parks Director the greatest resistance to development of a boat launch on the waterfront came from Mayor Williams. The reasons for his opposition are not known. One theory is that he was being influenced to oppose public activity there by his wife, who was the long-time office manager of Bellingham Tug & Barge at the Whatcom Creek waterway. Bellingham Tug & Barge had been purchased by Foss Tug & Barge in Seattle in 1949; its subsidiary, Bellingham Boom Company, owned some of the soon-to-be-targeted waterfront and had extensive log booming operations at the site. It was also possible that he was simply reflecting the long-held community belief that waterfront should be devoted to industry. To his credit, Williams eventually came to see the wisdom of the project. The record shows that it was he who finalized the purchase negotiations for the gas works site a year later.

Ann Rose, a former president of Eco-Action and later a long-time member of the Bellingham Planning Commission and the Bellingham City Council, recalls that YWCA Eco-Action had two major agendas—the requirement of double-hulled tankers for Puget Sound, and the preservation of the waterfront views along the Boulevard. She recalled meeting with me to solicit my aid, and the aforementioned meeting at the Yacht Club to pass the torch to the Rotary Club. Eco-Action had enjoyed little success in persuading City Hall to join their cause. Their new tactic was to involve Rotary, which they believed would have the influence and political clout to bring the view preservation issue to the attention of the City and the community at large.

Rotary Commits

Eco-Action's efforts were successful. The next Rotary *Tattler*, (reporting on the Monday, December 10, 1973 meeting), contains this announcement under the heading, Follow-up on Boulevard Beautification:

> "The Board of Directors, at its special meeting last Monday, instructed the Community Service Committee to proceed in its investigation of creating more scenic viewpoints along the Boulevard. Jim Fickel will be primarily responsible for this effort."

Now Rotary was committed. The considerable influence and power of the Rotary Club of Bellingham would ultimately play a large role in guiding this community park to completion. Many years, much frustration, and a great deal of hard work lay before the members. The club committed to the project in late 1973. It would be the summer of 1980 before the park would be completed.

Waterfront Included

Initially the club's intent was only to protect the views from the Boulevard by acquiring control of the views from the high land along the road and uphill from the railroad track. That was soon to change.

The author recalls stopping along the Boulevard near the old gas works site several weeks after the Rotary fireside meetings and looking down at the former mill site on the waterfront. At the time, the large flat area of filled land was entirely unused except for a U-shaped road at the north end, where log trucks dumped logs into the bay to be sorted and placed into the large log booms moored to the shoreline. As I watched a load of logs splash into the water it dawned on me that the abandoned mill site would be the perfect place for much needed public access to the water. The large expanse of flat waterfront land was separated from the Boulevard view property by a steep

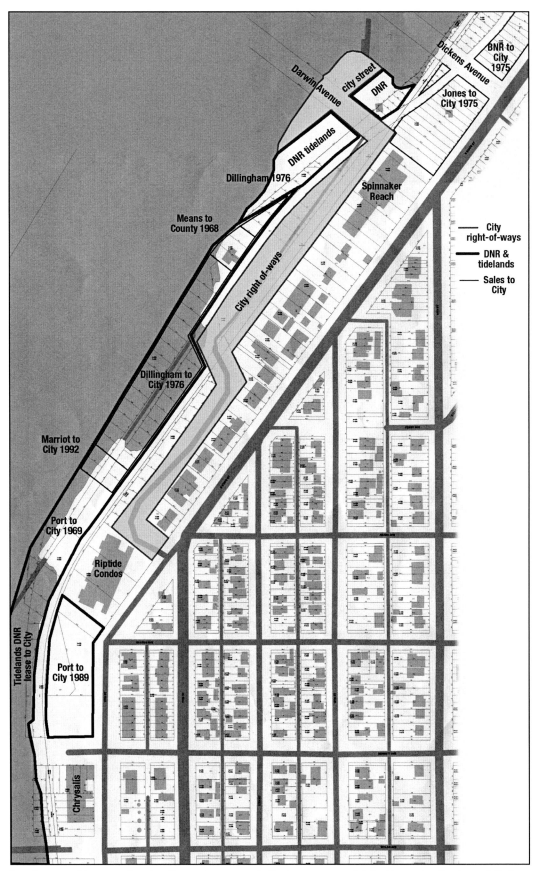

Land ownership map showing the various parcels that were consolidated to make Boulevard Park.

bank and the main line of the Burlington Northern Railroad; but a nearby city street, Bayview Drive, provided access. I determined to try to broaden the Rotary commitment to include the waterfront land.

I framed my vision in a letter to the club Board of Directors and to Bob Moles, pointing out that the club had a unique opportunity to get waterfront access for the community and that an expanded waterfront vision went hand and glove with preserving the views along the Boulevard. Moles recalled his committee receiving the letter, agreeing with it, and acting upon its suggestions by including the waterfront parcel in a new proposal to the Rotary Board.

The Rotary Board concurred and approved the broadened plan enthusiastically. Armed with that approval the committee rolled into action, beginning the process of identifying and making the first contacts with property owners.

Land Assembly

There were eight separate ownerships to be dealt with in piecing together Boulevard Park. Fortunately four of them were public entities. The Whatcom County Park Department, The City of Bellingham, The Port of Bellingham, and The State of Washington Department of Natural Resources (DNR).

The private ownerships included the Estate of Rogan Jones, Catherine Jones executrix; The Dillingham Corporation (which had recently bought Foss Tug & Barge); The Marriott family; and finally, Zuanich, McBeath and Livesey—the would-be developers who held the long-term lease on three entire blocks of the Burlington Northern Property north of the gas works site.

The Rotary Committee headed by Jim Fickel began their task, recognizing that perhaps their greatest challenge, surely their first, would be to convince a conservative mayor and City Council that the City of Bellingham should take on the financial and administrative burdens of such a large park and that it was prudent to remove that section of waterfront from potential industrial use. The challenges before Moles, Fickel and the committee were large. By February of 1974, after weeks of planning and investigation, the committee was prepared to make their report to the Rotary Board of Directors.

The Board minutes of that month contain the following.

"Bob Moles and Jim Fickel, Community Service Committee Chairmen, presented their committee's recommendations on the development of Marine Parks along the Boulevard (see recommendation attached.) It was asked from the Board that the committee meet with the railroad and find out what our capabilities are regarding leasing the property for the street-level

Phase 1 of the parks, and report to the next board meeting in March. Phase 2 of the committee's recommendation was to lease the Jones & Dillingham property for 18 months. It was moved and seconded by the Board that the committee investigate the cost of option of these properties and report back to the board as soon as this amount is determined. President Pete Gaasland gave Bob Moles authorization to seek help from the general membership in his investigation."

The committee recommendation to the board is printed in its entirety herewith.

February 14, 1974:
To: the Board of Directors of the Rotary Club of Bellingham
From: Bob Moles, Chairman, Community Service Committee
Subject: Marine Parks
Dear Sirs,

In accord with the meeting held Tuesday, February 5 at the Leopold Hotel, we are recommending to the Board of Directors that the Rotary Club spearhead a drive to establish a marine park on Bellingham Bay.

We recommend the properties now owned by the Burlington Northern Railway, the Dillingham Corporation and the Rogan Jones Estate be optioned for purchase, plans be formulated for adding these properties to the County Parks lands contiguous to the Dillingham Property and the package be submitted to the appropriate agencies and the public for purchase and development.

It is unlikely the property now owned by the Burlington Northern Railway can be purchased, but it could be leased and made part of the whole system.

Preliminary estimates of the likely cost of purchase of the properties:
Dillingham $40,000 per acre,
Jones $70,000 low, $105,000 high.

We recommend the Rotary Club finance this project by spending $500 to option for 18 months the Dillingham property, and $500 to option the Jones property subject to negotiations with the respective owners. It is anticipated the Burlington Northern lease would be minimal.

It is our understanding the present forty-year lease of the Burlington Northern property is likely to be cancelled. This would have to take place before this property could be leased by us or the County Parks.

We further urge preliminary development of the Burlington Northern property as follows: Clear brush and trees and rubbish for a clear view of the Bay. Fence as required by Burlington Northern, plant grass and landscape scrubs, purchase and place 10-15 benches for public use, urge the city to establish parking along the Boulevard, urge the city to provide proper sanitary facilities for the area.

Estimates of these costs are;

Fencing, chain link:	1200 ft @5./foot	$6,000
Landscaping:		$2,000
Benches:	15 @ $80.00 each	$1,200
Total		$9,200

This is a very rare opportunity that we have to gain control of perhaps the last property available around Bellingham Bay for public use. There are many groups and individuals interested in this Marine Strip Park concept and we will have widespread support for this project.

The Chairman of the Whatcom County Parks Planning Board and the Director of the Whatcom County Park Department are both enthusiastic about the idea and have promised to work toward this goal.

We strongly urge the Rotary Club to make every effort to bring this idea to fulfillment.

Respectfully
Robert Moles, Chairman
Community Service Committee

The Board of Directors unanimously approved the proposal. With strong support from the board and the membership, project chairman Jim Fickel was free to begin his work in earnest. His challenge was substantial. He must find a way to persuade the lease holders of the all-important three blocks north of the gas works to abandon their lease. He must convince the Burlington Northern to re-lease or sell the property to Rotary or to the public agency building the park. He must convince Catherine Jones, the executrix of her husband's estate to option and ultimately sell the gas works site to Rotary or the public agency that would build the park. He must do the same with the giant Dillingham Corporation with its home offices in Hawaii. He had to deal with the Marriott family which owned a narrow lot bisected by the Northern Pacific right-of-way along the water, and not the least of his challenges was to persuade either the Port, Whatcom County Parks, or the City of Bellingham to be the lead agency which would own and operate the park.

At this point in the project it was not at all clear that the City would sponsor the park. City government, neither the executive nor legislative branch, had shown en-

Ken Hertz, Whatcom County Parks Director at that time, looking over the railroad right-of-way that he had just purchased from the Northern Pacific Railroad, and the Joe Means property that he had recently acquired. The site of the E.K. Wood Lumber Mill.

thusiasm for the idea. Perhaps the county might be a stronger candidate. Ken Hertz and the Whatcom County Parks Board had been pushing for public development on the waterfront for several years and had completed three key land acquisitions that were absolutely essential to a successful park on that site. Their most important achievement was a remarkable negotiation by Hertz that resulted in the Northern Pacific Railroad selling to Whatcom County Parks their entire right-of-way for a token $5.00—including the railroad trestles which would eventually be developed into walking paths. This right-of-way penetrated the very heart of what would become Boulevard Park from north to south.

A year previously Hertz had negotiated the purchase of the Joe Means property at the tip of Pattle's Point. This purchase included the only surviving building of the E.K. Wood lumber mill which had burned in 1925. The concrete structure was repaired and leased to Whatcom Community College (the college without a campus) for use as a pottery studio.

Hertz had also negotiated with the Port of Bellingham for a large piece of land on the waterfront just beside and below the Riptide Condominium, which included what is commonly known as Easton Beach.

Perhaps inter-agency competition played a part in determining the lead agency. The City of Bellingham owned significant portions of the land in the proposed park in the form of street right-of-ways. The combined area of the Bayview Drive, Darwin Ave., and Railroad St. right-of-ways made up almost forty percent of the total area of the lower park; while the State Street right-of-way and the bisecting street right-of-ways off of State Street constituted a substantial percentage of the proposed upper park. The fact that the park would be within the heart of the city would also become a factor.

Mayor Williams and the Bellingham City Council had not been enthusiastic about public use of the waterfront several years previously when Hertz was trying to develop a boat launch on the Joe Means property, which would become the pottery studio. Former County Park Director Hertz related (when interviewed in 2006) that Williams had attempted to deny the public road access over Bayview Drive, and had gone so far as to ask Burlington Northern to prevent the public from crossing its track in his opposition to the boat launch idea being promoted by County Parks.

The Rotary proposal of a waterfront park was also resisted by Mayor Williams. Terence "Terry" Wahl, a member of Hertz's county parks board at the time, recalls an unexpected visit from mayor Williams in the basement of Wahl's Department Store, which Wahl managed. Williams tried unsuccessfully to enlist Wahl in an effort to kill the park. Wahl, when interviewed in 2007, remarked with some irony that it took about a year before public enthusiasm for the park concept made Williams a keen supporter. In fairness to his memory, it must be stated that much later when Boulevard Park land acquisition was underway, Williams successfully participated in important land purchase negotiations.

A final consideration determining which entity would own and develop the park was, of course, financial. Land purchase and development would cost considerable money. Either the City or the County would have to find the necessary funding.

All of these challenges were faced by Rotary's Fickel and his committee, and one by one they were overcome. At this juncture of the story let it suffice to say that all parties were eventually brought to the bargaining table and finally consensus was reached. The City chose to become the park developer and owner—although it was not until nineteen months had passed from the date of Rotary's involvement that they made that formal decision. The City was successful in getting a 1976 state grant for outdoor recreation to help purchase property, the County agreed to loan their properties to the City via interlocal agreement, the DNR agreed to provide their lands by interlocal agreement, and Rotary was able to secure options on private lands and to convince the leaseholders to give up their forty-year lease on the Burlington Northern tracts.

The single hold-out property owner was the Marriott family, who could not be convinced to sell the waterfront part of their long lot. They had built their brick home on South State street on a lot that ran west, over the street right-of-way, over the bluff to the track, and beyond the track to the water. Fortunately their property was not essential to the park because it was bisected by the old Northern Pacific Railroad right-of-way, which had been included in Hertz's $5.00 purchase. The walking path on the old railroad right-of-way was in county hands while the Marriotts owned on both sides of the path. The Marriotts continued to own the waterfront portion just north of Easton Beach until 1992 when the City Park Department was finally able to purchase it with Greenways' funds.

Rotary Club Records

A review of Rotary records will shed some light on the long and rather torturous process of developing the park.

June 14, 1974. Board Minutes: "The progress of the waterfront park has slowed down because of problems with the purchase of the Dillingham Property."

July 18, 1974. Board Minutes: "Jim Fickel reported on the progress of the Waterfront Park. He said things are going great guns now."

July 22, 1974. *Tattler:* "Jim Fickel will be meeting with City and County officials to discuss the future of a park along the Boulevard."

Nov. 14, 1974. Board Minutes: "Jim Fickel reported on the progress of Waterfront Park. The option we have will be up soon and Mayor Reg Williams is working to help get the ball rolling."

January 9, 1975. Board Minutes: "Jim Fickel reported on the progress of Waterfront Park. The Mayor was able to commit Mrs. Jones to selling her property for $95,000. The Park Department was to decide by January 10, 1975. It looks like the Foss (Dillingham) property may be able to be settled by negotiation."

February 10, 1975. *Tattler:* "Congratulations and a pat on the back to Bob Moles and Jim Fickel for progressing successfully on the proposed waterfront park."

February 13, 1975. Board Minutes: "Jim Fickel reported that Foss has received their property back and is willing to sell for $90,000. $5,000 option for one year. The board commended him for a job well done on this project."

April 7, 1975. *Tattler:* "On April 28 the City Council will hold a hearing on the future of a waterfront park. The Parks and Recreation program currently lists this development as Number One priority. PUBLIC SUPPORT is greatly needed, so we encourage you to attend this upcoming meeting. Any further questions, contact Bob Moles or Jim Fickel."

May 8, 1975. Board Minutes: "Jim Fickel reported that the City Council has approved Boulevard Park."

July 18, 1977. *Tattler*: "Al Williamson's Waterfront Park Committee has been revived under the co-chairmanship of Jim Fickel and Howard Mills Jr. We thought the club might be interested in the progress to date so we talked to Jim Fickel about it. Park Director, Bill Hutsinpiller has assigned 14 CETA employees to clear brush along the Boulevard, and our park committee will be seeking Board approval soon to begin development of a portion of the park by the Rotary Club. Rotary work crews will be recruited for late July and August. Jim says we can expect a more complete report to the club in the next few weeks as things come a little clearer in focus. It is clear that now is the time for us to act, not only to insure the reality of the park itself, but to gain some recognition for the part Rotary has played in the genesis and evolution of the project."

August 22, 1977. *Tattler*: "Jim Fickel reported on the progress of the Waterfront Park as it relates to us. The City Council is deliberating on the 3.7-million-dollar bond issue proposal, $350,000 of which is earmarked for the Waterfront Park. The August 22 meeting of the Council will decide. It was the feeling of the Board that the $350,000 should be separated from the rest of the bond issue, but the Board has decided against taking a position at this time. City Park Director Bill Hutsinpiller has left for a position in Seattle. They hope that the interruption in continuity will not delay plans already in motion for the waterfront park."

By the time Hutsinpiller resigned, Bellingham had a new mayor, Ken Hertz. As the director of Whatcom County Parks, Hertz had laid much of the groundwork for a waterfront park when he secured three vital pieces of land from Joe Means, the Milwaukee St. Paul R.R., and the Port of Bellingham. He was an active advocate for the park and the Parks bond issue.

Hertz hired a new Park and Recreation Dept. director, Byron Elmendorf, who started with the City in April of 1978. Elmendorf recalls that his first duty was to put together and promote the big bond issue of 1978 that would provide 2.2 million dollars for city park development. Included in the bond issue were funds to add to Civic Field and the adjoining baseball diamond, and $350,000 for what by that time was being called Boulevard Park. Elmendorf was also busy applying for a State of Washington matching grant of $350,000 for Boulevard Park construction.

The twin attractions of civic field improvements and a waterfront park were enough to convince the taxpayers of Bellingham. The bond issue passed. The State approved the matching grant and Elmendorf was able to begin.

The City hired the Bellevue landscape architectural firm of Jongejan, Gerrard

& McNeal to design the park. Terry Gerrard, a principal of the firm, led the effort. Gerrard was to have a considerable aesthetic influence on Bellingham in future years for he also designed the downtown street improvements of 1980 which introduced Bellingham to bollards and street trees.

Park Department employees were busy on the project months before the contract was let to a general contractor. John Ivary—who had worked for Elmendorf in Vancouver, Washington, for six years—was persuaded to move to Bellingham by the new park director. Ivary reported for duty in 1978 and his first assignment was to get two stalled art projects underway.

The City had contracted with Tom McClelland for his art piece, titled "Conference Table". The work had been finished and stored in an old Fairhaven fire station for six months while the artist and a crew of CETA employees were working on its installation footings. Elmendorf was frustrated with the slow progress. The other project, Michael Jacobsen's Western Rock Garden, was ready to be installed. Ivary was successful at getting both installed before any other work on the park was begun. In what seems to be a reversal of the usual process, the park was built around the previously installed art.

The big challenge for the City occurring before the general contract was even bid was the removal of the steel gas tanks from the old gas works. Both tanks and some of their supporting framework were in place when the City bought the property. The City was not pleased to find that the tanks contained large quantities of an oily coal residue accumulated over years in the coal gasification process. They had little trouble removing the older of the tanks, which dated back to 1890. The coal residue was in the second tank. Ivary recalls that when they started on the larger tank with the concrete base, they pumped and pumped until they had removed thousands of gallons of coal residue spending a "significant" amount of money. In his memory, it was more than $100,000. Running out of budget funds they finally decided to simply fill the concrete base with dirt absorbing the remaining coal residue. The circular concrete base was then capped with a thick layer of asphalt and the Rotary Shelter was built on top.

Now the Boulevard Park project could be put out to public bid. The contract was won by J.I.J. Construction of Bellingham with a bid of $637,500.

John Ivary has some interesting remembrances of building the park. He reports that the waterside park site was essentially level and filled with demolition debris. The tops of innumerable wooden piles could be seen protruding amongst and above the rubble. The rubble consisted of a great number of red bricks, concrete slabs, and cut pieces of Chuckanut stone. His recollections confirm the urban legend that the grand and imperial Fairhaven Hotel found its grave under Boulevard Park. When the hotel was razed in 1955, the debris was dumped among the old piling of the burned out

Photo Port of Bellingham Records, Washington State Archives; Northwest Regional Archives, Bellingham.

Above: Aerial view of site showing log booms, the old gas works, and hundreds of pilings on the E.K. Wood mill site. Below is a more recent photograph of the beach—the lines of cut-off piles are evident, as are the stacks of lumber which fell through the dock during the 1925 fire.

E.K. Wood Lumber Mill. The numerous red bricks and large amount of Chuckanut stone surely point to the truth of the old story. A fitting use for the bones of Fairhaven's old Victorian palace it seems to me.

Ivary continued, "The rubble and slabs of concrete visible around the shoreline were not brought in to stabilize the shoreline, they were there when the park project began. There was no additional heavy fill rubble brought in for the park project. The contractor did haul in load after load of dirt with which to fill and plant grass and build berms such as the high berm that the play structure sits on. The site had scores of wooden piles protruding from the water and protruding between the rubble on the uplands. The piles on the uplands were largely covered by the truckloads of soil brought in, but the piles out in the water were simply cut off as low as possible at low tides."

Terry Gerrard, the landscape architect, selected the few piles to be spared the chainsaw. Several years after the park was completed the land under the walking path near the dock began to settle. As it settled the heads of piles began to press up under the asphalt of the path until there were numerous pie-sized lumps rising under the asphalt. Ivary related that park workers dealt with the lumps by digging up the asphalt walk around each pile and sawing them off again.

The J.I.J. contract accomplished most, but not all, of the park improvements that we see today. They brought in the top soil, built the parking lots and pathways, planted the grass, built the dock and the restrooms. The largest part of the job was building the tower and bridge over the railroad track connecting the upper park with the lower waterside park.

By June of 1980 the contract was completed. This landmark project—envisioned for so many years by forward-thinking citizens, prompted by threats of loss of the views, begun as a serious project by the Rotary Club of Bellingham, supported by a slow-to-be-convinced city government, and built with the tax dollars voted by Bellingham's citizens—with generous support from the state—was a reality at last.

The women of YWCA Eco-Action had provided the initial effective spark in the long effort to create Boulevard Park. Full credit must be given their vision and foresight. Their role was recognized by the City in a certificate presented to them at the park dedication ceremonies on June 14, 1980.

"The City of Bellingham, Washington, in deep appreciation acknowledges the service and effective contribution of Eco-Action YWCA to the preservation of the land for public use at Boulevard Park."

Byron Elmendorf, Park Director, and Ken Hertz, Mayor

The dedication ceremony was held at the park and presided over by Mayor Ken Hertz whose early land purchases had been so crucial to the final success. One of the City Council members in attendance was Ann Rose, a leader of YWCA Eco-Action, whose group had started all of this eight long years before.

The picnic shelter built atop the old gas storage tank base.

At the ceremony, Mayor Hertz also presented a certificate of appreciation to Rotary in recognition of its pivotal role, for it was the Rotary Club of Bellingham that provided the muscle, and the influence, and the dedication to bring the Park to fruition over the long gestation period.

Rotary, wanting to leave a physical legacy on the park, donated $17,000 to construct the picnic and viewing shelter on top of the old gas works circular tank base. At the entrance to that shelter is a bronze plaque commemorating their involvement. As the brass band played, ending the ceremony, the community had their waterfront park at last.

Bronze plaque at picnic shelter honoring Rotary's role.

Chapter 3

The Park Grows

BOULEVARD PARK has been a work in progress from its beginning. The initial bond issue receipts and state grant funds were not adequate to build it out to its original design. The developed park at its dedication in the summer of 1980 stopped at the water's edge where the wooden boardwalk now begins. There were no funds to renovate the old trestle and convert it into the present wooden walkway. The trail along the sandstone prominence to Easton Beach remained an old railroad grade and there was no money to restore the steam turbine generator building that stood on its ancient saw mill site.

The most recent construction of the boardwalk connecting the original park to Taylor Avenue Dock and the renovation of the dock itself was not even contemplated at that time.

The community was delighted and satisfied with its new playground by the sea. The Boulevard Park of 1980 was a huge accomplishment for the city, but Byron Elmendorf and Ken Hertz wanted more. They were both energetic and forceful young men, new in their jobs and determined to complete the original vision. They worked at finding funds and help. They found a good measure of it in the Comprehensive Employment and Training Act (CETA), a U.S. government program designed to assist economically disadvantaged, unemployed, or underemployed persons. Enacted in 1973, CETA provided block grants to state and local governments to support public and private job training.

The Bellingham-based Northwest Youth Services organization applied for and received a CETA grant. They hired a young inexperienced work crew and two experienced union journeyman carpenters and committed them to the Park Department's Boulevard Park. The youthful 12-person crew had two goals—to convert the old railroad trestle to a walking bridge and to restore the concrete steam turbine mill building to a functional structure that would meet city building codes. Elmendorf and the Park Department were able to scrape up enough money to supply the materials and Elmendorf assigned John Ivary as project supervisor.

The wooden trestle walk, Pattle's Point and the steam turbine building at the far end.

The trestle came first. It was badly deteriorated, but it had been built for the tremendous weight of a laden railroad train and contained an excess of heavy timbers. Over the many years of its disuse people had scavenged many of its large beams and there were several major gaps in its span. Supervisor Ivary said that the bridge was built many times heavier than it would need to be to support the walkers and bicycle riders it was soon to carry. Landscape Architect Terry Gerrard was able to redesign it for the lesser load and salvage many of the excess beams, moving them to empty spots to fill the gaps in the structure. After several months the walking trestle and pathway were completed and the public could now walk to Easton Beach. The crew then turned its attention to the building.

The Whatcom Community College Pottery Studio

The Whatcom County Park Department had leased the steam turbine building to Whatcom Community College, which was using it for a pottery studio. When the Boulevard Park plan came together and the City committed to being the lead agency, the Park Department decided that they wanted to tear the building down. It had numerous building code violations and the cost of renovation to code exceeded what the City wanted to spend.

It was not going to be *that* easy. The artists and crafts people who used it, taught and learned there, were outraged at the thought of its destruction. The arts community, the Park Department and the community at large entered into a protracted and heated dispute over what to do with the pottery studio. The fiercely debated 'dustup' resulted in the coming together of the arts community to save the building and its crafts operation—and ultimately resulted in the formation of Allied Arts, still a major player in the art scene of Bellingham.

The pottery studio, originally the steam turbine building of the E.K. Wood Lumber Mill, now The Woods Coffee shop.

Eventually the artists prevailed and the City Council voted the funds to renovate the building. Elmendorf was directed to negotiate a new lease with Whatcom Community College, which at the time proudly proclaimed its policy of not having a campus, but of leasing all of their classroom space. The "College Without a Campus" continued in the building for many years, conducting pottery classes and earning the building's nickname 'the pottery studio'.

In 1980 when the work began, the building was in tough shape. Ivary related that to rectify the numerous code violations practically an entire new frame building was built within the concrete walls of the old structure. The building was re-roofed, and a loft with stairs leading to it was constructed. The restroom wing was constructed. An extension to the north was added. On June 1, 1981, a new lease with Whatcom Community College took effect at a monthly rental rate of $1,038.

At the date of this writing it has been announced that the city has leased the building to a coffee shop operator and I imagine that over the ensuing years its use as a pottery studio will be forgotten. One day it will be known as the coffee shop. In an ironic case of name similarity the new lessee of the old E.K. Wood building is The Woods Coffee shop. I am assured by its owners that they are no relation to the Wood of lumber mill fame. Hopefully, its historic origins—as a part of the old E.K. Wood mill at the site of William Pattle's homestead, and the Eldridge and Bartlett Mill—will be remembered and acknowledged as park visitors sip their coffee and watch sunsets over Bellingham Bay.

With the completion of the wooden walkway toward the south the park was provided with a pleasant and popular extension. The rejuvenated wooden trestle crossed the water to the small rock promontory which the railroad grade had cut through so long ago and made a perfect walking trail. The trail ended abruptly at Easton Beach, that delightful small sandy beach long enjoyed by Bellingham's southside kids, now a public property to be enjoyed by all.

Repair and maintenance are an ongoing difficulty for any park department. Boulevard Park was no exception; in 1990 vandals set fire to the timber walkway across the water. Firemen promptly brought it under control, but apparently a few hot spots were missed. During the night, after the fire department left, the flames rekindled and with the help of a brisk breeze did considerable damage to the old trestle. A major reconstruction was required; and while they were in the process of repairing the fire damage, the City replaced all of the old piling under the bridge. It had been showing serious deterioration.

Acquiring The Can Factory Site

Another park property that would wait many years for development was the large upland piece which fronts on 10th Street between the Chrysalis Hotel and the Riptide Condominium. This land originally held a large brick canned salmon warehouse. The warehouse and the land were sold to the Port of Bellingham by George Jeffers in 1965. The Port demolished the warehouse, and eventually transferred the land to the City of Bellingham in a land trade containing a proviso that the property would revert to the Port if it were not developed into a park by a certain date ten years hence.

The Park Department acted to preserve their rights the year before their deadline expired. This upland addition to Boulevard Park has now been improved with walking trails and benches at several view sites, thereby validating the original terms of the land transfer agreement from the Port of Bellingham.

The Boardwalk

The renovated Taylor Avenue Dock and its connecting Boardwalk are proving to be a most popular addition to Boulevard Park. No one knows exactly why and how this all steel and concrete structure began to be called the Boardwalk, but it appears that shall be its moniker from this day forward. Completed in 2006, the old bridge over the railroad track was repaired, extended a bit and then attached to a substantial

The site of the old can factory.

broad concrete walkway which approximately follows the original Bellingham Bay & Eastern (later Northern Pacific) railroad trestle right-of-way north to connect with the trail at Easton Beach.

The Taylor Avenue Dock will receive intense historic scrutiny in a later chapter. For the purpose of this chapter it need only be reported that the most recent addition to the park is the small overlook park complete with restroom at the foot of Taylor Avenue. The overlook park was completed in the summer of 2006. This little park which beckons the walker to enter the Taylor Avenue Dock, lies adjacent to the Reid Boiler Works property and north of the Fillmore Avenue right-of-way.

Boulevard Park now extends from Reid Boiler in the south to exactly where State street meets the Boulevard in the north a distance of 4,650 feet or almost nine-tenths of a mile. The 1969 dreams of those college student park proponents have surely been satisfied, as a person can now walk from Fairhaven Village Green along the bay trail to Taylor Avenue Dock, through Boulevard Park, back onto the Bay trail all the way to the downtown at Depot Market Square a distance of three-plus miles. Bellingham's trail system and commitment to parks and walkways has reached its finest proportions along Boulevard Park.

The Taylor Avenue Dock entrance park.

The boardwalk looking north. Easton Beach and the Riptide Condominiums are on the right.

The log train right-of-way.

Future Possibilities

There is a possibility that the park might one day add one last leg to its water walk with the construction of another boardwalk over the water. There is thought being given to building a walkway to the north, along the line of piling that marks the railroad trestle that used to support log trains which dumped logs into the booming grounds.

In the days of log booming, huge rafts of logs lined the entire shoreline from Boulevard Park, north to the site of the Bloedel Donovan Mill at the foot of Cornwall Avenue. The loaded log cars would stop at the appropriate place along the length of the trestle. The logs would be tipped into the water directly from the trestle to be graded and sorted, then placed in the massive booms to await their fate in the surrounding lumber mills.

That final connection could join Boulevard Park with public spaces in an adjacent dump/landfill and a renovated Georgia Pacific site. Should that connection ever be made, Bellingham will indeed have reclaimed its waterfront.

If history tells us anything it tells us that change is constant and ongoing. The remarkable and ceaseless changes that have occurred to the shoreline spanned by Boulevard Park since the arrival of European man illustrate that truth emphatically. The rest of this book will illustrate and recite those changes. I hope you will walk the pathways of Boulevard Park with book in hand, envisioning past structures and activities (both human and industrial) at the very place you stand. It is my desire that your knowledge of the past will fire your imagination and allow you to envision the future.

Port of Bellingham Records, Washington State Archives; Northwest Regional Archives, Bellingham.

Bellingham Boom Company log booms. Note the log truck dump located at the site of today's boat dock. Loaded railroad cars can be seen on the trestle waiting to dump their logs into the boom. The gas works sits above the log dump and the N.P. right-of-way that is now the South Bay Trail. Photo circa 1949.

The 1891 *Fairhaven Birdseye.*

Chapter 4

The Southside

THOSE OF US WHO WERE RAISED in Bellingham's most southerly neighborhood feel a special connection to that area broadly described as the "southside". The sense of nostalgic community that we share certainly rises from what we perceive as a unique and distinctive historic background rich in story and nuance. That special "southside" feeling becomes an intangible part of the history of the area. As I wrote and researched the story of the park I finally concluded that I must broaden my focus if I were to properly transmit to you, the reader, the true history of this part of Bellingham. This chapter will introduce you to some of the rich background and flavor of the southside even though little of it deals specifically with Boulevard Park. Perhaps it will contribute to your feel for southside history.

Much of the southside's mystique begins with Daniel Jefferson (Dirty Dan) Harris who arrived at the sheltered beach by the mouth of Padden Creek in 1853. He moved in with the tubercular John Thomas who, in that year, had filed a donation land claim on what was to become Fairhaven. After Thomas' demise in 1854, it was Harris who took up the land claim, who platted Fairhaven, and who named its main street and the waters of the inlet in front of the cabin after himself. Harris was a former seaman and he had a seaman's eye for good anchorage. The small bay at the foot of Harris Avenue was such an anchorage

Fairhaven's Boat Haven

The deep waters of Harris Bay, sheltered from the prevailing southerly winds and protected by the high land of Dead Man's Point, made the logical boat moorage area on Bellingham Bay, exceeded in protection only by the excellent anchorages of Chuckanut Bay to the south.

Port of Bellingham Records, Washington State Archives; Northwest Regional Archives, Bellingham.
Fairhaven's Boat Haven, circa 1940.

Harris Bay thus became the logical and natural place for the development of the canneries of Pacific American Fisheries and the Bellingham Canning Company, that same area now occupied by Fairhaven shipyards, the Alaska Ferry Terminal, and Arrowac Fisheries.

For the same reasons it was logical at a later date that the Port of Bellingham would build its small boat harbor there. In the bight of the bay, at the foot of Knox and Mill Avenues, a block or so south of Douglas, the Port built a simple boat harbor behind a protective seawall of wooden piling driven closely together into the sea bottom. The piles were needed to protect the marina from the occasional strong westerlies that every three or four years would roar across Bellingham Bay from the direction of the Nooksack River mouth, and from the winter northeasters howling down the Fraser River gorge and across Whatcom County from Sumas.

The good weather westerly winds were the greatest threat. Winds would build up on the straits of Georgia, whistling down from Canada, during clear and sunny days in the late summer. With the long fetch of the Straits of Georgia offering no resistance, great waves would pound at the beach at Sandy Point. The wind would rise over the low lands west of Ferndale and sweep across the seven miles of Bellingham Bay with real ferocity, surprising all who had been lulled into a sense of safety by being so nicely protected from the prevailing south winds. Severe westerly storms occur rarely, but when they do hit they wreak significant havoc and put unprepared boats up on the beach with astonishing force.

By the 1940s, the days of the southside's boat haven were numbered. Its piling breakwater was showing signs of deteriorating. The Slav fishermen who moored their seine boats there knew the next big westerly might fatally damage the rickety old protective wall. They were watchful on that September day in 1945. The day dawned clear and bright. A large high-pressure cell began to develop strong winds in the Georgia Strait between the British Columbia mainland and the high mountains of Vancouver Island. As the day warmed, the western winds built and soon waves were pounding on the beach at Sandy Point. The waves on Bellingham Bay had turned from their customary southerly course to a robust northwest, straight across the bay from the Lummi Reservation.

As the seas built in Bellingham Bay the word passed quickly among the Croatian owners of the twenty or more purse seiners moored behind the breakwater. As the old piling began to give way to the power of the storm, Martin Kuljis went to the moorage with his father and boarded their *New Moon* just as the breakwater gave way. In his words, "somehow we were able to get out, and get across the bay to the little harbor owned by Clift Marine near the mouth of Squalicum creek." Kuljis recalled that the larger seine boats were able to power out of the disintegrating marina and make it to the protection of the north shore. The quick action of the commercial fishermen undoubtedly saved their fishing fleet.

The smaller pleasure boats did not fare as well. Their owners were likely unaware of what was happening at the Boat Haven. At the peak of the winds, a large section of the pile breakwater collapsed from the force of waves and wind and chaos reigned.

Without the protection of the stout piles, boats were wrenched from their moorings and thrown violently up against the rock ballast of the railroad bed lining the shore. Many small pleasure boats were badly damaged. The storm marked the end of the Fairhaven Boat Haven. Boats were soon transferred to a makeshift boat harbor north of the present Port Ocean Terminal adjacent to pulp mill land, until Squalicum Harbor could be constructed.

The Croatian Community

At the beginning of the twentieth century times were difficult in Europe. The lands east of the Adriatic—then called Croatia, Slovenia, Serbia, and Bosnia—were all protectorates or outright possessions of the Hapsburg Dynasty's Austro-Hungarian empire. In Croatia, off the shoreline north of Dubrovnik, lies an island archipelago of great beauty. One of the islands, Vis, was the home of a hearty and hardworking race of fishermen mostly living in the fishing villages of Komisa and Vis. Times were hard on the island. The future for a young man was not apt to be easy or any different than all of those generations of his family before him. The ever-present threat of being conscripted into the armies of the empire further clouded his future.

It was the period of mass migrations from Europe to an expected brighter future in the new world. The fishermen of Vis were not immune to the hope of a better life and escape from service in the emperor's seemingly ceaseless wars.

A cannery in Brookfield, Oregon, a small town on the Columbia river, sought fishermen from the Adriatic Coast and advertised there. The advertising worked. It is thought that the first of the Slavs to immigrate to the west coast fishery were Nick Bozanich and Barto Fadich. The first Croatian to settle in Bellingham was probably Antone Glenovich who came in 1896. He found work in one of the numerous mills that lined the Bay. Like so many immigrants of that era, he wrote home to tell of the beauties and opportunities of this new land. Each year more and more Croatians came—finding employment during the summer in the fishing industry and in the lumber mills during the winter. These people were attracted by the waters and islands, apparently not unlike those of the Adriatic. Their letters home describing life and opportunities in this new land attracted others. Many of the young men returned to the old country to marry and promptly bring their brides back to Bellingham Bay, meanwhile having spread the word of its advantages to their friends and relatives back home.

Before very long a large area on 11th, 12th, and 13th streets spreading out behind the Taylor Avenue Dock was occupied mostly by people of Croatian descent. The Swedes and Norwegians of Happy Valley and the folks living above them on the South Hill called them Slavs. They called themselves Slavs, proud of their heritage.

The old 14th Street School, the predecessor to Lowell School, had a large number of students whose names ended with *ich*—names such as Evich, Zuanich, Elich, Zorodovich, Kostolanovich, Zankich, Radisich, Susulich, Brozovich, Kinkovich, Valich, Derpich, Vitalich, and strangely enough Kuljis. Historically Roman Catholics, they worshiped at the Sacred Heart Catholic Church at 14th and Knox Avenue and were proud to also call themselves *Southsiders*.

In the early years the men hired out to the canning companies as fishermen or salmon trap workers. They rowed or sailed the small fishing boats of the various canneries, beach seining along the coast at Cattle Point on San Juan Island, bringing their boats ashore for the night at the fish camp patched together on that long beach. In later years as boats became motorized and too large to beach, the fishermen returned through Cattle Pass each night to anchor in the protected inlet of Fish Creek just around the point.

In 1935 the diabolically efficient salmon traps were outlawed in Washington State as a salmon conservation measure. Purse seining became the most productive way of catching the huge migrations of silvery fish. The experienced Slavs were leaders in the new fishery with probably 90 percent of the several hundred purse seiners operating in Washington waters operated by Slavs. In Bellingham, Nick Pecaric, Andrew Martisich, Dick Kink (Kinkovich), Mote Evich, and Dominick Zuanich were among the first of the Slavs to own their own purse seiners. To this day some of the most successful fishers in Washington and Alaska are the fourth generation descendents of those first Slavic immigrants from Croatia and the island of Vis.

They have made their mark on their community in many ways. Kellie Kuljis Linville is a veteran Washington State Legislator from her home district. Peter Elich, the grandson of pioneer Slav groceryman Andro Martesich, is the recently retired Dean of Arts & Sciences at Western Washington University. And one of his sons, Matthew, is a district court judge in Whatcom County. Mitch Kink has long been a respected teacher in the Bellingham School District and was a long-time State Legislator. Peter Zuanich who played a large role in the creation of Boulevard Park was not only a highly respected leader in the fishing industry, but a long-time commissioner of the Port of Bellingham.

Easton Beach.

Easton Beach

In the old days—before the condominiums, before the boardwalk, before the gentrification of the area—there was one secluded and all-but-secret place where you could enjoy the waters of Bellingham Bay and do so in private. Tucked into a little corner between the railroad tracks, in the shadow of a large outcropping of sandstone, protected from the south winds by the large warehouses that spawned the tin rock, lay Easton Beach.

Above: Easton Beach recently.

Left: Generations of Southside kids carved their mark into the sandstone cliff behind Easton Beach. Here the class of 1954 is prominently memorialized.

For generations the Slav kids from the fishing families of Fairhaven claimed it for their own. Many of them have fond memories of warm summer evenings when they would head to the beach, change to their swimming suits behind the big rock on the west side of the beach, and enjoy the cool waters of the bay and the fine sand warmed by the sun and the heat radiating from the sandstone cliff. It is even said that from time to time as the sun went down, some of the boys would bring Mason jars filled with Zinfandel wine tapped from their fathers' wine barrels. A bonfire would be lit and the party would go on into the night.

Martin Kuljis, born in his aunt's home at 808 11th Street in 1927, recalls walking the path down the Easton Avenue right-of-way to the beach, past the garbage dump located where the Riptide Condominium now stands. The Croatian community taught its kids to swim in the waters of Easton Beach and many of them enjoyed family picnics there. Kuljis recalls that the water was none too clean. In the thirties before the age of sewer treatment plants, the city sewers simply drained into the bay. One of the South Hill sewers emptied a few hundred feet south of Easton Beach. Additionally, during the canning season the two large salmon canneries just across Harris Bay were dumping their offal directly into the water. Kuljis remarks that their less-than-clean swimming waters didn't seem to harm his generation. Most of them have continued to live long healthy lives.

Winemaking

Many of the Croatian immigrants, true to their cultural roots, made wine each year. In the earlier years, all who wanted to make wine would place their grape order with a selected cadre of Slav elders. When each winemaker had decided how many pounds of grapes he wanted in the fall and the money had been paid, two or three of the most trusted elders would be sent with the cash by train to the wine growing country of California. Their mission, and their responsibility, was to select and bargain for the best Zinfandel grapes they could find. When the selected grapes had ripened to the proper point they were picked and sent by rail to Bellingham.

In later years an Italian vegetable dealer would go up and down the streets of the Southside taking grape orders. In the fall, the big truck from California would drive the alleys behind 11th, 12th and 13th delivering the 25-pound boxes of grapes. The basements of the Southside would echo with the happy sounds of the crush, for almost every household made wine. Many Slavs had their own hand-cranked crushers and manual grape presses, but there was much sharing and convivial good times. Soon the crushed grapes were in the fermenting vats and the yeasty smell of fermenting grapes wafted along the alleys and byways of the lower South Hill. The fermented wine was pressed into big oak barrels and the Slav community eagerly waited for the maturing wine to be ready.

Each family made enough wine to last them through to the next grape harvest. Most of them had at least two large oak barrels in the basement. Some families had ordered as much as 100 25-pound boxes. A glass or two of wine was a part of the evening meal. I remember fondly my annual visits to several Slav families to review and renew their insurance. I quickly learned to make my visit at the end of the day, because I would always be offered a glass of wine as an act of hospitality. Sitting in the kitchen sipping a glass of Zinfandel with those friendly people was a nice way to end the day.

Times have changed. The unique and closely connected ethnic community of fishermen on the South Hill is essentially just a memory. There are still a few folks living along those streets whose last names end with *ich*, but nothing like the 1920s, '30s and

The Welsh Mansion at 17th Street and Taylor Avenue.

'40s when virtually every house for a three-by-six-block area was occupied by a Slavonian fisherman with ties to the island of Vis.

Times have changed for the beach as well. Easton Beach is now constantly exposed to public view by the hundreds who walk the boardwalk daily. It is unlikely that there will be any skinny dippers at the beach these days. The beach remains a charming and pleasant place to while away a sunny afternoon or even enjoy a dip in the cold waters of Bellingham Bay, but if you have a Mason jar in your pack filled with a tempting drink, remember—no alcohol in the public park.

The Great Toboggan Ride

Taylor Avenue itself was a bridge across the socio-economic gap in Bellingham in the early part of the 20th century. Recent Croatian immigrants who fished and worked in the mills lived at the lower end, the captains of industry lived at the top of the hill. Beginning at the dock and headed uphill you passed the 11th, 12th and 13th Street homes of the Croatian fishermen. Continuing slowly up the steep hill at 14th, 15th and 16th, you encountered an economic level that improved with each ascending street, until finally, at the very top of Taylor Avenue stood the imposing Tudor mansion of the Welsh family. Owners of canneries, possessors of the good life in the eyes of all us onlookers, the Robert Welshes were the second generation owners of the Bellingham Canning Company, which shared the Harris Bay waterfront with PAF. My family rented a smallish home on 17th street, just catty-corner from the Welsh mansion. We neighborhood children looked upon the opulence of their existence with envy and amazement.

Built in 1929 by Robert Welsh II and his handsome wife Jeanice, the Welsh home was widely admired and the Welshes appeared to be the very cream of society.

The Welsh home and possessions spoke of two generations of accumulating wealth garnered in the harvesting and processing of the silvery hordes of salmon that passed through their family canneries. Their five children—Bob, Barney, JoAnne, and the twins Bill and Barbara—possessed the best of toys and everything else, establishing them in our post-depression world as a different class from the rest of the kids in the neighborhood.

Proof of their status was evidenced each winter when the older Welsh boys, Bob and Barney, would appear at the first snowfall with their varnished toboggans. The rest of us had never seen toboggans before; only the Welshes had them: long, sleek,

hardwood rockets. The largest toboggan was an 'eight man' as I recall. Eight large teenagers could
climb aboard and launch themselves down a snowy hill with incredible speed and control. They
were the envy of the slopes.

Taylor Avenue has always
been the best sledding slope on the
South Hill. It is consistently steep,
each block down to 10th Street being about the same steepness with
good visibility at each cross street,
so that car watchers could safely
observe and stop cars for the sled-
ders. For generations of Southside
kids, Taylor has been the place to
be at the first snow fall.

Taylor Avenue hill looking westward down to the
dock.

One winter, in the late 1930s
or early '40s, there was a terrific
January snow storm. On a Friday
night the snow piled up on the streets to a depth of two feet, and Saturday morning
the South Hill streets blossomed with kids complete with mittens and mufflers, sleds
and skis and anything a person could possibly slide on.

Most of us in those days shared one family-owned steel-runnered sled. Some kids
used garbage can lids or scraps of oil cloth. Not the Welshes, they had store-bought
toboggans made of wood and incredibly fast. The eight seater was the exclusive vehicle
of Bob and Barney and their high-school-aged friends.

As cocky boys of that age will, one of them proposed that they load up the toboggan and take on the entire length of the hill—the entire seven blocks of the precipitous
Taylor Avenue chute from 17th to 10th. Actually another block could be squeezed in
by starting up the trail to what is now Highland Drive. It was then just a pathway entering the woods. The decision was made. The eight-seater was pulled up the trail a
block above 17th Street and eight bold teenagers squeezed themselves on. Eager push-
ers gave them a running start and the laden toboggan burst across 17th and lowered
its upswept nose to the hill. Faster and faster it went crossing 16th and 15th like a blur.
The fabled ride was on, the toboggan had reached maximum speed as it approached
14th and was still handling well going straight down the middle of Taylor.

Car watchers poised at the busy 14th Street intersection waved them on, not that the boys could have stopped by that time. Thirteenth and 12th Streets flashed by, but now they were concerned about the trolley running along its tracks on 11th (South State). As they rocketed over the tracks they were relieved to see the trolley still a half block toward town. They had avoided that peril, but now a new one loomed.

How would they stop their juggernaut? Their goal had been to reach 10th Street at the head of the Taylor Avenue Dock, but they were going so fast they could not turn or stop. And they were going too fast to roll off. Their rocketing toboggan was speeding directly toward the steep incline of the dock itself. Flashing across 10th, the toboggan perfectly centered on the opening to the dock, and now looming before them was the icy cold water of the bay.

Hooting and howling, the now frightened boys held to each other until the last second, and then in last chance desperation rolled off the speeding toboggan just as it reached the flat dock. They rolled and slid on the soft snow, stopping before the heavy toe-rail of the dock. But the now-unburdened toboggan had less luck. It smashed into the heavy timbered toe-rail, did a graceful flip in the air, and fell to the waiting waters of Harris Bay twenty feet below. The shattered toboggan slowly drifted out into the Bay as the excited and relieved boys started the long trudge back up the Taylor Avenue hill to tell their story and establish a neighborhood legend.

I had heard the toboggan story so many times, and I was so young when it happened, that I sometimes wondered if I was just telling an urban legend. I was very pleased when I learned that Bob Welsh still lives at this writing, at age 80, in Vancouver, B.C. His sister and my classmate, Barbara Welsh McCullom, called him to check on the story. To my great pleasure he confirmed it in every nuance.

Chapter 5

Unionville-
Bellingham-Fairhaven

To understand the history of the land spanned by Boulevard Park we must go back to the very beginning of the European settlement of Bellingham Bay. 1852 was the pivotal year. Trappers, the occasional timber cruiser, and certainly traders from the Hudson's Bay Company headquarters in Victoria had wandered the shores of this bay before that time.

Perhaps the first of them was the legendary "Blanket Bill" Jarman, who got his nickname from his experience of being a captive of the Nootka Indians and having been ransomed by the Hudson's Bay Company Factor, Governor Douglas, for a pile of blankets equal to his height. Blanket Bill may have visited the bay for the first time as early as 1848. Surely another of the very first was William Reed Pattle, an Englishman and sometime employee of the Hudson's Bay Company. Pattle was licensed by the Hudson's Bay Company to cut timber and also was a master mariner. He was cruising the area seeking replacement spars and masts for sailing ships waiting in San Francisco.

Hundreds of sailing ships were moored in the Bay City recovering from the trip around Cape Horn on the way to the booming gold fields east of San Francisco. Replacement masts and other rigging were badly needed and the tall straight trees of the Pacific Northwest were perfect for the purpose. Everyone was attempting to cash in on the incredible economic surge brought on by the California Gold Rush of 1849.

Pattle apparently had explored the economic opportunities to be found along the shores of Bellingham Bay. In 1852 he came across two adventurers in the pioneer town of Fort Townsend (deemed important as a military site before it became Port

Townsend). The two Americans, Henry Roeder and Russell V. Peabody, were looking for a site to build a saw mill, planning to ship lumber back to the ravenous San Francisco market.

Pattle revealed the location of a large stream rushing over a falls into the salt water of a bay (Bellingham), and he offered to guide the budding industrialists for the whopping fee of $1000, the equivalent of $26,780 in 2006 dollars. This astonishing sum persuaded Roeder, a penurious German immigrant, and his partner to hire a couple of Indians and their dugout canoe and search for that bay and its waterfall themselves. It is not recorded what they paid the two Indians on that fateful December 15, 1852, when they landed at Whatcom Creek, but you can be sure it was a great deal less than $1000.

Roeder and Peabody were to be the first white men to settle on the bay, building their mill on the east side of the creek where it spills into the salt water. They brought water from above the falls in a wooden flume to power the mill-wheel, which they had built at tide water. The two men became influential and essential founding fathers of the community that has evolved to be called Bellingham.

William Pattle knew of another economic opportunity to be found on Bellingham Bay. Coal! San Francisco needed coal and was willing to pay good prices for it. During his earlier explorations he had been told by the Indians of "black fire dirt," to be found along the shores of the Bay. It is thought that in October of 1852 he had visited the Bay on the Hudson's Bay Company steamer, *Beaver*, and had found a coal outcropping along the shore in a location described as near present-day Taylor and Bennett Avenues. Pattle shared this information with two friends and co-workers for the Hudson's Bay Company, James Morrison and John Thomas, and the three of them were quick to take advantage of a short-lived but generous act of the United States Federal Government.

The Donation Land Claims

In an effort to encourage settlement of the far reaches of the West—and perhaps to help in the U.S. and British dispute over ownership of the Oregon country—the United States Congress passed a unique law called the Oregon Land Bill. The new law provided that a single man could make claim to 160 acres of government land (twice that for a married couple), and after meeting requirements of building on it and living on it for a certain period of time the land would be his.

The Oregon Land Bill, commonly called the "Donation Land Bill," was enacted in 1850 and repealed in 1855, but in that five-year period all of the land around Bellingham Bay was taken up by the early settlers; and consequently, all of the present titles to land around the Bay rest upon those early donation claims.

My research findings, among the very earliest records in the Washington State Regional Archives at WWU, make it clear that Pattle, Morrison & Thomas were not settlers in the usual sense, but opportunists hoping to make a quick dollar in the donation land claim game. Four early documents tell the story. First there are the three Donation Land claims made by the men. Pattle's is dated first, April 1, 1853 and he claimed 320 acres for himself and his wife. The property is described as "commencing at a blazed cedar tree on Mineral Point being on the east side of Bellingham's Bay, running thence in a northerly direction one mile, thence east one half mile, thence south one mile, thence west one half mile to the place of beginning". Little is known about Anna Pattle's claim. She apparently gave it up, as the land she claimed was finally claimed by C.C. Vail. Perhaps she died, or the Pattles divorced. After the initial claim was made in 1853 the record holds no further mention of Anna Pattle, and Pattle's claim was reduced to 160 acres.

Morrison and Thomas dated their claims the next day, April 2, and each of them claimed 160 acres. Morrison's document includes: "this claim is made in virtue of settlement thereon on or about the 1st of December 1852". This date would make Morrison the first settler on the shores of Bellingham Bay, beating Roeder and Peabody by a full ten days.

The three speculators filed their claims on the same day in Coveland, on Whidbey Island, the county seat of Island County. The claims were all recorded on April 18, 1853.

The Oregon Territorial legislature established Island County in 1853. At the time Island County included the future Island, San Juan, Whatcom, Skagit, and Snohomish counties. Coveland, a tiny settlement at the very end of Penn's Cove, Whidbey Island, was designated the county seat. The first commissioners' meeting was held there on April 4, 1853. It was not until ten years later that the county seat was moved to Coupeville.

Just a week previously, April 11, 1853, the three men had been in Olympia where they had penned a deal with F. Rogers Loomis, a San Francisco agent for a group of coal speculators that called themselves the Puget Sound Coal Association. They had negotiated and signed a lease of the mineral rights to all of their described lands for the princely sum of $75 per month each until such time as their government land patents (deeds) were received under the Donation Land Act. Upon receiving the patents, each of the partners was to receive $2,500, (in today's dollars the equivalent of $66,275). Even the $75 per month was today's equivalent of $1,950, not a bad deal for a trio of roughnecks. The catch to the whole thing was that they got nothing until they had shipped 100 bags of coal to the office in San Francisco and the coal was judged acceptable. If it was not acceptable the lease would become void.

I have included the text of the lease as Appendix #2. It makes interesting reading

Border marker. Bellingham,
Fairhaven/Sehome.

and leaves the strong impression that Pattle, Morrison and Thomas had little interest in mining or settling, but just wanted to stay long enough to get their government patents, cash in, and move on.

The documents prove another interesting point, that these early donation land claimers were able to lease and sell their land in the pre-patent period. In a very real sense they did not yet own the land, but they dealt in pre-patent rights, sometimes posting bond to guarantee their performance once they did receive the patents. (See the wording of a bond given by Pattle to guarantee a deal with Reuben L. Doyle in 1855, shown as Appendix #3.)

Apparently seeking to bracket all the coal possibilities along the southeastern shore of the Bay, the three men filed adjoining claims.

Pattle's claim of 158.20 acres was the farthest north. It began at what became the southern border of Sehome and is now marked by a double granite memorial marker on the Bay Trail. His claim then proceeds to the south, ending at a line which bisects the concrete pottery studio building, on the point of land that became known as Pattle's Point, but was first called Mineral Point.

William Morrison's claim of 165.18 acres adjoined him at that point and ran south to the center line of what is now Douglas Avenue. The twin granite marker there denotes the original north border of Fairhaven, and is the exact spot where Morrison's claim ended and John Thomas' began. Thomas' claim ran south to Cowgill Avenue, four blocks south of today's Harris Avenue, where the property of Fairhaven Middle school begins.

In a historical side-note, we must point out that Thomas built himself a crude shack behind the beach of the protected bay on his claim, and soon welcomed another pioneer who rowed in from Victoria, Daniel Jefferson (Dirty Dan) Harris. Harris moved in with Thomas in 1853 and may have helped him build the cabin. Unfortunately Thomas died in May 1854, a victim of tuberculosis. Thomas was buried on his claim, the first recorded white man to die on Bellingham Bay. Harris was able to buy Thomas' donation land claim from Thomas' heir (a brother). Harris (who earned his nickname "Dirty Dan", because of his unsavory personal hygiene) eventually founded and platted Fairhaven, naming its main street Harris Avenue, and the bay in front of the shack, Harris Bay.

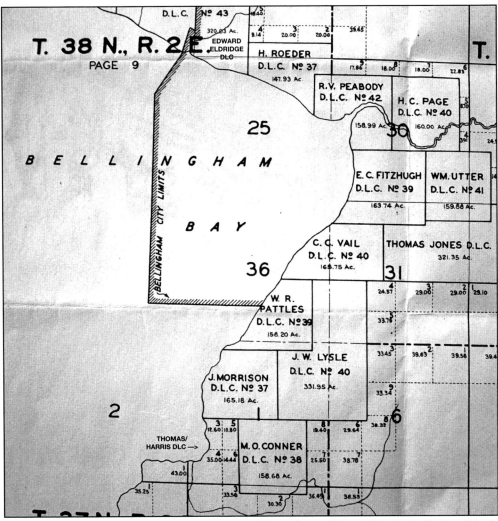

Donation Land Claim map.

Jeffcott Collection, Center for Northwest Studies, Western Washington University.

At Thomas' death his friend Morrison gave an affidavit testifying to his end. Percival R. Jeffcott in his book, *Blanket Bill Jarman*, quotes that affidavit:

"In January 1853 he had a claim which he occupied and on which he erected a dwelling and built a cooperage. He died in 1855. He sickened and died and was buried on said claim where his grave now is."

Pattle was also subpoenaed, but the sheriff reported that "he had left for parts unknown". Jeffcott goes on to confirm that: "Thomas died of tuberculosis and Harris helped him build his cabin and succeeded to his claim in 1861."

There is no explanation of the conflicting years of his death; however, most historians believe it to have occurred in 1854, not 1855.

Early Coal Mining

The most promising coal opportunity was found on Morrison's claim where Pattle had first seen the outcropping. There, close to the shoreline, above the bluff between present day Taylor Avenue and Bennett Avenue, they found a vein that seemed worth serious effort.

The lease, which Loomis had quickly assigned to the Puget Sound Coal Mining Association, was just the first of a host of deals that were to be made for the coal that was found on Morrison's claim. Almost immediately, Dec. 8, 1853, one of the Association owners, John A. Peck of San Francisco, sold his 2/15ths share of the Associations stock to James H. Ray, another San Franciscan for $7,000. The next year, on Feb. 17, 1854, Ray sold that same stock to an O.B. Merrill, perhaps having learned that the quality of the Bellingham Bay coal was not very good. He took a substantial loss selling it for $3,000.

The Association apparently started a mining operation on the Morrison claim. It is thought that they built a warehouse and other buildings and dug a shaft, removing some tonnage of coal before ceasing operations. Perhaps they finally tested the coal and found it wanting, thereby voiding their lease with Morrison, Pattle and Thomas. For whatever reason the deed record has no further mention of the Association nor of the property until March 1, 1861, when James Morrison sold his entire claim (land, mineral rights and all) to Seth N. Doty for a mere $3,000. Morrison may have been discouraged by its prospects, but Doty and his friend Charles E. Richards were not.

Further evidence that the Association lease had been voided is found in the activities of William Reed Pattle. On the tenth of June, 1855 he gives 1/16th of the coal mining rights on his claim to a James Houston in return for "labour done by him for me".

Then on December 15, 1855, Pattle binds himself in the amount of $5,000, in a bond, to Reuben L. Doyle of San Francisco, guaranteeing to deliver to Doyle upon receiving his patent deed from the USA, an undivided 1/4 interest in the coal mining rights to his donation land claim. The bond specified the mining rights to the northerly 1/4 of the claim with equal frontage on the east and west sides.

Next, on June 21, 1856, Pattle sold one half of his donation claim, to Kenneth McLea of San Francisco for $2,000. The next year he gave McLea his power of attorney to sell his remaining half of the claim.

On May 1, 1860, McLea succeeded in selling the entire 160 acre land claim to another San Franciscan, Robert Simson and his wife Jeanette for $10,000. Strangely enough, the deal was signed at Saint Johns, Newfoundland.

Pattle had made his claim in 1853, presumably received a little monthly rent from the Coal Mining Association, sold mining rights to Reuben Doyle for $5,000, traded mining rights for labor, and finally received a total of $7,000 for his claim from McLea and Simson. His patent deed was not delivered from the U.S. Government until 1870. Erastus Bartlett bought the Pattle donation claim in that year for $2,000 in gold. A final transaction saw Bartlett paying Robert Simson $3,500 to clear his title to the land on August 3, 1893.

Eldridge & Bartlett

Edward Eldridge had come to Bellingham Bay because he was a friend of Henry Roeder. They had met when Roeder was captaining a commercial ship on Lake Erie and Eldridge had served under him as second mate. Eldridge was born in Saint Andrews, Scotland, on December 7, 1829. He was an orphan raised by his grandparents. Always adventurous, he ran away to sea at age eleven. There was an unconfirmed story that Eldridge was not his real name at all.

The story goes that the youthful runaway was trying to get on the crew of an English ship. At ship's muster a previously signed-on cabin boy named Eldridge failed to show up. When his name was called, our runaway orphan answered to the Eldridge name with an, "aye Sir", was signed on, and he used that name for the rest of his life. Whatever the truth of the story, Edward Eldridge was at sea for 12 years and rose to become a licensed navigator. He made his first trip to America in 1846 where he came inland to work as a sailor on the Great Lakes. There he met Captain Henry Roeder.

Eldridge sailed with Roeder on Lake Erie for a time, but he soon went back to salt water. October of 1849 found his ship, the *Tonquin*, putting into San Francisco at the beginning of the gold rush. Gold fever took control and Eldridge signed off of the ship to try his luck in the gold fields.

Whatcom Museum of History & Art
Edward Eldridge

By 1851 he had met and married Teresa Lappin and their first child had been born. In a great coincidence Eldridge had run into Roeder briefly in Sacramento during their time in gold country. The California gold fields had not panned out for either of them. Eldridge determined to try mining again, this time in Australia. He and his wife and baby were waiting for a ship in San Francisco that would take them to Australia, when once again he ran into Captain Roeder. Henry Roeder by that time had found Bellingham Bay. He was in San Francisco buying supplies for his new lumber mill on Whatcom Creek.

Roeder convinced Eldridge of the great opportunities that awaited him and his family on Bellingham Bay and succeeded in hiring Eldridge to come north and help with the new mill. They immediately sailed north. Teresa Lappin Eldridge became the first white woman to settle on Bellingham Bay.

The Eldridges were to have a profound influence on the towns that would rise on the shores of their pioneer outpost. Together they took out a 320-acre donation land claim on the north side of the Bay, west of Whatcom creek. Their land fronted on the bluff on what is now Eldridge Avenue. Eldridge was a classic entrepreneur, a man of energy and vision, but like most of the pioneers on the Bay, very short of cash. He needed a financial backer for his many ambitions and ideas and he found one in Erastus Bartlett of Augusta, Maine, later San Francisco. Eldridge and Bartlett were to be partners in many enterprises on the bay. Their story is vital to our history of Boulevard Park.

Very little is known about Erastus Bartlett, the man. I have been able to find neither a photograph of him, nor any description of his appearance or personality. We do know, from numerous citations in the title company records and the Whatcom County deed records, that he was a major financial influence on Bellingham Bay from at least 1866 to his death in 1902, and even beyond. The 1860 U.S. census finds him living in Augusta (the capital of Maine) with his wife Helen L. Bartlett (age 36), and two children, Augustus L. (age 18) and Anna M. (age 15). Also in the household are listed two female servants and two six-year-old girls, not related. He was apparently a person of means even then, as his home's value is listed at $10,000 and his personal possessions at $5,000—large sums when compared to the economic listings for others on the census documents.

I could not find him in the 1870 census, but he turns up again in the 1880 census as a single man living as a lodger on Hayes Street in San Francisco. His occupation is listed as "capitalist" and his place of birth, Maine.

We know that he was living in Boston, Massachusetts in the early 1870s, as he uses that as his address in a Whatcom County deed dated April 4, 1870, and again on October 25, 1871. He skips mention in the 1890 census, but we find him again in 1900 at age 89 living in the home of his cousin Richard B. Ayer on 6th Avenue in Oakland, CA. Ayer lived in the house with his mother Caroline and his stepfather Converse J. Garland, and his elderly cousin Erastus Bartlett. Of interest is the fact that Garland will come into our story again as the man contracted by Eldridge and Bartlett to construct and operate their Bellingham Bay Mill at Pattle's Point in 1884 (see page 138).

Bartlett also had significant real estate interests in San Diego, buying in 1890 a large tract of land that would become one of downtown San Diego's first suburbs, South Park. Smyth's *History of San Diego*, published in 1906, records that Bartlett

"…had purchased the land from W.H. Curtis and E.A. Chamberlin. That he had arrived from Augusta Maine, via the Cape of Good Hope, landing in the San Francisco area in 1850. Already wealthy, he proceeded to make another fortune in the shipping industry. He began purchasing land in the San Diego area in the 1860s. He convinced his daughter Anna and her husband and family to move to San Diego, where the family was to become important in the development of that city."

Bartlett died on July 24, 1902, at the age of 91. He left an estate valued by the probate court at $530,000 (*Fairhaven Times*, Nov. 7, 1903), $289,000 of it in Whatcom County investments. (Expressed in 2006 dollars, Bartlett's estate was worth $12,526,140 at his death, $6,830,290 of it in Whatcom County investments.)

His will, a copy of which is in the Washington Regional Archives at WWU, stipulates generous bequests to his daughter and his four grandchildren, the widow of his deceased son Augustus, lesser amounts to several relatives, and the remainder to be divided equally among his daughter and four grandchildren. This remainder would have totaled approximately $490,000 ($11,580,770 in 2006 purchasing power). The survivors apparently agreed to keep the assets intact and working, as they used them to capitalize the Bartlett Estate Company.

Grandson E. Bartlett Webster became the President of that company. For at least a year Webster lived in Bellingham, managing the company's assets in Whatcom County. The 1906 city directory shows him living at the S.W. corner of North Forest and Pine Street. Returning to San Diego, Webster guided the Bartlett Estate Company in its development of the South Park suburb and the development of a streetcar company. While we do not have a photo of his grandfather, we do have this photo of E. Bartlett Webster.

E. Bartlett Webster, President of the Bartlett Estate Co. and of the South Park and East Side Railway Co.

The partnership of Eldridge and Bartlett ultimately purchased the donation land claims of both James Morrison and William Pattle, consequently owning the entire stretch of waterfront that we now know as Boulevard Park. Their lands stretched from the center of Douglas Avenue to the south, to the Sehome border about where State Street comes down the hill to meet the Boulevard; and they were to strongly influence what was to happen on this key stretch of waterfront.

Unionville

The Morrison land that began at the center line of what would become Douglas Avenue and extended north to Pattle's Point was to change names several times, successively to be called Unionville, Bellingham, Fairhaven, and finally Bellingham again. Unionville got its name from the cluster of small buildings that sprang up around the Pattle coal mine, which for a brief time was to be called the Union Coal Mine.

Lelah Jackson Edson in her excellent book, *The Fourth Corner*, tells the story of Charles E.R. Richards, whose enterprise founded Unionville. It was he who in 1858 built the first brick building in Washington Territory at the corner of Astor and E streets. Richards, operating as T.J. Richards & Company, built his two-story structure of bricks that had been made in Philadelphia and shipped around Cape Horn. The bricks had been off-loaded in San Francisco, where Richards trans-shipped them north along with iron, glass, hardware, groceries and clothing—stock for the store that he was to open. The Fraser River gold rush had begun and the red brick building on the beach at Whatcom creek was sure to be a success selling supplies to the miners.

Unfortunately for Richards, Governor Douglas in Victoria wanted the business from the miners in his city, and enacted rules making entry to the Canadian gold fields from Bellingham Bay inconvenient. He simply decreed that a mining license had to be purchased in Victoria. The stampeding gold seekers camping on the beach near Richards' store soon disappeared and thereafter entered the gold fields thru Victoria. Richards and his partner John Hyatt persevered selling groceries and provisions to the locals, they advertised warehouse space, and survived there until May 7, 1863, when they sold the building to Whatcom County to be used as its first courthouse. The building had cost $8000 to build and the failed merchants sold it for $2000, payable in county warrants (which they then sold to a William Moody at a great discount).

The old building was used as a court house, a jail, a newspaper office and a drug store, all at the same time. A January 4, 1889, article in the *Bellingham Bay Reveille* reports more dramatic uses:

> "The court house in Whatcom was the first brick building erected in Washington Territory. It was 25 x 40 feet, two stories high, plastered, had iron shutters, a tin roof, and was built in 1858. It was a very fortunate thing for the early settlers that this building was constructed of brick, and that iron shutters were put over the window exteriors. During an Indian outbreak in 1862, the handful of people sought refuge in this building, and the savages made a fierce onslaught during which bullets drummed against the walls, and one ball penetrated an iron door shutter. Several persons were killed in front of the door."

The building was to have many subsequent uses. In 1903 the County Commissioners sold it to The Woman's Relief Corps to be used as a lodge hall by that organization, and the Grand Army of the Republic (GAR), a Civil War veterans organization.

In later years, Carl Akers operated his taxidermy business in the building. Akers has recently given the historic old building to the Whatcom Historical Society which is currently planning a restoration.

Storekeeper Turned Miner

Richards decided to try coal mining in the hope of recouping his losses. The Sehome coal mine, just a mile north up the bay, was reported to have made $300,000 in 1860, its first year of operation. Richards was confident that the old Pattle mine had not been properly tested. He assumed the mine near present-day Taylor Avenue would do as well as the Sehome mine, and he determined to buy it. Edson reports that he wanted to remain unknown in the negotiations so, "He engaged Seth N. Doty to make the deal." Morrison sold the land and mineral rights to Doty for $3000 on March 1, 1861, and according to county records, Doty the next day conveyed a 3/4 interest in the land to Richards for $3,750. It would appear that Richards may not have been so skillful as a businessman.

In a curious turn of events, on the following day, March 3, 1861, Doty, for the sum of one dollar, conveyed back to James Morrison one square acre in the "extreme S.W. corner" of the claim. Perhaps James Morrison's cabin was located on that one acre on the beach and the conveyance was an act of kindness by Doty; or, perhaps, the occupancy requirements of the Donation Land Act, required Morrison's presence and his continued working of the land to validate the claim. The U.S. patent deed to the claim was not to be awarded until June 16, 1866. Doty may have been simply protecting his interests. Whatever the real reason, this acre of land where Reid Boiler Works now stands was to remain in the ownership of Morrison or his estate until April 18, 1888.

The Union Coal Company was immediately organized with Richards as president. Edson reports that, "The sum of $40,000 was raised by the company and expended in opening the mine and in constructing wharf, storehouse and other buildings.".

A small community to be called Unionville came into being adjacent to the coal mine. Speculation was rampant among its organizers. Almost immediately, on March 13, Richards sold an undivided 1/4 interest in the claim for $1,000 to Alexander H. Bailey of San Francisco. A month later Doty sold a 1/3 interest in his 1/4 interest to a David Leach for $2,000, and finally in June of 1861, Leach bought the remainder of Doty's interest for another $3,000. In August Richards sold another undivided 1/4 to Alexander Bailey for $1,000.

The next February, in 1862, Alexander H. Bailey sold his 1/4 interest back to

Richards for $10,000, mine prospects must have been looking up temporarily. Seth Doty, however had given up and moved to California. He finally sold the last of his original 1/4 interest to Richards on December 11, 1855. The price was a mere $500.

Edson remarks in *The Fourth Corner*, "The Union Coal Company mine was opened by a 100 foot shaft (probably an incline), the vein worked was but two feet thick; also thicker beds occurred on the claim. 2500 tons of coal were mined and shipped to San Francisco and then the mine was closed."

The mining adventure had clearly been a failure, but C.E. Richards and a new partner James S. Doyle of San Francisco were able to bail out. On Dec. 16, 1865, they were to sell the entire Morrison claim, mine, works and all to a Robert Vance of NewYork for $10,000.

In August of 1866, Erastus Bartlett appears on the scene. He was interested in the land and not the coal. He bought from Vance half of nine-tenths of the Morrison Donation claim for $5,000.

Neither Unionville, nor the Union Coal Company, had a long or successful run. The mine had closed after a disappointingly short life. Unionville and its few buildings were then entirely destroyed in the devastating forest fire of 1868. The diary of Sheriff James Kavanaugh has this entry.

> "September 23, 1868, I find Unionville coal works, houses, etc., all laid in ashes, Whatcom and Sehome were saved by force of numbers and great exertion. The whole country is afire, such a continuation of dense fogs the oldest inhabitants had not seen before."

Erastus Bartlett was not discouraged by the fire. He was interested in the real estate and the fire had not damaged the land. On October 25, 1871, he paid Robert Vance $1,000 for the remainder of his interest. Now Bartlett had the entire claim, except for the one square acre at the extreme S.W. corner of the claim which still belonged to Morrison.

Bartlett had staying power. In 1875 Morrison failed to pay the county property tax, in 1888 the county sold the one acre in a sheriff's sale. Bartlett bought the acre for the delinquent taxes and costs totaling three dollars. He had consolidated the entire Morrison donation land claim, paying a total of $6,003 for it. He would later deed 1/4 of it to his partner Edward Eldridge, and together they would eventually profit handsomely from Morrison's old claim.

Now both the Pattle and Morrison donation claims were owned by those two entrepreuners, Edward Eldridge and his Maine-born partner, W. Erastus Bartlett. The pair would continue to accumulate land. They bought the Maurice O'Conner donation claim which bordered Dan Harris' land on its eastern edge. One series of 14 deeds found in a Whatcom County Book of Deeds in the Regional Archives catalogs a series of US patents wherein the partners bought 4,798 acres of land in the year in the year 1889 alone.

The Unionville land lay fallow for years after the fire. Apparently the mine entrance was filled with rubble and eventually forgotten. Unionville was but a ghostly memory. The land and the memory of the village were essentially forgotten there in the midland between Sehome and Fairhaven.

A few homes had been built on lots sold by the partners Eldridge and Bartlett. There was an exciting flurry of optimism in 1871 when it appeared that the Northern Pacific Railroad was going to bring its line to salt water on Bellingham Bay, but a world-wide economic panic caused by the onset of the Franco-Prussian war stymied the railroad's plans.

In 1871 or 1872 the Bellingham Hotel was built in anticipation of the Northern Pacific coming. The hotel was built on the corner of Front Street and Broadway, streets that are now named 10th Street and Bennett Avenue.

We are not sure who built the hotel, but it is established that it was eventually owned by Erastus Bartlett. The Bellingham Hotel was the center of social life in the Fairhaven area for a period. An indication of this is found in a few entries from a now-lost guest register of the old hotel that was published in a *Bellingham Herald* article of 1906.

> "Friday, December 26, the height of the holiday season is now on. A grand dance was given in the parlors last evening. Many of the guests arrived at the docks early, on the steamer *Monroe*, Captain Brownfull."
> "Monday, February 9, 1885. Bark *Columbia* arrived today for lumber, twenty-four days out from San Francisco, Sailed on the 26th."
> "November 22, 1888. J.J. Donovan arrived from Tacoma."
> "September 22, 1888. E. Bartlett, owner of the building, registered today, San Francisco."

The fate of the Bellingham Hotel was sealed with the coming of the Fairhaven boom in 1890. Business activity moved south a few blocks making the Harris Avenue axis the place to be and leaving the old hotel six blocks to the north far out on the edge of the action. The small wooden Bellingham Hotel paled to insignificance beside the glory of the huge brick and stone Fairhaven Hotel. Soon after the turn of the century the old hotel was empty and in serious decay. It was demolished in about 1912. The site is presently occupied by the modern Bay Shore Arms Condominium.

Galen Biery Papers and Photographs #1412, Center for Pacific Northwest Studies, Western Washington University.

The Bellingham Hotel, built in anticipation of the arrival of the Northern Pacific Railway in 1871.

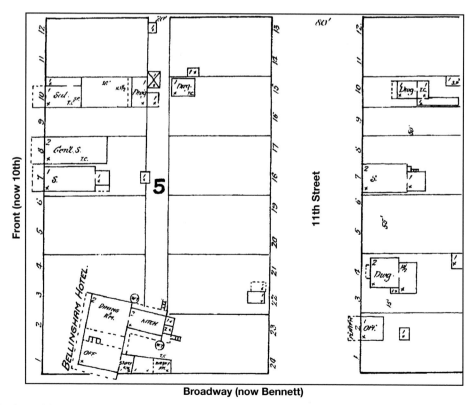

Sanborn Map of 1890 showing the Bellingham Hotel sitting askew on the lot. The hotel was built before the land was platted.

Bay Shore Arms, built on the site of the old Bellingham Hotel.

Thomas E. Monahan

In an historical side-note, a review of the Sanborn Map of 1890 establishes that across the street from the Bellingham Hotel, on the southeast corner of what was then Front and Broadway, was the saloon of Thomas E. Monahan. Monahan was a well-liked leader of the Harris Bay communities and was re-elected year after year as a Fairhaven city councilman. As Fairhaven boomed in the early 1890s, Monahan moved his business to the heart of the "Imperial City", building a new saloon in the center of the block on 11th Street,

The Monahan Building, 2006.

that he advertised as The Turf saloon. Those who remember the old movie house, The Picture Show, or shop at Fairhaven Runners on 11th street in Fairhaven, will know well the Monahan Building, which Monahan built in 1890. He proudly had his name cut in stone at the peak of the building front and it is still there announcing the Monahan Building to all who pass by.

The Monahan family lived on the second floor above the saloon. The building survives as one of Fairhaven's classic boom period originals.

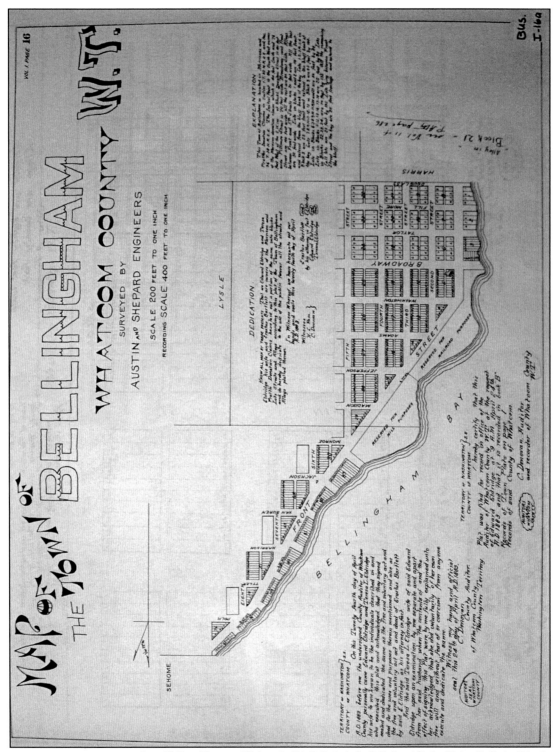

The Plat of Bellingham, 1883. Austin and Shepard were the surveyors of the town of Bellingham, for which a plat was filed for record on April 24, 1883.

Bellingham Platted

With the area beginning to show some signs of life it must have appeared to Eldridge and Bartlett that it was time to create their own town. On the 24th day of April 1883, Edward Eldridge and his wife Teresa, acting for themselves and as Attorney in Fact for Erastus Bartlett, their partner, platted the little town of Bellingham on a portion of their land. In the plat document they state that they are the owners of the Morrison and Pattle donation claims. Lots were laid out along what they called Front Street, but would be later called 10th Street. The plat provides for the land at and around Pattle's Point to be reserved for "Mill Purposes," while the waterfront just to the south was reserved for "Railroad Purposes".

It is interesting to note that the shoreline both to the north and south of these two large pieces of industrial reserve are platted with small narrow lots typical of dwelling lots. Perhaps Eldridge and Bartlett were enlightened urban planners before their time and planned for residences along the water, but I rather doubt that. It was simply not the planning style of the time. Note that all of the streets with the exception of Douglas, Fillmore, Taylor, and Adams were renamed at a later date. It is also interesting to note that the plat did not lay out lots very far up the hill. Starting at the water it went up hill only to what is now 14th Street.

Fairhaven Land Company Buys Bellingham

The new town progressed slowly, A few lots were sold and a few houses built. Eldridge and Bartlett built a lumber mill to give Bellingham an industrial economic base. The mill had problems of its own. The Fairhaven land boom, when it came, must have looked like a windfall for Bellingham's owners. Railroad millionaire Nelson Bennett came to town in 1888, intent on cashing in on the expected arrival of the Northern Pacific Railroad to Bellingham Bay.

Later in the year, Nov. 26, 1888, Bennett and E.M. Wilson, E.L. Cowgill, Charles X. Larrabee, and Samuel Larrabee incorporated the Fairhaven Land Company with capital of $250,000. Their plan required land, lots of land.

First they bought Fairhaven from Dan Harris; actually, Bennett and Larrabee as individuals bought out Dan for $75,000, and then sold Fairhaven to their Fairhaven Land Company for $205,000, presumably making a quick personal profit of $130,000, an incredible fortune in 1888.

Then, on May 12, 1890, they joined forces with two other prominent land-owners by incorporating the Bellingham Bay Land Company. The new company was capitalized at one million dollars. The signatures on the articles of incorporation tell the story. The incorporators were Edward Eldridge, Erastus Bartlett and Nelson Bennett.

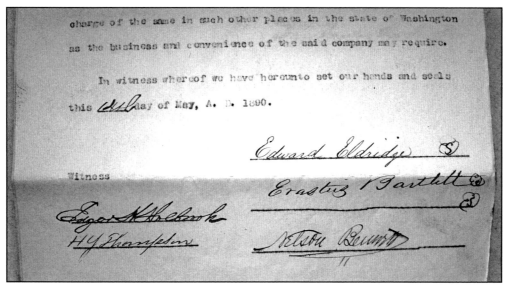

A photo of the incorporation document of Bellingham Bay Land Company showing signatures of the three land moguls of Bellingham and Fairhaven—Eldridge, Bartlett and Bennett.

The other stockholders were those stalwarts of the Fairhaven Land Company, E.L. Cowgill, E.M. Wilson and C.X. Larrabee.

On May 16, 1890, Eldridge and Bartlett sold their Bellingham and Fairhaven holdings to the Bellingham Bay Land Company. The sale included their unsold Bellingham lots, and unplatted land totalling some 2000 acres. The price was the incredible sum of one million dollars, presumably much of it taken as shares in the new

C.X. Larrabee

Edward Merton Wilson

company. This land included all of the Morrison and Pattle donation land claims, as well as the Maurice O'Conner donation claim, which adjoined the eastern edge of the Thomas/Harris claim in Happy Valley. The sale did not include Bellingham's land along the waterfront, platted as the "Railroad Reserve". That was sold to the Fairhaven Land Company in a separate May 16, 1890, sale for one dollar, apparently a part of the negotiation between the parties. The sale also did not include the "Mill Reserve", containing the Bellingham Mill Company.

An undivided one half of the Mill Reserve and the mill itself had been sold to the Fairhaven Land Company a few weeks earlier, on April 5, 1890, for $40,000. Eldridge, Bartlett and their new partner, The Fairhaven Land Company, would sell that land and mill to the E.K. Wood Lumber Company ten years later.

One million dollars in 1890 was the equivalent in purchasing power of 26 million 2006 dollars. Dan Harris, hearing about the sale, must have felt he got short shrift—having sold Fairhaven two years before to Bennett and Larrabee for a total of a mere $75,000.

Bennett, the Fairhaven Land Company, and the Bellingham Bay Land Company soon merged Bellingham into Fairhaven, extending that booming city's borders all the way to Sehome.

Presumably Eldridge and Bartlett's financial problems were eliminated with the sale and they were ready for other adventures. Sehome and Whatcom soon merged, and eventually in 1903 the two surviving entities, Whatcom and Fairhaven joined to become modern Bellingham.

Most of the land between the predecessor towns gradually filled with homes and commercial buildings until it was almost impossible to recognize that they had once been separate political subdivisions. Today, the only remaining physical evidence of Douglas Avenue being the border between Fairhaven and Old Bellingham is found in the fact that along that old border some of the streets meet with an awkward jog. 11th, 12th and 13th Streets at Douglas take an odd jog to the west in order to meet their northern counterparts. The streets have to jog because the two pioneer towns failed to lay out their streets to meet.

The street connections on the north side of present day Bellingham on the historic borders of Whatcom and Sehome are similarly misaligned making modern Bellingham notorious for strange street layouts, all a legacy of our ancient history of platting four separate towns around the Bay and connecting them years later.

The Widow Richards

The 1890 boom brought a visitation from the ghost of C.A. Richards, in the form of his widow Henrietta, who appeared in 1890, the year of his death, to claim her rights.

The *Fairhaven Reveille*, in September of 1890, reported under the title "That Lawsuit," the following.

> "It is said that Mrs. Henrietta C. Richards claims a dower right in Morrison donation claim, which includes the townsite of Bellingham (which is now part of Fairhaven). Bellingham Bay Land Company's first addition to Fairhaven, Bellingham mill tract and railroad reserve. It covers about 1,200 lots. Richards purchased the tract while here about 1860. At the time he was a member of the firm of Richards & Hyatt. He afterwards went east and was married to a young wife by the Rev. Dr. Newell, of New York City. Mr. Richards died in May, 1889. Mrs. Richards is now 47 years of age. Mrs. Richards did not join her husband in the deed when the property was sold, and has never disposed of her interest. Harris, Black & Leaming, her attorneys, are now serving notices on the different parties in possession, and will shortly commence proceedings in the United States court for Washington to have Mrs. Richards' interest set off to her filing a *lis pendens* to protect her rights."

The widow Richards apparently was claiming that her deceased husband's purchase from Doty in 1861 and eventual sale to Robert Vance was not legal. She evidently failed to prove her case and the various land owners retained their property. The ghost of C.A. Richards was put to rest, and his opportunistic widow went home.

The southside land that had begun as the donation land claims of Pattle and Morrison—briefly been called Unionville, then Bellingham, then merged into booming Fairhaven—was finally to return to its present and final name Bellingham.

Chapter 6

Scorched Earth

THE INDUSTRIAL AREA JUST SOUTH of the Taylor Avenue dock was the scene of several spectacular conflagrations in the 20th century.

Murchison Mill Fire

Title company records confirm that Fairhaven Tidelands lot #47 was owned by H.W. Templin, who operated a lumber mill there in 1893 & 1894 (see photo on page 77). We know that the "Murchison Mill," owned by the Bellingham Lumber and Shingle Company, was built on those lots and the adjoining lots 48 thru 55 to the south in the summer of 1902.

Title Company records show that lot #47 and several other of the tideland lots were leased by Murchison and his Bellingham Lumber & Shingle Company. Cyrus Gates was the lessor on lots 49 thru 52, and Roland Gamwell on lots 54 & 55. While we have no photo of the lumber mill that was built there in the summer of 1902, it is safe to presume that it was a large one. On March 6, 1903, the mill caught fire and burned in a huge conflagration that was cited at the time as the worst industrial fire that had ever occurred on Bellingham Bay. It is perhaps ironic to recall that just a few hundred feet to the south another huge industrial fire occurred, nearly 80 years later, when the Uniflite boat-building plant burned to a total loss.

The Murchison Mill fire started late at night during a high wind. It raged for 550 feet along the waterfront destroying everything in its path. An article in the *Fairhaven Times* the following week reports:

> "The mill was totally destroyed, as was the Hill-Welbon wharf, two vestibuled passenger coaches of the Great Northern Railway, one freight car of the Northern Pacific loaded with shingles, both the trestles of the

Great Northern Railroad along the shore, and several hundred feet of the Northern Pacific Railroad trestle out over the water. It came very near burning the Sehome cannery, the old Steele cannery building, the N.P. freight house, and the sheet metal works, all of which were saved by effective fire-manship. The fire consumed everything along the shoreline from the center of Douglas Avenue to the north side of Taylor Street. The financial loss was reported at $100,000 only $30,000 covered by insurance."

The Murchison Mill never was re-built. Soon other businesses were to occupy the land. The *Fairhaven Blade* of February 3, 1904 announced:

"A new enterprise started up Monday. The new industry is the factory of the Pacific American Tar Company. The plant is located on the waterfront at the foot of Taylor street in South Bellingham. From fir wood, particularly the stumps, will be manufactured turpentine, tar, pitch, tar oil, gas and charcoal. The refinery is 50 by 84 feet and four stories high. The building is filled with huge and peculiar machinery for the extracting of the various commodities of the wood. Nearly all the stock is owned by Bellingham people and the enterprise might be said to be a home concern. The operation of a plant of this kind here will

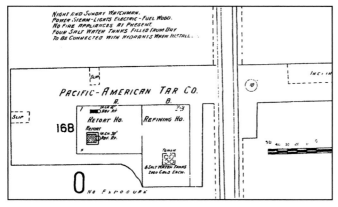

1897 Sanborn Map. Taylor Avenue borders the north edge of the building. The railroad track is shown running from top to bottom.

undoubtedly prove a boon to farmers and mill men as it handles that portion of the tree that is undesirable for lumber, also makes a market for the stumps that the farmer most wishes to be rid."

This intriguing news is confirmed by this old Sanborn Map detailing the Tar Factory.

Reid Brothers Boiler Works

An industry that did move to the scorched earth between Douglas and Taylor Avenues was the Reid Bros. Boiler Works. The Reid brothers, Robert Albert Reid and Thomas Reid, first began their pressure vessel business in Missoula, Montana. Seeking a better business climate for their specialty they moved to Fairhaven in 1898 to manufacture

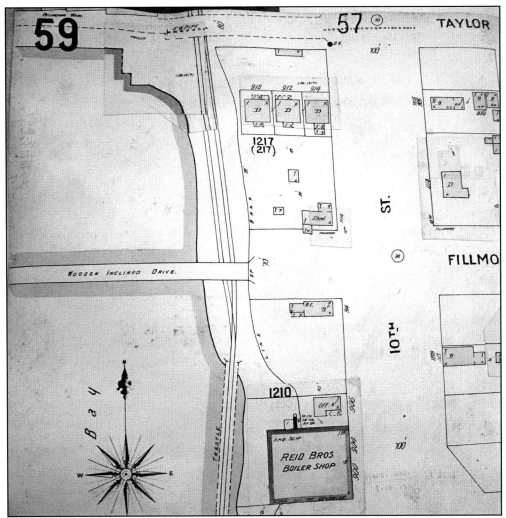

This photo of the Sanborn Map shows a narrow dock leading from the bluff at the foot of Fillmore Avenue. It is labeled only "wooden inclined drive". That is a dock leading to the Northern Pacific freight terminal located on the trestle. The Roth history speaks to Hill-Welbon's presence at Taylor Avenue with this quote, "In April 1894 Wallace Brothers of Kalama, Washington, bought the Bellingham Bay Fish Company's properties at Fairhaven and also leased the Hill-Welbon wharf, foot of Taylor Avenue."

boilers and retorts for the mills and canneries of the local area and Alaska. They initially set up business in a building at the foot of Harris Avenue. In 1904 their building burned. They rebuilt at that site, but in 1912 they moved to Front Street (now 10th) and constructed the building in which Reid Bros. Boiler Works still operates, making and repairing pressure vessels.

The pioneer business is now owned and operated by Robert Reid, the grandson of Robert Albert Reid. The buildings occupy valuable view land just south of the uplands park entrance to Taylor Avenue dock. The 1904 Sanborn Map shows on page

59 of that book the framed, metal-clad building. "Reid Bros. Boiler Shop". The office building is shown detached from the shop building. Modern additions now join it to the boiler shop structure.

The Uniflite Fire

The Uniflite fire of 1980 was Bellingham's great conflagration of the modern era. It occurred on that same ill-fated industrial area just south of Taylor Avenue and Boulevard Park. The United Boat Company, commonly known as Uniflite, is one of Bellingham's great success stories. The roots of the company go back to The Bellingham Shipyard, which built minesweepers for the U.S Navy during the 1940s and '50s. Art Nordvedt was the general manager of Bellingham Shipyards. Under his leadership the shipyard became a pioneer in the fiberglass boat industry with its Bell Boy Boat Division, begun in 1952.

In 1957 Nordvedt left Bellingham Shipyard to found his own company, United Boat Company. Nordvedt relates that he started with only $39,000 of capital, some of it from Willard Rhodes, Bill Muncey, and Ted Jones of Seattle hydro-plane racing fame. He quickly grew the company into a large national manufacturer of quality fiberglass boats, both for the pleasure cruising market, and for the U.S. military.

In 1959 Uniflite moved into a 100,000-square-foot former plywood plant on the fill in Fairhaven. The large wooden building had been built in 1937 by Bellingham investors who had formed The Bellingham Plywood Company. The building was built on piling over the landfill and was positioned just to the south of the Fairhaven Boat Haven. Peeler logs were dumped into what is called Padden Lagoon, where they rose and fell with the tide, contained by the railroad trestle. From there they were hauled up a log ramp into the peeler to eventually become plywood.

The Bellingham Plywood plant was eventually sold to Georgia Pacific Corporation. At some point in time the land had come under the ownership of the Port of Bellingham. When Georgia Pacific ceased plywood operations they simply left the site and deeded the building to the Port.

Tom Glenn, retired Port Manager, recalls the Tuesday evening in 1980 when a phone call interrupted the regular Port of Bellingham Commissioners' meeting announcing that the Uniflite plant was ablaze. The meeting was quickly adjourned and the Commissioners all repaired to Glenn's home on 13th Street, from which they could observe the spectacular fire.

The 43-year-old wooden building, with crawl space beneath the floor, laden with fiberglass, resin, acetone and other flammable chemicals virtually exploded in a huge conflagration that lit the night sky and was visible from miles around. Unlike the 1903 Murchison Mill fire, damage was confined to just the Uniflite building, which was a

The still smoking ruins of the Uniflite boat plant.

total loss. Even though Uniflite was able to continue production in their East Coast plant at Swansboro, North Carolina, the fire was the beginning of the end for the company. In 1984 Uniflite was sold to Chris Craft.

The area occupied by Uniflite, and now the Port of Bellingham's light industrial business park, has been the location of a long succession of lumber mills and business operations. The names ring in Fairhaven history; Heacock's Mill, Frankenberger's Sawmill, Earles-Cleary Mill, Bellingham Lumber & Shingle Co. (*aka* the Murchison Mill), Washington Loggers, the Fairhaven Boat Haven, and Uniflite, each one a significant force in the economy and history of Bellingham's southside.

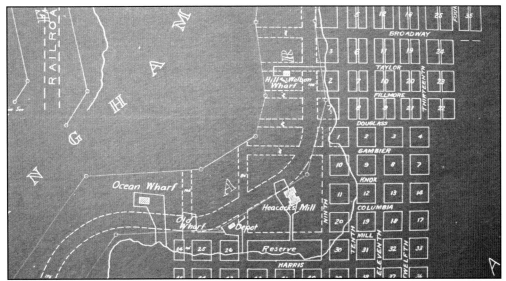

Heacock's Mill on piles over the water, Hill-Welbon and Ocean Wharf. Note original shore line circa 1889.

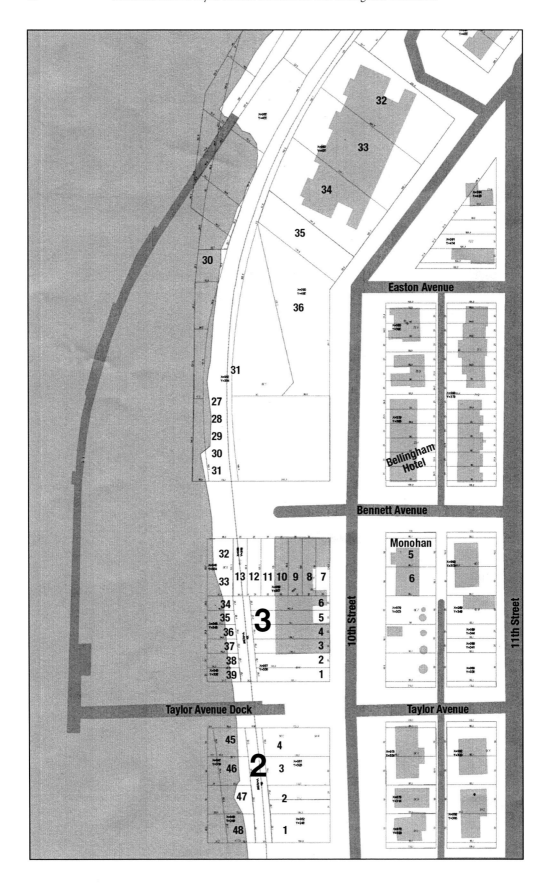

Chapter 7

The Old Dock

THE TOWNS ON BELLINGHAM BAY relied on water transportation for almost everything in the three-plus decades before the railroads arrived. Docks and wharves were of extreme importance to their very existence. Not much is written however, about when these wharves were built or by whom.

The Unionville Wharf

I rely on a quote from Edson's book, *The Fourth Corner*, to identify the first wharf on the waterfront that now comprises Boulevard Park. Mrs. Edson, reporting on the organization of the Union Coal Company in 1861, writes, "The sum of $40,000 was raised by the company and expended in opening the mine and in constructing a wharf, store-house and other buildings". The Union wharf, sometimes known as the Unionville Wharf, was built by the Union Coal Company at the foot of Broadway, now called Bennett Avenue. That would have placed it close to the mine entrance. The earliest pictorial evidence we have of the wharf is an image in the 1890 Sanborn Map which shows the first part of the wharf and a notation reading "190' to end of wharf". The 1897 Sanborn also shows it set just north of the Broadway right-of-way and angled off toward the north at about a forty-degree angle from the street. The notation reads "Wharf (old)". A small building labeled "Who." (warehouse) sits on the land beside the wharf.

The Taylor Avenue Dock

The Taylor Avenue Dock is believed to have first been constructed by E.B. Hill & Company. E.B. Hill was a native of Montpelier, Vermont. He arrived in Fairhaven around 1887, where he joined with H.L. Moreland and J.P. Lewis to form his trading company. They

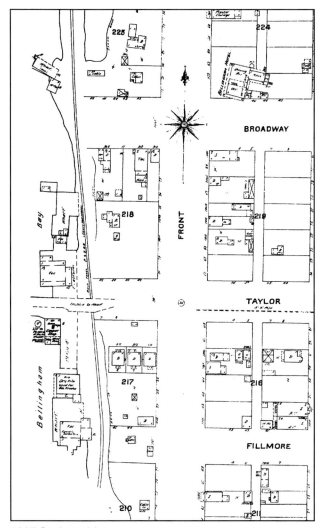

1897 Sanborn Map.

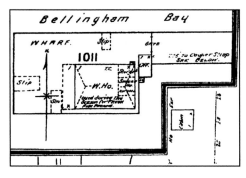

are described in the *Fairhaven Illustrated* published in 1890 as Commission Merchants and Shippers. A drawing published in that same publication clearly shows the long dock extending far out into the bay with a large building at its end and a side-wheeler steamer tied to the dock. On the roof of the building are the words "E.B. Hill & Co., commission merchants and shippers, wharfage & storage, building materials, hay and grain."

The wharf is described as "running out 525 feet into the bay, and being 90 feet in width, at the end of this wharf are two warehouses, one 50x100 and the other 40x60 feet. This wharf was erected at great expense, and at an exceptionally fine location, and it is safe to say that it is one of the strongest on Puget Sound, the piles being two feet in diameter. At low tide there is 27 feet of water, allowing the largest ocean-going vessels safe berths."

The 1897 Sanborn Map not only shows the wharf (marked "incline to wharf") but a building labeled "cooperage", on the water just south of the wharf. It also shows a separate image of the wharf end supporting a large warehouse and a notation, "225' to cooper shop". Whether it was 525 feet or 225 feet, it was still a long dock.

It is difficult to establish the exact date of the dock construction. An early photo from the Gordon Tweit collection may show the dock under construction. The

Fairhaven Illustrated, 1890. Whatcom Museum of History & Art

View showing wharf and warehouse of E.B. Hill & Co.

clues to the date of this photo are the existence of the 14th Street School seen on the hill above the dock and known to have been built in 1880, and the absence of the Fairhaven and Southern R.R. track which was cut along this shore in 1890. If this is a photo of the dock under construction, its date must be in that decade before 1890. Also of interest in this photo is the large cut in the bluff which would have contained a gradual ramp-way up to the street level on top of the bluff. An inclined bridge from the top of the bluff would not be built until the arrival of the railroad. The cut is now filled with rubble under the inclined bridge leading from Taylor Avenue down to the boardwalk, and can be seen to this day. The large warehouse on the bluff to the right of the cut was likely owned by E.B. Hill.

Gordon Tweit collection.

Hill-Welbon Dock under construction? Before railroad, circa 1885. Note 14th Street School (with its central tower) on the upper right hilltop in the background.

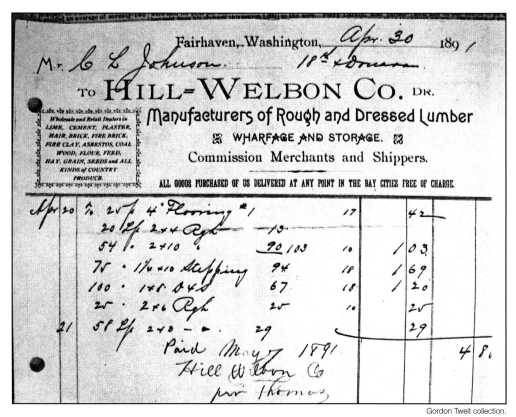

Photo of Hill-Welbon invoice.

E.B. Hill and a lumberman named W.H. Welbon joined forces in 1889. The warehouse at the end of the dock was soon to have its roof sign changed to Hill-Welbon Co., and the new company would now promote itself as "Hill-Welbon Co., manufacturers of rough and dressed lumber, wharfage and storage, commission merchants and shippers"; and their invoice would list among their products: "lime, cement, plaster, hair, brick, fire brick, fire clay, asbestos, coal, wood, flour, feed, hay grain, seeds and all kinds of country produce."

Welbon had a lumber mill out in the woods four miles from Fairhaven, but along the Fairhaven and Southern track which had been built in 1888-89. The mill was pictured in the 1890 *Fairhaven Illustrated* and described as follows, "This is certainly one of the most lucrative mills of its size in the Bellingham Bay Country; an almost exhaustless supply of immense fir, cedar and spruce trees stand at its back, and although the mill is sawing away at the rate of 40,000 feet per day, the inroad upon the majestic forest surrounding it is scarcely perceptible. The shipping facilities are of the best as a side track runs down from the main line of the railroad to the mill and cars are loaded on the spot. The owners are E.B. Hill and W.H. Welbon."

Whatcom Museum of History and Art

This remarkable photograph was taken from the top of Dead Man's Point, as evidenced by the grass in the foreground. It shows the Hill-Welbon wharf with its name emblazoned on the roof. The earliest Pacific American Fisheries Buildings are in the center foreground and Dirty Dan Harris' Fairhaven Hotel is in the right foreground. Across the Bay, behind the top of the Taylor Avenue dock, is the Bellingham Hotel distinctive because of its size and its colonnaded porch. Off to the left around the point, are seen the twin smokestacks of the E.K. Wood mill, and large piles of lumber stacked on the lumber wharf.

The Hill-Welbon dock at Taylor Avenue was used for many purposes over the years. It had been built as a shipping-storage warehouse. The April 13, 1893 edition of *The Bellingham Bay Express* reported, "A Sash & Door factory is being erected on the Hill & Welbon Wharf. The company will manufacture clear dressed cedar for the

Fairhaven Illustrated, 1890. Whatcom Museum of History & Art.

Illustration of Hill-Welbon Mill.

Fairhaven Illustrated, 1890. Whatcom Museum of History & Art.
Illustration of Welbon Home, Knox Avenue.

eastern market. Roth's *History of Whatcom County* says that in April of 1894 it was leased by the Wallace Brothers of Kalama, Washington, who had just bought the Bellingham Bay Fish Company. The building was used for fish processing during the season. The business was evidently successful as Welbon built a large and imposing home on Knox Avenue. The house was later to be occupied by Cyrus Gates, and is currently the home of Don and Carol Salisbury. The *Fairhaven Illustrated* of 1890 contained this drawing of the home.

The Fairhaven *Birdseye*

Among the first images we have of the old dock is the remarkably accurate historic illustration, the Fairhaven *Birdseye*, published in 1891. The *Birdseye* is a lithograph commissioned by the Fairhaven Land Company as a sales aid during the great Fairhaven land boom. It is an artist's rendition of Fairhaven as though seen by a bird flying overhead. The complete *Birdseye* measures a generous 28 x 42 inches and depicts with remarkable accuracy the Fairhaven of 1891. Shown here is just a partial section of the much larger original.

These *Birdseyes* of Fairhaven are very rare. There are presently only fifteen known to exist. The public can examine an original, framed and hanging beside the elevator on the bottom floor of the Village Books store in Fairhaven. Prior to 1971 there

From the author's collection.

Cropped photo of Fairhaven *Birdseye*.

were only three of these historic documents known to exist according to Bellingham's prominent historian, the late Galen Biery.

In 1971, upon the death of Elisabeth Newman Clausen, my wife and I bought the Thomas Newman home at 1027 16th Street. Thomas Newman was a Fairhaven attorney prominent as a lawyer for the Fairhaven Land Company and in local Republican Party activities.

Elizabeth Newman Clausen had lived in the 1890-era house until she died in her late eighties. The house had been almost continuously occupied by the Newman family and contained a treasure trove of old Victorian artifacts and Fairhaven history. High in the attic rafters of the old house we found a large cardboard tube containing eleven of the old *Birdseyes*, most of them in pristine condition. A consultation with Biery confirmed the rarity of the find. A fifteenth *Birdseye* has been identified in recent years in the possession of the pioneer Larrabee family. The wonderfully detailed old illustrations are a unique and valuable depiction of our community history.

The Taylor Avenue dock is shown in the upper left hand corner of the lithograph with a ship moored to its north side. The accurate details of this hand-done work tell us much about early Fairhaven. North along the shoreline is seen the smoking Eldridge & Bartlett Mill with a sailing ship tied to its lumber dock. That mill site would soon become the E.K. Wood Mill, and eventually the heart of Boulevard Park.

The Hincks Map

We clearly see the dock again on the excellent map of 1892 prepared by Edward Hincks. The Taylor Avenue dock stands out prominently from the shore-line.

The Quackenbush *Birdseye*

Another view of the dock is to be seen from another *birdseye* prepared as a promotional piece by the pioneer real estate firm J.J. Quackenbush & Co. of Sehome, W.T. (Washington Territory).

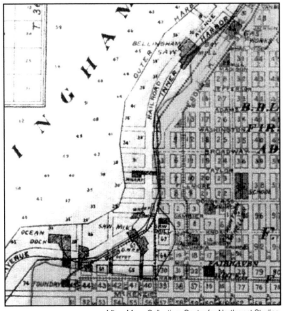

Misc. Maps Collection, Center for Northwest Studies, Western Washington University.

Hincks Map, circa 1890.

The Quackenbush *Birdseye*

The old illustration is printed both front and back, a *birdseye* view of Whatcom, Sehome and Fairhaven on the front and the realtor's advertisement for "The Sehome Addition to Sehome and Whatcom" on the back. This was printed in pre-statehood days, so it has to be older than 1898. It presents an interesting view of Bellingham and Fairhaven from the west with the Taylor Avenue dock in the approximate center. It also shows the Eldridge & Bartlett Bellingham Mill/E.K. Wood Mill with smoke pouring from its twin stacks and two lumber schooners at its dock.

The Dock Survives

The old Hill-Welbon, Taylor Avenue Dock may have been largely destroyed in the Murchison Mill fire of 1903, however, it is possible that the inclined bridge over the railroad track survived only partially damaged to last into the present day. Parks Department officials reported finding evidence of charring on some of the large timbers of the bridge when doing the retrofit for the "boardwalk" project. The Taylor Avenue dock was to survive in other forms to serve the community in future decades and in a future century.

Galen Biery Papers and Photographs #1403, Center for Pacific Northwest Studies, Western Washington University.

The 14th Street School is distinguished by its central tower which shows high on the recently logged hill. The old school was built in 1880 and served until it was replaced by Lowell School in 1914. The 14th Street School stood on the west play field of the present Lowell School. Lowell was constructed behind it and then the old school was demolished.

P.R. Jeffcott Collection, Washington State Archives, Northwest Regional Archive, Bellingham.

This photo (circa 1891), taken from the Hill-Welbon Wharf at Taylor Avenue, shows the 14th Street School, the Gamwell house, and Wardner's Castle. The trestles of the Fairhaven & Northern Railroad (later Great Northern, and now Burlington Northern) are evident.

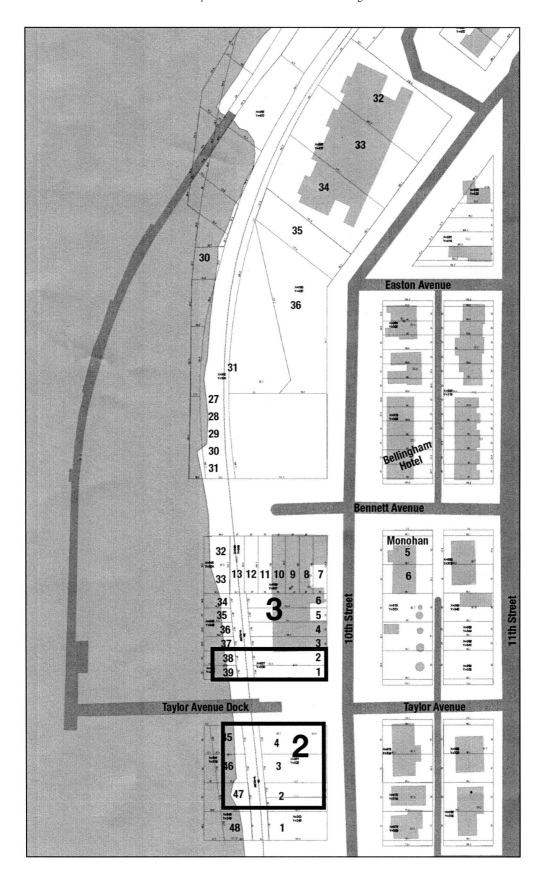

Chapter 8

Taylor Avenue
& The Oil Industry

THE HISTORICAL BACKGROUND of each of the various sections of waterfront spanned by Boulevard Park will be examined closely. The reader is encouraged to review the map at the start of each chapter. We will examine each highlighted section one after another from south to north.

Let's begin at the most southerly end of the park with lots 2, 3 & 4. In block 2, the first Bellingham Plat, those lots now contain the Outlook Park with restrooms adjoining Taylor Avenue. The chain of ownership of these lots (that the new entrance park sits on) is an interesting one. They were within the boundaries of the original donation land claim of William Morrison in 1853.

Morrison sold the land to Seth Doty in 1855, Doty sold to Richards. Several other owners are involved until Erastus Bartlett and Edward Eldridge consolidate their ownership in 1871. Eldridge and Bartlett platted Bellingham in 1883 and sold these lots individually. Then the lots were sold and resold many times, mostly for residential or speculative purposes.

At the turn of the century these three lots south of Taylor Avenue were owned by the Hill-Welbon Lumber Company and probably supported the activities on their wharf that extended out from Taylor Avenue. Several of the Sanborn Maps and old photos show that over time several small dwellings were built on the lots. Eventually the lots were consolidated into one ownership by Pacific Realty.

With the advent of the automobile and the increasing popularity of internal combustion engines, the need for petroleum products in Bellingham and Whatcom County grew dramatically. The most efficient way of transporting petroleum products in those days was by sea via barges or oil tankers and the Taylor Avenue dock was identified as an excellent off-loading location.

Gilmore Oil Company

In 1938 the three lots south of Taylor were sold by Pacific Realty to the Gilmore Oil Company. Gilmore built their office and storage tanks on the bluff just south of the Taylor Avenue dock. Gilmore Oil Company was a pioneer California gasoline retailer that had its beginning at the dawn of the automotive industry in the early 1920s.

Roar with Gilmore emblem.

Arthur Gilmore moved his family from Illinois to the Los Angeles area in 1870. He bought a huge 365-acre ranch on the edge of town and built a successful dairy operation. In 1901, being short of water for his cows, he hired a drilling rig to dig to the aquifer he imagined to be beneath him.

Some people have all the luck! It would appear that Gilmore was one of them. He didn't find water, instead Gilmore's drill rig struck oil and the Gilmore Oil Company was born. He and his son Earl grew the company to be the largest retailer of automotive gasoline on the west coast. Earl invented the 'Gasoteria,' the first self-service gas station known. Their chain of franchised stations grew to 11,000 stations, all marketing gas under the red roaring lion insignia. The Gilmores' economic success enabled them to start a famous automobile race track and build Gilmore Stadium, the first National Football League stadium in America. "Roar with Gilmore" was their slogan, and the roaring red lions were a common sight on the 'banjo signs' above their stations throughout the west.

Pat McEvoy, whose father's Texaco consignee location was just across Taylor Avenue, relates with nostalgia that the local Gilmore distributor, a man named Von Gruenenwald, even kept a live lion caged at its 10th and Taylor facility for a time. Apparently the manager was a flamboyant character and had somewhere found a lion to use in promotions. Who could now imagine the Gilmore lion once roaring where today the Boulevard Park walkers enjoy a rest stop at the Taylor Avenue uplands park.

In 1940 the Standard Oil Company (Sonoco) affiliate, General Petroleum, bought Gilmore Oil. They continued the Gilmore operation and trade name for five years. Gilmore's roaring red lion trademark was finally retired after the end of World War II.

The Haggen Brothers

By 1974 General Petroleum, which by that time had changed its name to Mobil Oil, ceased operations at the site. They had built a new tank farm on the east side of 10th Street and then sold it to Glen Keith who operated it as Keith Oil. The original site on lots 3, 4 & 5 was sold to a Carl Goodwin in 1974. On December 20, 1974, Goodwin sold those three lots, plus lots 1 & 2 in block three north of Taylor Avenue, to Don and Rick Haggen, the owners of the Haggen Food chain.

The Haggen brothers had considered someday building a water-view restaurant on the land. They held it for a number of years, but the capital and time demands of their rapidly growing supermarket chain prevented them from acting on their restaurant venture. The land sat empty and unused.

California Petroleum

Several oil companies were to establish oil storage tanks and distribution points at the dock on both sides of Taylor Avenue. California Petroleum, which took over the old flour mill site in 1926, was the first to take advantage of the location. They were bought out by the Texas Company in 1928, and the Texaco brand operated on the location through their Texaco Distributor, McEvoy Oil Company, until 1996.

California Petroleum had purchased the Taylor Avenue flour mill property on lots 3, 4, 5, and 6, and tideland lots 34 thru 37 in 1926. They may have demolished the buildings and the dock before they sold to the Texas Company in 1928, or it is pos-

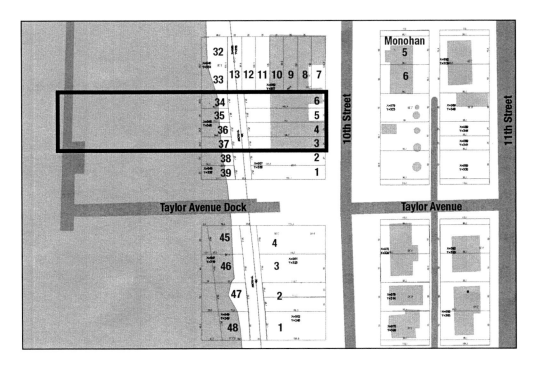

sible that the Texas Company did the demolishing in the year of their purchase. Using their marketing name Texaco, the Texas Company built a finger pier onto the railroad trestle beside the old dock and placed their office on it. From that facility they not only received petroleum products from barges for their bulk tanks on the bluff behind them, but they sold gasoline and diesel oil to the fishing and pleasure boats that came to their dock.

Texaco built a pipeline from the dock to their storage tanks on land. The pipeline was placed on concrete piers. The piers are still there to be seen (six of them directly in front of the Chrysalis Hotel), leading from the shore to the trestle and paralleling the Taylor Avenue dock. Pat McEvoy recalls the installation well. A walkway was built on top of the pipeline installed on those piers. He walked it many times while operating the pumping system transferring fuel from the barges up to the storage tanks.

Texaco operated through a consignee who was an independent dealer using Texaco's property, selling their products at Texaco's proscribed prices, and being paid a commission based on his sales.

Origins of McEvoy Oil Company

Charles McEvoy had a brother, John, who was a successful executive with Bloedel Donovan Lumber Company in Bellingham. In 1927 John McEvoy urged his brother

Gordon Tweit collection.

McEvoy Oil Company.

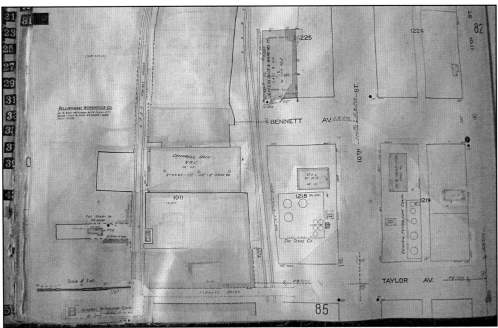

Sanborn Map.

Charles to move to Bellingham to become the purchasing agent for the giant timber company. Several years after his arrival McEvoy learned that the existing Texaco consignee wanted to sell his business. McEvoy borrowed money here and there and was able to purchase the business. Charles McEvoy became the consignee in 1932.

Patrick McEvoy joined his father in 1953 and bought the business from him in 1964 to become the new consignee. In 1979 Pat bought the land and physical plant from Texaco and became a distributor. As distributor he now owned the land and equipment, bought the product from Texaco and set his own prices.

McEvoy Oil enjoyed a substantial business selling marine fuels to the commercial fishing boats and pleasure craft conveniently moored in the port's boat haven just south of them; as well as delivering fuel oil to homes and businesses and servicing the Texaco gas stations in their area.

The aerial photo (on page 112) taken in the late 1930s shows many interesting features of that time. Note the box car on the trestle track. Pat McEvoy explained that heavy canned greases were delivered via the railroad, which was still able to use the trestle by entering it from the north. The trestle south of the Taylor Avenue Dock had been demolished and removed many years before.

McEvoy operated the business at his 10th Street location until selling the property in 1996, to move the business to a more modern location in the Irongate Business Park.

Pattle's Mine

McEvoy was soon to sell the land to Fairhaven landowner and developer Kenneth Imus. McEvoy's sale of the old Texaco site was contingent on his removing the old bulk plant with its storage tanks and piping, and because of the environmental laws, testing of the land for petroleum pollution. Strider Construction Company was employed to remove the building, tanks and various concrete supports. As a large Strider backhoe was digging out a concrete support for one of the oil tanks, it exposed a great gaping hole in the ground. The yawning cavity seemed to go deep into the earth and it was filled with water. No one knew what they had uncovered until checking with the geology department at Western Washington University and the US Bureau of Mines. Realization dawned.

They believed they had uncovered the entrance to the old Pattle Mine, begun so long ago by Pattle and Morrison and the Puget Sound Coal Mining Association. While called the Pattle Mine by its discoverers, this was more likely the entrance to the Union Coal Company mine of 1861. Pattle's mine of 1853 had been opened 100 feet north and closer to the beach.

Neither McEvoy nor the Texas Company before it had any idea that one of their huge oil storage tanks had stood exactly over the entrance to the old mine.

G. Mustoe photo. Whatcom Museum of History & Art.

Pattle's Coal Mine, 10th & Taylor Avenue, Fairhaven. 1/12/1996. Professor R.S. Babcock in foreground. WWU Geology Department. G. Mustoe photo.

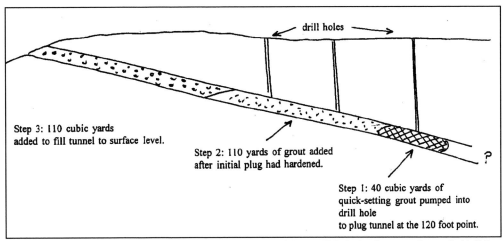

Step 3: 110 cubic yards added to fill tunnel to surface level.

Step 2: 110 yards of grout added after initial plug had hardened.

Step 1: 40 cubic yards of quick-setting grout pumped into drill hole to plug tunnel at the 120 foot point.

drill holes

?

G. Mustoe, WWU Geology Department. Courtesy Patrick McEvoy.

Method of sealing the mine.

The discovery of the old coal mine was obviously to become a major problem for McEvoy's sale preparations. His first challenge was to determine depth and size of the mine. He hired GeoTest Inc. to begin the investigation. Complicating the study was the water that filled the shaft almost to the level of the surface.

The mine shaft angled into the earth at a decided slant to the northeast. The Chart of Mine Entrance shows its location and the direction of the shaft. An adventurous scuba diver was hired to plumb its depth, he dove until at 120 feet he had had enough. He had no idea how much deeper it might go, but he knew he had no desire to go deeper.

The engineers attached a camera on a long pole and tried to plumb the depths electronically; that was not successful.

Consultations with engineers determined the final solution. They would drill three vertical holes down to the shaft to the east of the entrance and pour quick setting grout down the vertical hole into the shaft to plug it. Then rubble and more grout would be dumped into the mine entrance, filling the shaft from the grout plug to the entrance. Finally it was done, the mine was plugged and safely sealed.

At considerable expense, McEvoy and the Texaco Company had completed the necessary environmental cleanup of the soil and resolved the problems presented by the discovery of Pattle's mine. With the ancient mine sealed up with grout, the site was ready for construction. The sale to Imus was finally completed.

The story of Pattle's mine remains a strange side-note to the history of the Taylor Avenue dock area.

Chrysalis Inn

Within months Imus re-sold the land to Ellen Shea, a woman with a vision and the determination to bring her vision to reality. Her dream was to create a high quality inn, spa and restaurant overlooking the waters of Harris Bay. The old McEvoy Oil Co. site fit her plans perfectly and she had sought out Kenneth Imus.

The property included all of block 3 with the exception of lots 1 and 2 adjacent to the north side of the Taylor Avenue right-of-way—the land that the City had purchased from the Haggen brothers when they exercised the option given to them by the Taylor Avenue Partnership. Shea's plans required a building that needed a little more land than was provided by the property she had purchased. Fortunately for both parties, about the time she was planning her construction, the City of Bellingham Park and Recreation Department had committed to their Taylor Avenue dock project and they had a need also. A *quid-pro-quo* arrangement revealed itself.

The Park Department desired a waterfront trail connection between their Taylor Avenue property and their (former can factory) uplands site north of Bennett Avenue.

The two parties negotiated an equitable agreement which solved each party's problem. Shea granted the Park Department an easement on the edge of the bluff which connected the two park properties, and agreed to build a public walkway across the front of her building. Its design put this walkway below the inn's floor level and is completely out of sight to inn patrons. She also agreed to improve a portion of Taylor Avenue for pedestrian use. In return the City allowed the inn to build its building virtually on its southern property line. The City required only that public access be maintained and that the strip of land along Taylor Avenue be used for access to the pedestrian walkway across the inn frontage.

This extremely civilized agreement has stood the test of time with each party enjoying the benefits of its terms and with no reported problems for either party. The Chrysalis has provided a much-needed upscale hotel to the community and its spa and restaurant have been popular and successful.

Old Texaco piers in front of the Chrysalis Inn.

The public access walkway in front of the Chrysalis Inn.

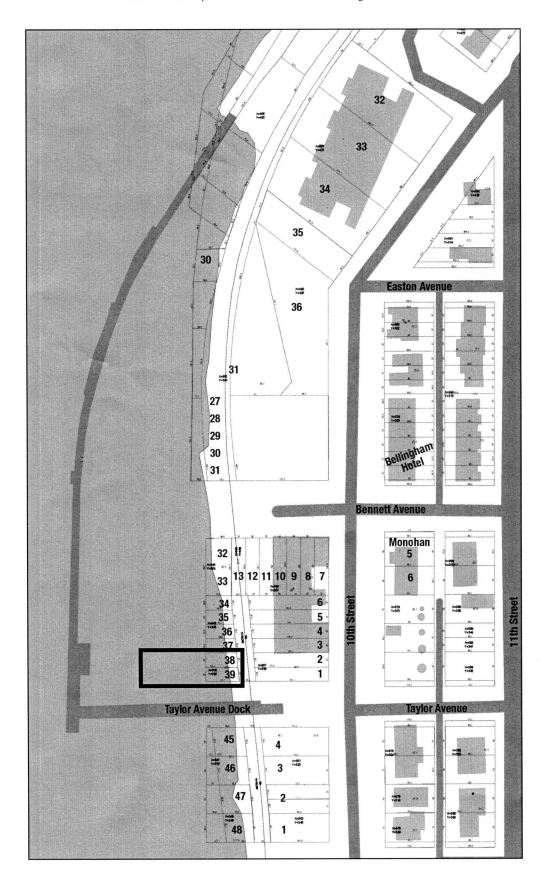

Chapter 9

The Salmon Cannery

THE LONG AND IMPORTANT HISTORY of salmon canning on Bellingham Bay began with a tiny and undercapitalized venture built at old Fort Bellingham, which failed in its first year. In 1897 the first cannery with serious economic potential was built at the foot of Taylor Avenue just north of the Taylor Avenue dock. The Sanborn Map of 1904 shows the wooden-frame building of the Fairhaven Canning Company adjoining the dock on the north.

The First Salmon Cannery

In 1895 a man named Oswald Steele came to Fairhaven to begin a business shipping fresh fish to the East Coast. It is daunting to consider how fresh a fish might be after enduring the rail trip from Bellingham to New York in the year 1895. Perhaps the implied problems of that long journey might be the reason that Mr. Steele opened the Fairhaven Canning Company just two years later. 1897 was to be the year of a big sockeye salmon run and Steele planned to cash in on its silvery abundance.

Capitalizing his company with $10,000 he built his one-line cannery on pilings on the tideland lots directly north of the Taylor Avenue dock. The photo on page 71 shows a small frame building just north of the dock, which I surmise is the cannery. If so, this might be the only photo of the Fairhaven Canning Company. The picture was taken before the railroad arrived and shows the dock without the present bridge necessary to rise over a track. It also shows a large cut in the bluff to provide entry to the dock from the street level above. That ancient cut can still be seen under the Taylor Avenue bridge, partially filled with rubble.

Steele hired Chinese labor, the first time that had been done in a local cannery and the first Chinese labor that had been used on the bay since Asian workers had been run out of Whatcom during the labor crisis of 1885. Prejudice against Oriental workers was to be a continued issue in Fairhaven.

The Fairhaven Canning Company completed its first year with moderate, but not outstanding, success. Cash was apparently scarce as Steele had to re-capitalize in 1898. He struggled along for several years and finally sold the business to the Pacific Packing and Navigation Company in 1901. Pacific Packing and Navigation Company had several other canning operations. They soon filed for bankruptcy and the Taylor Avenue operation was separately sold to investors from Chicago. Those investors included E.B. Deming. The new owners renamed the cannery the Sehome Canning Company, which would eventually morph into being a part of the giant Pacific American Fisheries, Inc. (PAF), of which Deming became president.

In 1898 two additional canneries were under construction across Harris Bay at the present site of the Alaska Ferry Terminal. Promoter Roland Onffroy was building the Franco-American North Pacific Canning Company cannery, which would soon be taken over by Deming and Gould and their Chicago investors to be re-organized as Pacific American Fisheries. Alongside Onffroy's cannery, B.A. Seaborg's Aberdeen

Port of Bellingham Records, Washington State Archives; Northwest Regional Archives, Bellingham, WA.

Bellingham Canning Company.

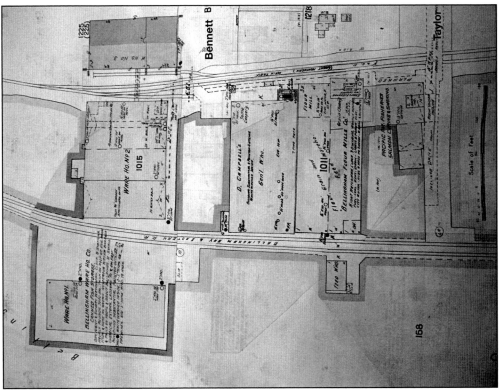

Sanborn Map, 1904.

Canning Company was being built. In 1904 it would be purchased by the Welsh family and renamed The Bellingham Canning Company.

The little cannery at the foot of Taylor Avenue would cease operations early in the twentieth century, but having been brought into the PAF organization, it would continue in use by PAF as a canned salmon warehouse and as their location for smoking and curing salmon. It is to that purpose that the Sanborn Map has labeled the building "Pacific. Am. Fisheries Salmon Curing & Smoking". It is interesting to note the indication on the map that there was a part of the building that extended under the Taylor Avenue dock itself. That extension is shown by the outline of the walls and the words "room under incline." The building encroaching on the Taylor Avenue right-of-way is also to be noted in the handwritten title records of the Chicago Title Co.

Curiously, at the other end of the building a line indicating a wall is shown penetrating the image of the adjoining flour mill. Is it possible that the cannery was built low to the water so that both the sloping incline of the dock and the large flour mill were both built over it? It is not known how long the old cannery was used nor when it was finally demolished. The two lots of tidelands next to the dock on which the cannery stood have never been built upon again.

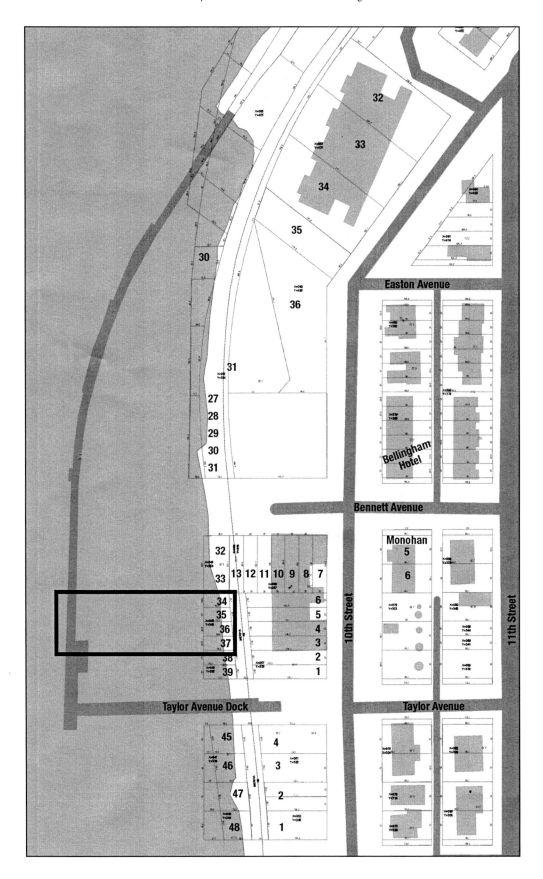

Chapter 10

George J. Hohl Waterfront Flour Mill

Bellingham Flour Mill Company

Alongside the old cannery building and occupying the four platted tideland lots to the north was the large flour mill operated by George J. Hohl. Finding the existence of a large flour mill at this site was a great surprise to me. I had never known or heard of a flour mill on the Fairhaven waterfront, but the surprises provided by George Hohl and his odyssey through life were just beginning with this discovery. I began to research the George J. Hohl Company by reading old city directories, certain that he must be the same Hohl that owned and operated Hohl's Feed & Seed at 1312 Railroad Avenue. His name lives on in that business which still operates at that address as of the date of this writing.

Hohl's Feed & Seed on Railroad Avenue has been a Bellingham icon for more than half a century. I was to find that the Hohl name has been connected with the local feed and seed business since before the turn of the 19th century. George J. Hohl was the son of German immigrants. He was born in Minnesota but it is not known when he came west to Fairhaven. The 1890 Fairhaven city directory shows him as a laborer at Heacock's mill on the Fairhaven waterfront. The 1899 directory shows him as a millwright living at 1532 19th street with his wife Nellie and son Ross.

He must have gone into the flour and feed business in 1899 because the City of Fairhaven city council minutes of Dec. 18th of that year contain a list of bills to be paid. Among them is the annotation "Geo. J. Hohl (feed for horse) $15.93." Those city records contain an annotation of a Geo. J. Hohl bill for every month thereafter, and the record of April 16, 1900, finally reveals the hay-burner the City was maintaining. The listing of bills to be paid includes, "hay and feed for the street commissioner's horse $8.33."

Those same City Council minutes provide us proof that George J. Hohl was also a politician. On December 4, 1900, the male citizens of Fairhaven went to the polls to elect their city government. The results are recorded in the city council minutes.

Mayor   John Cloab   267 votes

            Geo. J. Hohl   302 votes

Hohl was apparently a rather straight-laced man. He wasted no time in asserting his beliefs. Shortly after his inauguration as mayor the minutes contain this entry.

> "Feb. 4, 1900:
> The Mayor addressed the council on the subject of gambling and ordered the Marshall to close all gambling houses tomorrow morning and to give the gamblers 24 hours in which to pack up their outfits and take them away, and also asked the council to endorse his action in closing the games.
> On motion of councilman Monahan, roll was called which resulted as follows: Monohan excused, Sorenson, Norman and Strickfadden voted *aye* to endorse the Mayor's action in stopping gambling. Martin, Atkins & Slattery voted *no*."

There is no further mention of the action in those minutes or any of the minutes of following weeks, so we cannot report whether the marshal acted or what the results of Mayor Hohl's morality campaign might have been. It might also be noted that the abstaining councilman, George E. Monahan, was a prominent saloon keeper and may have had a game or two going in his establishment.

Hohl must have found himself in a challenging new role. Another notation in the February 1990 Council minutes reads:

> "Petition of D.J. Slattery and about 50 others asking that the japs and chinise imployed at the cannerys be confined to certain limits in the city, was read and referred to the Street, Sewer, & Waterfront Committee. All voting *aye* except Martin who votes *no*."

Perhaps Hohl found that the pressures of running a boom town were more than he needed. He must have quickly had his fill of politics. In 1902 he did not run for re-election. Now his name again appears each month on the list of city expenses that the

city must pay, "Geo. J. Hohl, feed for the road commissioners horse."

The 1900-1901 *Polk City Directory for
Fairhaven* shows a listing for the Geo. J. Hohl &
Co, flour, feed, hay & grain located at 1710 12th
Street. That address is probably a typographical error, as it would place him in the block just beyond
the 12th Street bridge on the south side of Padden
Creek. The directory also shows a personal listing
indicating he was president of that business. The
1902 and 1903 directories are missing, but in the
1904-05 Polk we find that his company is now listed at 1308-1310 12th Street, and we know that to
be an accurate address. Hohl is also listed in that
directory as president of the Bellingham Brick and
Tile Co., so he apparently was a busy man with his hands in at least two businesses.

Whatcom Museum of History & Art

George J. Hohl

Another probable address error in the Polk directory of 1899 shows George H.
Hohl living at 1532 19th Street, while the 1904 Polk shows George J. at 1132 19th
Street. The old city directories are infamous for typographical errors. I am confident
that both Hohls mentioned were George J. Hohl, living at 1132 19th Street, a pleasant house at the corner of 19th and Mill Avenue that is still there.

Checking the 1904 Sanborn Map reveals that the business address, 1312 12th

George J. Hohl's home at 1132 19th Street.

Street, is the address of Fairhaven's historic Waldron Building. Sanborn proves to us that Hohl was indeed occupying the main floor of that historic building by labeling the drawing "hay, feed, seed." The prestigious Waldron Building seemed an unlikely location for a feed and seed store. Only an understanding of the economic times can give us a reasonable answer.

The Waldron Building

Charles W. Waldron came to Fairhaven from Wisconsin as the boom hit Fairhaven. He started his Bank of Fairhaven in 1889. In 1891 he was able to move the bank

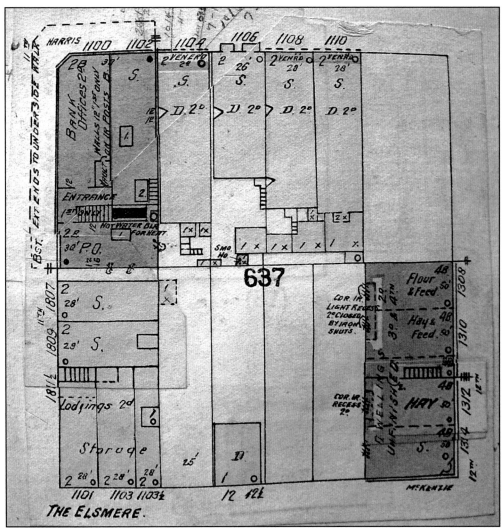

Sanborn Map, 1904. Waldron Building (lower right hand corner) after the Bank of Fairhaven had failed. This image of the map shows a large portion of the ground floor used as hay storage and grain and feed sales in the remainder.

into in his new stone and brick building at the corner of 12th Street and McKenzie Avenue. The Waldron Building began life with a ground floor and two upper stories containing a hotel or apartments. The bank was located in the southeast corner of the ground floor.

The building started enjoying an aura of success with the ground floor occupied and the two upper floors completed and operating. It is said that some of the Fairhaven notables including Roland Gamwell used to play a regular game of Whist in a room on the second floor. Fairhaven pharmacist and historian Gordon Tweit recalls that he had an uncle, Ole Tweit, who lived on the second floor for a short period. A notation found in the July 1, 1893, Fairhaven City Council minutes records that Charles Waldron offered to rent rooms in his building for the Fairhaven municipal offices. Fairhaven did not have its own city hall building at that time and rented offices for its city government. The council turned down his offer, choosing to stay in their present quarters.

This evidence clearly debunks the long-held urban legend that the upper floors of the Waldron building had never been finished.

The true story is that Waldron was so convinced of the grand economic future for Fairhaven (and for his new building) that in 1894 after completing and occupying the building, he decided to add an additional floor. Workers tore off the original cornice down to the top of the third story windows and began laying up the bricks for the fourth floor. They were working in the cold winter months of 1894 and were having trouble getting their mortar to set up properly. It was necessary to bring in a heat source to warm the mortar. The contractor set up burn barrels or stoves on the fourth floor and built fires in them. The outcome might have been predictable. The burn barrels ignited the building and the upper three floors were gutted by the fire.

The following story was printed in the Tuesday, January 23, 1894, issue of *The Daily Reveille*.

> "Sunday evening (January 21) at 7 o'clock the Waldron block at Fairhaven was destroyed by fire, entailing a total loss estimated at from $30,000 to $50,000. The alarm was given, the fire boys rallied, the churches were forsaken, and a great portion of the population was soon at the conflagration. At 8 o'clock the firemen, under the direction of Gibbons and O'Dell, had the fire under control. The steamer working nobly, but the water pressure from the hydrants had been left open to prevent freezing. At 9:30 the fire was out, but the building was a blackened ruin above the third storey. It was a four story building and one of the finest in the city, valued at $35,000. The walls are yet standing, but should a gale arise will probably fall... The fire

started in the fourth story, where a fire was kept to dry the work and it is supposed that the fire caught from this stove. The block was built in 1891 as to three stories, and a fourth story was lately added. It has been occupied for banking, residence, store and office purposes. The Bank of Fairhaven being the principal tenant. The owner of the building, Mr. C.W. Waldron, was seen by a reporter, and stated that the building would be rebuilt as soon as practicable. He was at Whatcom when the fire occurred and has no theory as to the origin of the fire, save that it must have been originated as before stated."

The Daily Reveille, January 24, 1894:

"T.A. Creighton gave the fire boys an oyster supper at Brown's restaurant Monday night to show his appreciation for the excellent work they did at the Waldron fire Sunday night."

Just to confirm the foregoing information, in December of 2006, I interviewed an Ebenal Construction Co. worker who had been working on the Waldron Building renovation project. He confirmed that they had indeed found evidence of a fire in the charred beams and timbers of the old building. These were especially evident in the southeast corner of the building above the old bank.

The Fairhaven legend that the Waldron building had never been completed in its upstairs stories is now laid to rest. The Waldron building, at least for a couple of years, was complete and functioning on each of its three floors.

Now Waldron was faced with rebuilding the upper floors. His timing could not have been worse. With inadequate insurance and dwindling funds he was just able to get the fourth floor walls up, put the roof back on the building and frame in the upper stories when the great Fairhaven Boom came to an end, a national financial panic set in and his Bank of Fairhaven failed.

The photo on page 99 shows the original completed building with its finished two upper floors. This nice drawing came from *The Fairhaven Illustrated* (published only once in 1890), a Chamber of Commerce production shamelessly boosting the opportunities and future of Fairhaven. You will notice the "Bank of Fairhaven" sign on the 12th Street side, and the fact that there are but two upper stories in the Waldron Building of 1890.

The next photo taken during the 2006 remodel shows that it now has four stories and that the fourth floor windows are of a different design.

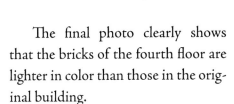

Gordon Tweit collection.

The original Waldron Building, illustration in the *Fairhaven Illustrated*, 1890.

Waldron Building remodel, 2006. Photo below shows different color bricks.

The final photo clearly shows that the bricks of the fourth floor are lighter in color than those in the original building.

The upstairs rooms lay unrepaired and unused for 115 years until 2006 when David Ebenal bought the building and began his luxury condominium and retail project.

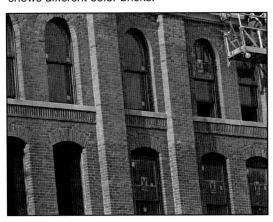

Hohl Moves to the Waterfront

Hohl apparently occupied the Waldron Building until 1906. The 1906 Directory shows the Geo. J. Hohl Company at the waterfront, at the foot of Taylor Avenue. Title company records show Hohl buying the waterfront lots of Fairhaven Tidelands on July 16, 1906, from a William Hedge. Hohl must have begun construction of his warehouse next to the old cannery in the late summer of 1906.

An October 19, 1907, article in *The Bellingham Herald* carries the headline "New Flouring Mills Rapidly Nearing Completion on Waterfront." The article speaks to the success of the new construction, but mentions the "old building on the right being the first structure put up by the present president of the new company." I suspect that the newspaper article tells us that Hohl built the first building at the Taylor Avenue waterfront in 1906 using his own money, but that he sold his company or at least part of it to outside interests in 1907 and the new Company, Bellingham Flour Mills Co., was financing the 1907 addition. Hohl was now the manager and president of the new company.

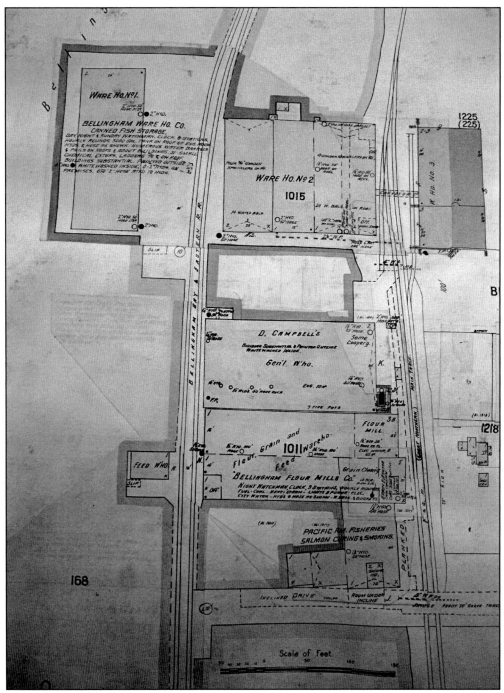

Sanborn Map.

The flour mill was built on four lots of the Fairhaven Tidelands Plat. Lots 34, 35, 36, & 37, each lot being 25 feet wide, the property width totalled 100 feet. The land was first purchased from the fledgling state of Washington on April 1, 1900, by

Galen Biery Papers and Photographs, #0093, Center for Pacific Northwest Studies, Western Washington University.

Bellingham Flour Mills Company.

C.X. Larrabee for the Fairhaven Land Company. They deeded the property to Erastus Bartlett two months later on June 1, 1900. Bartlett died two years later. The title company records show his will filed on August 25, 1902. His heirs transferred their rights to the Bartlett Estates Company in 1903 and the Estate Company sold the lots to a William Hedge on July 16, 1906. Hedge gave a deed to George J. Hohl on that same date. Hohl sold the four lots just eleven months later to Bellingham Flour Mills Company. The exact date of the deed was June 8, 1907.

The Sanborn Map shows the mill and grain elevator as a three-story building on the shore beside the Great Northern track and beside the grain elevator. The rest of the structure is a one-story warehouse stretched out to the west on piling, the huge warehouse is labeled "flour, grain and feed warehouse". The 22,000-square-foot, wooden-frame warehouse was built over the water on piles driven into the sea bottom and spanned the entire distance from the Great Northern main line on the shore to the Bellingham Bay & Eastern trestle (later to be the Northern Pacific R.R.) 220 feet off shore.

This configuration meant that it could be served by two railroads. The facility would have been able to serve the marine and offshore economy through the "Feed

Warehouse" shown on the small dock seaward of the trestle. The dock would have stood in deep water capable of mooring the largest vessels of the day. A double railroad track shown on the trestle allowed for a sidetrack for loading and unloading. I would guess that the railroad on the trestle provided the primary service to this facility as Sanborn shows the office at the southwest corner of the warehouse beside the B.B. & E. / Northern Pacific trestle.

Polk City Directory listings for the George J. Hohl Company remain the same until 1908, when the business name is shown as Bellingham Flour Mills Company. It is probable that Hohl sold his business at about that time to an Everett company who would own and operate it using the Bellingham name. It is also probable that the Everett milling company provided much of the financing for the second phase of construction of the huge facility and was a co-owner or a total owner from the beginning of that second construction phase. The aforementioned *Herald* article makes mention of "the present President of the new Company," which in this article is called The Bellingham Flour Mills Company. I suspect that the true owner at this point might have been Everett Flour Mills Co. dba Bellingham Flour Mills Company.

The year 1911 must have been a tumultuous one for the Bellingham Flour Mills Company. The city directory of that year shows that it has a new president, and George Hohl is out. The new officers are Frank Gibson, President; W.W. Harden of Seattle, Vice President; and W.E. Simonton, Secy Treasurer.

Whatever happened to cause Hohl to leave Bellingham Flour Mills we do not know, but we do know that he managed to stay in the feed and seed business. He is now listed as the manager of Whatcom Flour & Feed with an address on Roeder Avenue at F Street. We also know that Whatcom Flour and Feed was owned by The Everett Flour Mills Company and represented by a R.G. Rusk. Interestingly, Rusk was also an officer of the Bellingham Flour Mill Company.

The Sanborn Map shows Whatcom Flour and Feed as the two one-story, wood-frame structures clad with corrugated steel siding and connected with a narrow mid-section. The building is clearly labeled "Whatcom Flour & Feed Mill" and a small two-story feed mill is indicated in the northeast corner. That old building is gone now and in its place are the

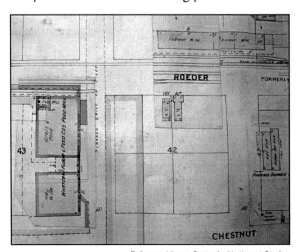

Reference Library, Center for Northwest Studies, Western Washington University.

Sanborn Map.

Hohl's house on G Street.

office and maintainance shops of the Sanitary Service Company. Paul Razore, president of Sanitary Service Company, told me that their building site (the old mill site), was covered with old pilings, evidence that the Whatcom Flour and Feed building was built on piling over the water or sand fill.

George Hohl and his wife Nellie left the southside for good in 1910 and moved to a handsome house at 2001 G street for a brief period. The next year they had moved again to 319 Magnolia Street, which is the block now occupied by Sherman Williams Paint Company and just a few hundred feet from the present Hohl Feed & Seed store on Railroad Avenue.

Back at the foot of Taylor Avenue, Bellingham Flour Mills Company must have remained in an agitated state. The year 1912 shows new corporate officers, G.W. Ford of Spokane, President; E.A. King of Portland, Vice President; and Frank Gibson of Salem, Oregon, Secy. Treasurer.

The 1915 *Polk Directory* lists R.G. Rusk as Secretary Treasurer of the Bellingham Flour Mills Company. We know him to be one of the officers of the Everett Flour Mill Company that also owned Whatcom Flour and Feed. By 1917 Bellingham Flour Mills Company disappears from the *Polk Directory* entirely, never to be shown again. Title company records show that the property at Taylor Avenue was sold on July 17,

1920, to Ford Grain Company. The Ford Grain Company was owned by G.W. Ford of Spokane, who was president of Whatcom Flour and Feed. In the fall of 1926 the property was leased by the Olympic Bell Marketing Company to Olympic CalPet Refining.

The future of the land was clarified when a warranty deed was registered to the California Petroleum Corporation on March 23, 1928. I am guessing that the mill and warehouse were demolished in that year and CalPet began the process of converting the site to a petroleum receiving, storage and distribution facility.

In the meantime George J. Hohl was still surviving in the feed and seed business. In 1918 he and wife Nellie had moved their home yet again to live at unit 1-B, Stephens Court Apartments. Here they would spend most of the rest of their lives.

He continued to manage Whatcom Flour and Feed until 1921. In 1922 he moved again, this time he is listed as the manager of Bellingham Feed and Seed Company at 1123 Railroad Avenue. That building now belongs to John Blethen and is the location of Blethen's cabinet shop, New Whatcom Interiors, and is across the street from the new Depot Market Square.

Railroad Avenue

In the year 1923, Hohl returned to ownership of his own business. In that year the directory shows him as president and manager of the Geo. J. Hohl Company at 1322-24 Railroad. He is his own boss again, his son Ross is shown as the bookkeeper and

Stephens Court Apartments.

Hohl is doing business in the exact same location that Hohl Feed & Seed occupies to-day 83 years later. His old companies, Bellingham Flour Mill Co., Whatcom Flour & Feed, and Bellingham Feed & Seed are never listed again. It is presumed that Everett Flour Mills retreated to Everett, perhaps finished in Bellingham because of a large debt owed them by a Bellingham bakery that they sued in 1923 and took into receivership. They had sold the Taylor Avenue flour mill to Ford Grain Company in 1920.

Hohl was now comfortably settled on Railroad Avenue in the ground floor of the Spokane Building that had been built in 1901. This was a rather famous, or perhaps I should say *infamous* address, made so by the shady reputation of The Spokane Hotel which occupied the entire second floor. The old hotel, more familiarly known as *The Spokane* by Bellingham's rakes, was a brothel. Railroad Avenue was a rough street in those days and The Spokane was one of the larger and tonier houses of ill repute on a street that sported many of them.

George Hohl may have actually first leased the Spokane Building in 1923; however, the The Chicago Title Company records confirm the lease with an entry dated March 20, 1925, between the building owners Edith W. Stimpson and J. Reid Morrison and the lessee, George J. Hohl & Company.

We are confident that the lease was for only the lower floor of the Spokane Building and that George Hohl had nothing to do with what went on upstairs. While Hohl probably benefited from doing business in such a well-known location, given Hohl's intolerance for gambling as mayor of Fairhaven, it would seem highly unlikely that he would have anything to do with prostitution.

Brothels were outlawed in Bellingham in 1948. It is likely that the Spokane was doing business up to the very end. Curt Smith, in his book *The Brothels of Bellingham*, shows photos of the never-remodeled upstairs of the historic old building.

George Hohl's long business career on Bellingham Bay came to an end in 1933. George was apparently in ill health. He and Nellie moved to Glacier and the business was sold to the Chas. H. Lilly Company, who installed Victor Wolfkill as manager. George died in 1934 at the age of 71. In the next year the City Directory shows Nellie Hohl as a widow. George's long and productive life was over.

The Hofeditz Era

In 1936 Tyrus Hofeditz, who was employed by the Chas. H. Lilly Co. in Seattle, was sent to Bellingham to take over the management of Hohl Feed & Seed. The Spokane Building was owned by Stimpson and Morrison until 1943, when both the building and the feed and seed business were sold to Sam Gelb.

Photo courtesy Hohl Feed & Seed.

Tyrus Hofeditz

In an incredible career of ten-hour, six-days-a-week work, Ty Hofeditz stayed on the job for 57 years. Including his three years with the Lilly Company in Seattle he worked for 60 years in the feed and seed business. Ty Hofeditz retired in 1994. He was followed as manager by his son Jack, who had been hired by his father in 1956. Jack Hofeditz worked for the Gelb family for 45 years, retiring in 2001. Interviewed in June of 2007, Jack Hofeditz recalled his father telling him that the brothel upstairs was operating in his early years at the store and it most likely remained in business up to the 1948 ban.

Whatcom Museum of History & Art

George Hohl in front of Waldron building feed store.

From a brochure from the Lilly Company, Hohl Feed & Seed collection.
Light Housekeeping Rooms.

Ty loved to tell about the lettering on the door to the upstairs establishment which advertised, "Light Housekeeping Rooms". Light housekeeping indeed!

By the time Jack joined the business in 1956 the upstairs rooms were a low-price flop house, with rooms being rented to itinerant 'knights of the road' for two and three dollars a night. He recalls it being known as the Lee Hotel at that time. The upstairs has been empty or used for Hohl Feed storage for many years.

The business is now owned by Sam Gelb's son, Charles Gelb of Spokane, and the building by Gelb and the Koplowitz brothers, Sam Gelb's two grandsons.

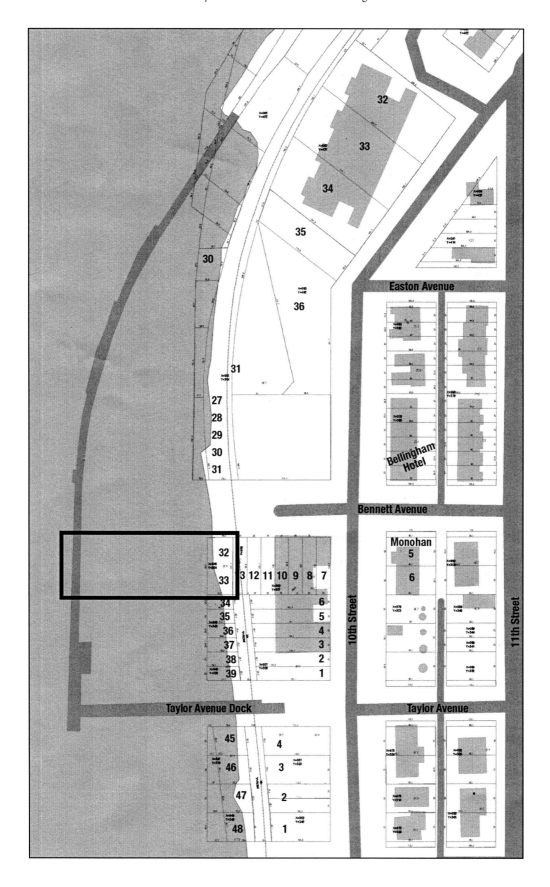

Chapter 11

Dan Campbell General Warehouse

JUST NORTH OF THE FLOUR MILL/McEvoy site, and in front of the northern part of the present day Chrysalis Hotel, there was another large wooden building erected on piles. It is shown on the Sanborn map as "D. Campbell's Gen'l W'ho". This building was largely used as a warehouse for canned salmon, although at times other commodities were stored there. Gordon Tweit remembers it used as a potato warehouse at one time during the Second World War. Eventually it was used as a manufacturing plant by cross arm manufacturer, R.J. Haley Co., and had a extension seaward of the railroad trestle occupied by Bornstein's Seafood.

Dan Campbell

Dan Campbell had bought the tidelands lot that the old buildings sat upon on May 7, 1907. He may not have built his warehouse until 1911, because that is the date the National Bank of Commerce recorded a mortgage on the land. Campbell owned it until 1930, when the deed was transferred to his Campbell Investment Company. The old warehouse was to remain in Campbell hands until August 22, 1963, when it was sold to Bornstein Seafood Co.

Dan Campbell came to the salmon canning and warehouse business through marriage. His father-in-law, a man named Kenny, owned the Astoria & Puget Sound Canning Company. Kenny bought the little cannery in Chuckanut Bay from its receivers after its founder Henry N. "Lord" Newton and partner John Baines had failed in 1898. He installed his son-in-law Campbell as superintendent. Apparently Dan

Dan Campbell house

had a talent for the business. The cannery in Chuckanut Bay ran continuously until 1934. By that time Campbell had a cannery at Excursion Inlet in Alaska, and he used the Chuckanut facility to store the salmon from his Alaska operations. It is presumed that the Taylor Dock warehouse was used for the same purpose.

Randolph Walker house

In 1948, after some 50 years of successful operation, Campbell sold all of his canning interests to the Columbia River Packer's Association, although Campbell Investment Company still owned the Taylor Avenue warehouse. Dan Campbell lived in a large brick and stucco home at 201 South Forest Street. Just a block away, his daughter Marjorie and her husband Randolph Walker, built

Gordon Tweit collection.

Can Company and Campbell Warehouse, see Bellingham Hotel in upper right.

their white frame mansion on the other side of the street at 115 South Forest Street. Randolph Walker died suddenly of a heart attack at the young age of 48, but Marjorie Campbell Walker continued to live in the home with her family for many years. Their children, Dan, Robert and Susie (Sudie) were all raised in the home.

The stately home was eventually sold to Dr. Edward Stimpson and his wife Catherine, and once again the house witnessed the raising of a family. The Stimpsons raised seven capable children in the home. The Stimpson progeny recently left a permanent mark upon the Whatcom County community with their gift of the Stimpson Family Reserve, a large timbered park in Bellingham's eastern outskirts. Matriarch "Kitty" Stimpson reigned for many years as a community leader and a prominent Democrat. The grand house with its huge living room was the scene of innumerable community meetings and election night parties and hosted many of our state's national figures, Henry Jackson and Warren Magnuson among them. The lovely house is now home to the family of Dr. Eric Laine.

Bornstein Seafood Company

In the early 1930s, Myer Bornstein and Charlie Hauser began a fish processing partnership. Taking advantage of the economic opportunities of the day they bought large king salmon from the canneries for 25 cents a fish. The big kings were too large for the canneries which wanted silvers and sockeye that fit their automated machines. The huge 20- to 40-pound kings were spurned. Bornstein and Hauser bought them for almost nothing in present-day terms, cut them up into marketable sizes, and sold

Bornstein's Seafood beside the Texaco dock.

them to anyone who wanted fresh salmon, wholesale or retail, from Blaine to Seattle. Thus a business was born that survives and thrives to this day. Incidently, king salmon is priced on the day that this page was written at $17 per pound. A 25-cent, 30-pound king salmon of 1930 would be worth $510 today.

Hauser was soon bought out, and Myer Bornstein's long record of success in the fish business began. Operations began in the smallish metal-clad building leased from Campbell Investment Company on the seaward side of the trestle. The company occupied that building and eventually the large warehouse building behind. Bornstein ultimately bought the entire property including some land above the bluff east of the railroad and operated there until the very early 1960s.

In 1952 Bornstein's opened their new facility on the I & J waterway and slowly began phasing out the Taylor Avenue operation, using it for seasonal operations during the crab and salmon seasons. The old piling and structures at Taylor Avenue were deteriorating badly and it was more economic to move to the protected waterway on the north side of the bay than to replace pilings, dock and building at their original site. Additionally, the only access to the Bornstein plant by that time was down the deteriorating Taylor Avenue dock, and then north over the increasingly dilapidated dock on what had been the railroad trestle.

The decision to move was made easier when a 14-year-old boy broke into the processing plant one night in the early '60s and set fire to its interior. Current Bornstein Inc. president Jay Bornstein comments that the arson ended the company's 30 year run on the southside. The deteriorated and charred old buildings were torn down, the Texaco Company abandoned its dockside operations in 1962, and the Taylor Avenue dock was left without a purpose or a function for the first time in perhaps 75 years.

Bornstein's apparently made the right move, as it continues as one of the Pacific Coast's largest processors of fish with operations in Bellingham, Astoria, Oregon, and in several locations in Canada.

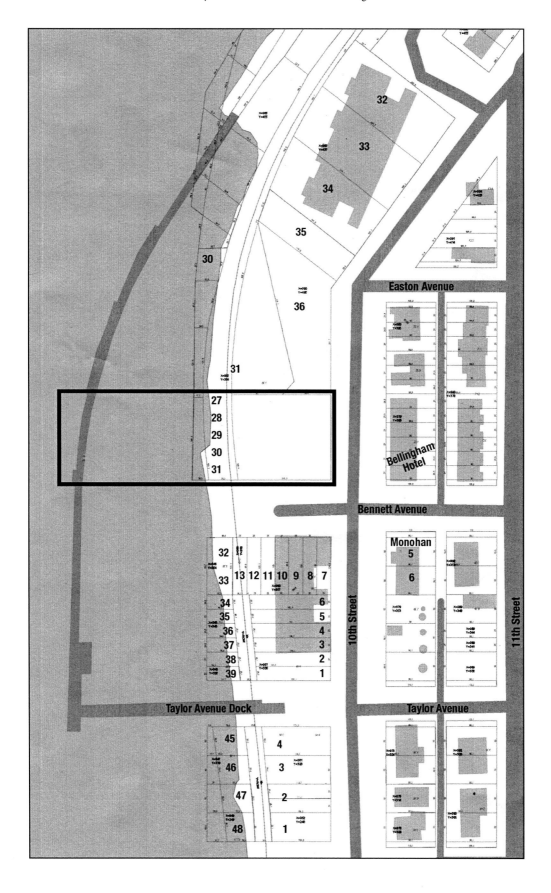

Chapter 12

The Can Factory

NORTH OF CAMPBELL'S WAREHOUSE building there was a large gap in the succession of structures. An 80-foot stretch of open water represented the city street right-of-way reserved for Bennett Avenue, which extended into the tidelands. On the north side of that 80-foot stretch of water, we quickly come to the three large wood-frame buildings of the Pacific Sheet Metal Company, manufacturers of salmon cans for the canneries of Washington and Alaska.

In 1898 the Fairhaven Branch of the Pacific Sheet Metal Works, Sydney M. Smith president, purchased the upland lots and built a three-story brick building on dry land east of the railroad track. The building was built into the cut-away bluff with its basement at the level of the Great Northern track. In this building Pacific Sheet Metal manufactured salmon cans for the burgeoning salmon canning business.

Apparently business was good for on June 6, 1900, the State of Washington sold tideland lots numbers 27 to 31 to Pacific Sheet Metal and the watery gap between the shore and the railroad trestle was soon filled with pilings on which three large wooden industrial buildings were built.

The photo on page 123, dated 1955, shows the original brick building connected to the later wooden buildings (built over the water) by an overhead "can-way" crossing the Great Northern track, seemingly penetrating the roof of the first building and extending to the adjacent roof. Pacific Sheet Metal operated the facility until 1902 when they sold it to the American Can Company. In 1907 the large buildings were purchased by Everett B. Deming and the Pacific American Fisheries Company. The facility was operated for many years as Bellingham Warehouse Company, a subsidiary of Pacific American Fisheries. Then in 1923 it was deeded directly to PAF.

The Tin Rock

Can manufacturing and canned salmon storage continued for many years at the Taylor/Bennett Avenue location by the successive companies. Evidence of that long service is found in the size of the "Tin Rock" which now sits alone in the open water on the north edge of where the buildings used to be.

Back in those unregulated days, industrial waste was disposed of in the most expeditious way possible. Each day of can production resulted in scraps of tin and unused but still molten solder. The day's waste was simply dumped into the water from the porch between warehouse #1 and warehouse #2. Year after year the pile of tin and solder grew as it rusted and fused together. Finally it began to show above the water surface. It grew and grew until even at high tide its rusty crown was well above the surface. The buildings remained until the mid 1960s, when they were demolished by the Port of Bellingham. But the Tin Rock is still there, a seemingly timeless, but rusting reminder of an earlier day on Bellingham's south side.

The Tin Rock.

George Jeffers' Friday Harbor Canning Company

At some time in the 1940s Pacific American Fisheries developed adequate canned salmon storage at its primary location farther south in Harris Bay. The buildings of the Bellingham Warehouse facility became surplus. In the early '40s George Jeffers purchased the Bellingham Warehouse buildings from PAF on a contract of sale. On December 20, 1956, the former can factory and warehouses were transferred by warranty deed to George P. Jeffers.

Jeffers first appears on the salmon canning scene in the early 1930s as the manager of the Carlyle Packing Co. Cannery at Village Point on Lummi Island.

The Carlyle Packing Company, owned by Frank Wright, had its own salmon trap just off the cannery and it successfully caught most of its own salmon in that trap. The

Beach Packing Company cannery, Lummi Bay.

Carlyle Cannery closed in 1934 when traps were declared illegal, but there was another cannery on Lummi Island in those years. The Lummi Bay Packing Company is first mentioned in title company records in 1911. It operated a cannery on the Hales Passage side, at the north end of what was then called Lummi Bay, or sometimes Fish Bay. The cannery was situated at the north end of the sandy crescent beach which terminates at Lane Spit. That choice property is now completely lined with summer homes.

Jeffers purchased the Lummi Bay Packing Company from its owner, the Spotswood Corporation, Karl Paulis, president. The date of purchase was November 23, 1935. His purchase included the cannery built over the water, a house, an office and storage building, the entire beach, the point and quite a bit of acreage. Jeffers and his wife, Aileen, continued to live in the old Pickering house which was the manager's house for the Carlyle Packing Company at Village Point, and their daughter Garreth was born in that house in 1937.

Jeffers renamed the Lummi Bay operation the Beach Packing Company, and operated the cannery until sometime in the early 1940s. Garreth Jeffers recalls that her parents moved to 17th Street in Bellingham in 1942 so that she could attend Bellingham schools, but it is probable it was not Lummi Island's one-room school-

Photo courtesy Garreth Jeffers.

Cabins on the beach on Lummi Island, Beach Cannery in the distance.

house that caused the move. It is more likely that the cannery was not doing well by that time. After World War II small independent canneries began an unending state of decline. The cannery and its valuable waterfront land were sold to D.R. Bourque on April 27, 1946. Jeffers paid off his mortgage to Seattle First National Bank and moved on to his next opportunity.

Pacific American Fisheries had a small salmon cannery in Friday Harbor on San Juan Island. The old cannery, complete with a superintendent's house, was situated within the city limits of Friday Harbor, nestled into the shoreline beside the present Washington State Ferry landing. The old cannery site is now occupied by a condominium development adjacent to the ferry landing.

Jeffers bought the cannery in 1942, and later, in 1952 moved his family to Friday Harbor and into the old house. He was to live there until his death in 1971.

The author can well remember his own father, Earle Griffin, chatting with George Jeffers while riding on the ferry *M.V. Vashon*. Jeffers was frequently heading home to Friday Harbor after doing business on the mainland. My family was frequently riding the *Vashon* on Friday evenings heading to our San Juan Island summer home. I remember Jeffers as a husky, energetic and friendly man.

Jeffers apparently was operating two businesses—packing salmon in his Friday Harbor cannery and acting as a salmon broker. Jeffers bought the large can factory warehouses from PAF, and operated as a salmon broker, selling both his own fish and the canned product of others on the world market.

History would eventually show that the salmon canning industry had long passed

Friday Harbor Cannery.

its peak. One by one, the old canning companies failed, as the once abundant salmon runs diminished and the world market for canned salmon shrank. Alaska became the last frontier for salmon packers. Soon Bellingham Canning Company, Alaska Packers, and even the mighty Pacific American Fisheries would close their doors.

George Jeffers was a man swimming against the tide, but he was also a creative and risk-taking businessman. As conditions in the salmon canning industry worsened, Jeffers decided to become a vegetable canner. His daughter Garreth, and the entries in the title company records, tell the story of his last desperate gamble.

San Juan Island had always been an agricultural island blessed with a large and fertile central valley which had sustained the island's farming economy for generations. Jeffers decided to convert his Friday Harbor cannery to can peas.

He mortgaged everything he had—including the warehouses in Fairhaven, the San Juan Canning Company, and some remaining assets from the Lummi Island days—securing a Small Business Administration loan of $250,000. The title company record on the Fairhaven property contains the following notations.

> 3-14-1958; deed and purchase agreement,
>   Friday Harbor Canning Co. to SBA.
> 1-13-1961; Sellers assignment-Beach Packing Co. to SBA.
> 6-24-1961; $250,000 mortgage-George Jeffers to SBA.

George Jeffers, second from left, next to the man with the *picaroon.*

Jeffers bet it all, putting everything he had into buying 250 acres of bottom land in the San Juan Valley and converting his cannery to can vegetables. The valley was planted to peas, and for a number of years he struggled to make his new venture succeed. Ultimately he met failure. He was unable to repay the SBA. The title company record tells the sad story in a terse notation:

> 5-18-1965; USA vs Friday Harbor Canning Company, Foreclosure.

George Jeffers' gamble had failed. The SBA took the valuable land in the San Juan Valley, The Jeffers family had to liquidate everything. By this time George Jeffers was a sick man. He lived on in Friday Harbor until his death in 1971.

One final entry in the title company record reveals the fate of the old Can Factory warehouses near the Taylor Avenue Dock.

> 7-7-1965; George Jeffers to Port of Bellingham.

Jeffers had lost everything, except by a strange twist of fate, the family home. The family was able to retain their Friday Harbor home because of an odd paperwork error. The foreclosure procedure revealed that the Jeffers family had never legally owned the SBA mortgaged house, even though they had been making payments on it for years. Since they did not own it, the government could not foreclose on it.

It seems that the original sale documents transferring the cannery and the house from PAF to Jeffers back in 1945 had described the cannery properly, but omitted any mention of the house. The Jeffers thought they had bought a house, and PAF thought they had sold a house; the SBA thought they had secured a house as collateral for their loan. They were all wrong.

Fortunately for the family, PAF was sympathetic to their plight. For the price of some minor legal fees the family was able to gain title to the house by Right of Adverse Possession. The house remained occupied by the Jeffers family after George's death and until the death of Aileen Jeffers in 1973. Garreth Jeffers sold the old house in 1976.

Back in Fairhaven, The Port of Bellingham became owners of the now dilapidated and obsolete old warehouses, and in 1965 contracted to have them demolished. The vintage 1898 bricks from the original building were cleaned and taken to Seattle to be sold. The wooden warehouses were salvaged for their lumber and their sheet metal sheathing. All that remains of their passing is the Tin Rock in the water and several stubs of piles in the mud of low tide. The site of the brick warehouse can be easily found by walking down the park path into the large basement excavation just north of the Chrysalis Hotel. The concrete floor of the basement can still be seen at the bottom of the old excavation on the level of the Burlington Northern Railroad track.

P.A.F. Sells to the Port

In 1966 Pacific American Fisheries (PAF) closed for good. Their extensive waterfront property holdings on Bellingham Bay were bought by the Port of Bellingham. Thomas Glenn, the Port's longtime manager, negotiated the sale with the president of the United Pacific Insurance Company, which had taken over the Bellingham assets of PAF as owner of its indebtedness. Glenn recalls that the negotiation was one of incredible civility. He and the insurance executive got along famously. Over a long period of discussions the asking price for all of the PAF land and buildings in Bellingham, which had started at two million dollars, was finally reduced at the point of purchase to a mere $675,000.

This substantial bargain included all of the land now occupied by Marine Park, the shipyards, Arrowac Fisheries, the Alaska Ferry Terminal, and around the bay to include the old Uniflite Boat site. Glenn reflects with pleasure that it was a pleasant and successful negotiation of lasting benefit to the community. It was surely one of the high points in his long and fruitful career as Port Manager.

The upland site of the now demolished 1898 brick salmon warehouse had gone to the Port earlier. Now the City wanted it for a park. The *Bellingham Herald* of May 25, 1975, contained a story about Mayor Reg Williams going to the Port to negotiate for the upland. The story caption read, "It's A Standstill At Present."

Eventually the Mayor prevailed, for on June 7, 1979, the Port made a deal with

Aerial view, May 4, 1955, shows Marriott home at curve of Bayview and South State. The iron ring in the rock along the path is established as the land anchor for the log boom by this photo. The steam turbine building is shown as a roofless ruin. The Croatian trail to Easton Beach is clearly visible across the present site of the Riptide condos on the right side of photo.

You can still see an interesting relic of the old booms that remains embedded in the hard sandstone of the Boulevard Park shoreline. A huge iron ring attached deep into the stone just 50 feet north of Easton Beach reveals itself at half tide. To that massive ring (and others that used to be along the shore) were attached the cables and chains which held the extensive rafts of logs in place. The iron of the ring is at least two inches thick, and has probably been embedded there in the live rock for more than one hundred years.

Whatcom Museum of History & Art

Aerial view of the four can factory buildings, dated May 4, 1955. Note the over-the-train-track canway from the old brick building to the waterfront warehouses. Gilmore Oil Co./Mobil Oil are still at location south of Taylor Avenue. Easton Beach is on lower left side of photo.

the City to trade this park land for property that the City owned in the Squalicum Harbor area. The deal required that the City improve it as a park within ten years or it would revert to the Port. It sat unimproved for many years, but the city hurriedly cleared the lot and planted some grass at the last minute in order to validate the agreement. Title passed from the Port to the City on January 16, 1990. In 2005 and 2006, in conjunction with the improvements at Taylor Avenue, the site was improved further with lawn, paths and seats which have added to the pleasant walking and water viewing opportunities of Boulevard Park.

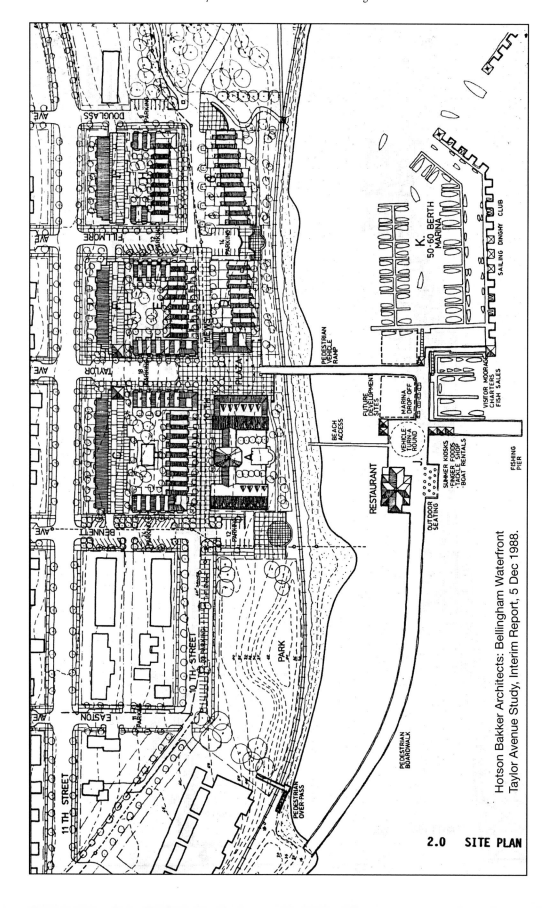

Hotson Bakker Architects: Bellingham Waterfront
Taylor Avenue Study, Interim Report, 5 Dec 1988.

2.0 SITE PLAN

Chapter 13

The Boardwalk

THE TAYLOR AVENUE DOCK was no longer needed or wanted. The Texaco Company wanted to relieve itself of the liabilities involved with fueling boats from an old wooden dock in need of repair. By 1962 its refinery at March Point near Anacortes produced the petroleum products that its Whatcom County consignee needed; and it was faster, cheaper and easier to simply truck the product to Bellingham. Bornstein's Seafood, which also used the dock for access, had moved their plant north to the I & J waterway. The Texaco office was removed from the dock, and a new office and storage building was built above the railroad track facing 10th Street. The dock became unused, was deteriorating, and becoming a greater liability with each passing year.

Joel Douglas, Entrepreneur

Joel Douglas was a young man seeking entrepreneurial opportunities. He had been born in Bellingham, did a stint in the Army, graduated from the University of Washington, and returned home as the local claims adjuster for the Unigard Insurance Company. He soon left that job and bought a share at the local plywood plant. With a small nest egg he began investing in land and business situations. His first purchase was Lairmont Manor.

In 1976 Douglas saw the Taylor Avenue Dock situation as an opportunity and he acted. Soon he had purchased Texaco's interest in the docks and their lease with the State of Washington Department of Natural Resources (DNR). Acting in his corporate name, Pacific Resources Inc, he negotiated a new lease with DNR.

The lease, signed on September 1, 1976, provided for a term of thirty years, subject to rent adjustments each five years. The annual rent represented six percent of the value of the leased property. The first year's rent was $1,236. A condition of the lease was that Douglas maintain the dock structures. Given their deteriorating condition that was not a small responsibility.

Adding complexity to the situation was the question of who owned what. DNR seemed confident that they owned the dock outward from the 'Inner Harbor Line,' which is approximately the low tide line. The question was, who owned the bridge over the railroad track and out to the 'Inner Harbor Line'. Was it the City? Had it been the Texas Company? The bridge was on the Taylor Avenue right-of-way. There was some confusing precedent, as it was known that in 1953 when the bridge and dock were re-planked the materials were purchased by the Dan Campbell interests, Texaco, Mobil, and perhaps other users; and the City provided the labor to install the planking.

Regardless, Douglas knew that the dock was of no use if you did not control where it touched the water, and Douglas' lease clearly put him into that control position.

He spent some money replacing the electricity and water service to the dock and then began seeking income-producing uses for it. The first and obvious use was boat moorage and he soon found several large boats that required moorage, among them a 40-foot catamaran and a big old tug boat. He had three or four renters most of the time. From time to time other opportunities appeared. There was interest from the owners of a derelict old ferry boat who planned to remodel it into a floating restaurant moored to the dock. That opportunity slipped away when the City of Bellingham was slow in considering a permit and the ferry boat folks moved on to another city.

In 1986, Ron and Wendy Thorpe of Sundowner Enterprises approached him, proposing to lease the dock to permanently moor their 180-foot vessel *Sundowner*. *Sundowner* was to be a bed and breakfast transient accommodation. Initial plans called for 6 to 10 rooms and a continental breakfast. Future plans included more rooms, a small coffee shop, a gift shop, and an art gallery. This proposal sounded promising and Douglas was making progress in his negotiations until word got to the Department of Natural Resources.

In a letter to William Geyer, Director of the City of Bellingham's Department of Planning and Economic Development, the DNR lease administrator wrote,

> "Unfortunately we were not advised of this proposal earlier since new residential uses of this nature can not be permitted to locate in harbor areas."

He cited the appropriate laws and formally objected to the City issuing any permit for the bed and breakfast. It is not known if the *Sundowner* ever became a bed and breakfast, but it didn't happen in Bellingham.

Not all of Douglas' tenants were savory characters. In the summer of 1981, he rented space to the lovely 65-foot converted trawler, *Tiki*. This handsome craft went to sea one morning only to return to Bellingham so laden with smuggled marijuana that she was difficult to steer. She was part of a large drug smuggling effort and was but one of several runner boats that had gone out to meet the mother ship, lying somewhere off the coast. Bales of marijuana were stashed in every available space, even packed so tightly in the engine room that the arresting federal agents could not see the engine. Three other vessels were seized at other locations; the total value of the confiscated marijuana was estimated at fifty million dollars. The overloaded *Tiki* rammed into the Taylor Avenue dock, knocking down her mast and dislodging her pilot house. There was minor damage to the dock. The waiting federal agents led the ship's crew away in handcuffs.

By 1988, Douglas had been leasing the dock for twelve years. Aside from a little moorage income he had not found much success with his investment. Its condition was going downhill and substantial maintenance would have been very costly. When the City of Bellingham approached him with an offer to take over his lease, Douglas was ready to listen. After appraisal and negotiation he sold his leasehold rights to the City of Bellingham for $35,000. The date of sale was January 4, 1988.

The Taylor Avenue Partnership

In 1988 the author developed a creative idea. I had been thinking about the inappropriate use of the excellent water-view property surrounding the by-then-decaying and virtually un-used Taylor Avenue Dock.

The commercial atmosphere of the area created by two oil storage and distribution plants and the old Reid Boiler works had apparently discouraged residential development on the otherwise choice view property in the area. The land immediately around the dock and up to South State Street was almost entirely empty except for the aforementioned commercial uses.

I concluded that if the commercial properties could be purchased, or their owners brought in as partners, it might be possible to build an 'Urban Village' on the site, centering on a town square at the head of the dock. Needing partners that would bring important skills, I shared the concept with prominent young attorney Steve Brinn, and a fellow Rotarian Robert I. "Bob" Morse.

Morse was a scion of the pioneer Morse family, a CPA, and the president of Morse Hardware Company. Griffin (myself), Morse and Brinn formed a partnership and each contributed $2000 of *getting started money* to the venture.

The partners visualized a small European-style village of two- and three-story buildings surrounding an intimate public square at the head of the dock and the 10th

Port of Bellingham Records, Washington State Archives; Northwest Regional Archives, Bellingham.
The land immediately around the Dock and up to South State Street was almost entirely empty except for the aforementioned commercial uses.

Street and Taylor Avenue intersection. We envisioned businesses around the ground floor of the square, and apartments or offices above. The back-lands, up the sloping hill to South State Street, would hold high quality apartments and town houses. The old boiler works building held promise as an interesting restaurant opportunity, while a renovated Taylor Avenue dock could provide access to a pleasure boat marina protected from the west wind by a floating breakwater that had recently been developed in Bellingham by Bellingham Marine Industries. A boutique hotel was envisioned on the bluff just north of the dock.

Realizing that we would need professional planning help to put our vision together, and having been impressed with the then-new townhouse developments in the False Creek area of Vancouver B.C., I contacted Norm Hotson, an architect who had done much of that Vancouver planning.

We also appealed to the Rotary Club of Bellingham to fund the architectural study and an economic feasibility study. The partners were of the opinion that their project was more than just a private development, but if successful would be a significant community improvement that merited Rotary support. In hindsight it seems a bit remarkable, but the Rotary Club of Bellingham agreed to fund the "Hotson Study" with a grant of $9000.

Hotson was hired to provide both an architectural study and a separate economic feasibility study. When Norm Hotson presented his completed report and accompanying economic study several months later the partners were delighted to see that the project appeared feasible conditioned upon the land being purchased at reasonable prices.

The Hotson Plan

The architect's vision included amenities which in an uncanny way presaged what we see on the site today (see page 124). He had sited the hotel the partners had envisioned exactly where the Chrysalis Hotel stands today. He had renovated the old dock and the dilapidated railway trestle and made it a pedestrian walkway just as we enjoy today. The partners had envisioned a marina accessed over the dock, but not the restaurant that Hotson placed on the dock where now stands a covered seating area. Encouraged and excited by the report and now armed with an economic study and a visible plan, the partners began the attempt to option the needed land.

The obvious key to success was to gain control of the waterfront owned by Reid Boiler Works, McEvoy Oil, and the former General Petroleum site just adjacent to Taylor Avenue. If those properties could be assembled it was hoped that the purchase of the backlands would follow more easily. Crucial to any successful development would be the elimination of the industrial atmosphere provided by oil storage tanks and the frequent use of the area by trucks and trailers servicing those businesses.

They approached Bob Reid of Reid Boiler, the Haggen brothers, Pat McEvoy of McEvoy Oil, and Sam Boulas (who was operating what had been Keith Oil across the street from McEvoy) with the suggestion that their businesses no longer needed waterfront locations and would be better suited on less valuable land elsewhere in the city. It was hoped that these ownerships would either join the venture as partners using their land as their capital investment in the project, or sell their properties outright.

The partners' spirits were soon dampened. Neither Reid, nor McEvoy, nor Boulas were ready to move their business, nor were any of them interested in the opportunity that the partners described.

Things went better with the old General Petroleum site. The Haggens were willing to sell. The capital demands of their rapidly growing grocery business, coupled with the management responsibilities they both carried, caused them to abandon the restaurant idea and agree to sell the property to the partners. An Option to Buy was purchased for $2000 giving the partners a six-month option to buy the land at the selling price of $300,000.

Renewed efforts with the other business owners were met with continued refusals to sell, and it became obvious that the project could not go forward.

The disappointed partners decided that it would be in the community interest to offer their option to the City of Bellingham. They had envisioned the project as both an entrepreneurial venture and also one of civic improvement. The Rotary Club of Bellingham had underwritten the Economic and Architectural study based on that premise. The partners considered that they had an obligation to offer the option to the City, and to do so at no cost to the City.

The author recalls calling on William Geyer, then City of Bellingham Community Development Director, in his office in City Hall and presenting him with the option and a copy of the Architectural Study. Geyer immediately recognized the site's potential for public use and eagerly accepted the option. He set in motion the city process. Geyer and Griffin presented the opportunity to the City Council Planning Committee, sharing the vision for the Taylor Avenue Dock.

After due process the City exercised the option and purchased the land. The date of sale was May 29, 1990.

Geyer, now a self employed developer, recalls that the Hotson Plan (showing the conversion of the dock and trestle to a pedestrian walkway) intrigued then Mayor Tim Douglas and Park Director, Byron Elmendorf, and was what began the city thinking about including the Boardwalk in their park planning. In Geyer's words, that plan showing the walkway to the north, inspired the cement walkway that we now enjoy. History was to prove that the partnership efforts and the Rotary Club investment had not been in vain.

The old dock which had served so many industrial purposes over the years was now being looked at for its public recreation potential. For several generations it had been enjoyed by southside families augmenting their diets with the plentiful Dungeness crabs caught in baited traps hung from the dock's stout toe rails. Now the City began to consider other recreational uses.

Plan to develop waterfront area goes under for lack of interest

By DEAN KAHN
of the Herald staff

A proposal to build condos, a hotel, shops and a marina in the Taylor Avenue dock area of south Bellingham is dead in the water.

Owners of key pieces of land in the area aren't interested in going along with the $22 million-plus project, said Bellingham insurance executive Brian Griffin, a proponent.

"I'm here today to report we have failed," he told members of the Bellingham City Council Planning Committee on Tuesday. "We're very sorry. It was a grand windmill to tilt at."

Griffin's effort may still bear fruit. The owner of about 20,000 square feet of land at the upland end of the dilapidated dock is willing to sell the property to the city for $300,000, Griffin said. He encouraged council members to buy the land as future access to the dock.

The city is investigating buying the land, Mayor Tim Douglas said.

The area between Bennett Drive and Douglas Avenue upland from the dock is one of the few stretches of underdeveloped waterfront properties in the city and thus a prime attraction to developers.

In 1988, the Bellingham Rotary Club, Griffin, Bellingham businessman Bob Morse and Bellingham attorney Steve Brinn commissioned a study of potential development in the area.

The consultant endorsed a major project featuring a small hotel, expensive condos or apartments, specialty shops, a marina with 50 to 60 berths and an over-the-water restaurant.

Besides upgrading the dock, the plan envisioned a pedestrian pier along an old railroad spur extending south from nearby Boulevard Park.

The city bought the dock, which served as a deepwater fueling facility, in 1986 for $35,000 from Harbor Lands Co.

Herald photo by Don Anderson
Proponent Brian Griffin explains development plan to City Council Planning Committee members.

Brian Griffin at City Council shown in a clipping out of the *Bellingham Herald*.

With the City now owning the Taylor Avenue uplands and the leasehold interest on the dock, Mayor Tim Douglas, Planning and Community Development Director William Geyer, and Parks and Recreation Director Elmendorf began to work on the possibilities of building a walkway over the old trestle right-of-way thereby connecting the main body of Boulevard Park with Taylor Avenue and its access to Fairhaven. The long process of planning, funding, permitting and construction of the modern boardwalk to Boulevard Park could begin.

The Boardwalk

The popular improvements to the dock, trestle and uplands (finally completed in 2006) were the results of more than 20 years of work by the City's Parks and Recreation Department. The idea to convert the old trestle and dock to a walkway to the park at the north end may well have been born with the Hotson Plan and the Taylor Avenue Partnership, but the achievement of the dream was an extremely complex and time-consuming effort which is a triumph of the City of Bellingham, Parks & Recreation Department, its advisory board, and several city administrations.

Before the approximately 4.2 million dollar walkway could be completed, years of planning and five years of permitting were required. Funding required the passing of a new Greenways levy and securing a grant. The project required a Department of Natural Resources lease agreement, a shorelines permit, Army Corps of Engineers Section 10 permit, a Hydraulic Project Approval from Washington State Fisheries, SEPA review, U.S. Fish & Wildlife review, Department of Ecology approval, National Marine Fisheries review, City of Bellingham building permits, and a construction agreement with the Burlington Northern Railway.

Finally the planning and permitting process was completed, and after bidding, the contract was awarded to Bergerson Construction of Astoria, Oregon. Bergerson got started by pulling out the creosote-treated railroad trestle pilings, and removing the surviving above-water trusses and steel railroad track that had been there for so long. The existing Taylor Avenue wooden bridge was strengthened and renovated to a condition that would allow people to cross over the railroad track and down to the walkway safely for many more years.

A primary concern was the protection of the extensive eel grass bed in the project area, some of the most significant eel grass beds in Bellingham Bay. Eel grass, which grows in narrow strips along the inter-tidal area, requires sunshine. In order that the boardwalk would not shade the beds, the Taylor Avenue dock was extended a bit; and the walkway structure was canted a little farther out than the original railroad trestle right-of-way in order to meet it. Work barges were required to move every three days to avoid shading the beds harmfully.

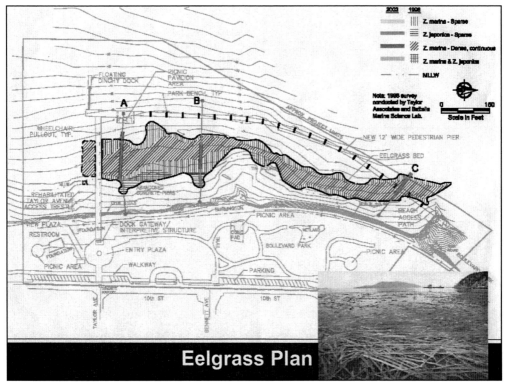

Eelgrass plan.

Bellingham Parks & Recreation Department.

The illustration shows the present position of the walkway in relation to the eel grass bed. In the first year of project completion the beds re-established themselves and expanded well beyond the predictions of the state biologists. Monitoring of the beds will continue annually.

A clean up of the sea floor to improve the health of the eel grass was one of the conditions of the permitting. More than 700 tons of debris were removed from the site. More than 1000 creosote-treated pilings were pulled. Tons of concrete slabs, rusty corrugated steel, old engines, tires, you name it, were removed from the sea bed. Let your imagine work on what might have been dumped off of those industrial docks and the railroad trestle over the course of almost 150 years. The sea bottom was covered with debris, total tonnage of all kinds was equal to that of 518 new Volkswagen Beetles. Here is the list of salvaged debris broken down:

submerged steel . . . . .5.30 tons
steel demolition . . . . .22.97 tons
wood submerged . . . . .60.05 tons
wood demolition . . . . .563.28 tons
concrete submerged . . . . .75.12 tons
total tonnage removed . . . . . . .726.72 tons

Taylor Avenue entrance to the Boardwalk seen here from uphill on Taylor.

The Taylor Avenue Entrance

The last piece of the Boulevard Park development story is the completion of the small uplands view park at the Taylor Avenue entrance to the boardwalk.

On this land where the Gilmore Oil Company lion once roared is built a small entrance park with view seating areas, and public restrooms. It was completed in the summer of 2006 by the City's contractor, Tiger Construction Co., and is graced by a wooden-arch dock entrance, the gift of the Bellingham Bay Rotary Club. The beautifully constructed fir-beam entrance structure was built by Gordon Plume Mfg. Co.

The Taylor Avenue area lends its great history to the southern end of Boulevard Park. It is a fitting balance to the equally interesting story of the park at the other end of the Boardwalk.

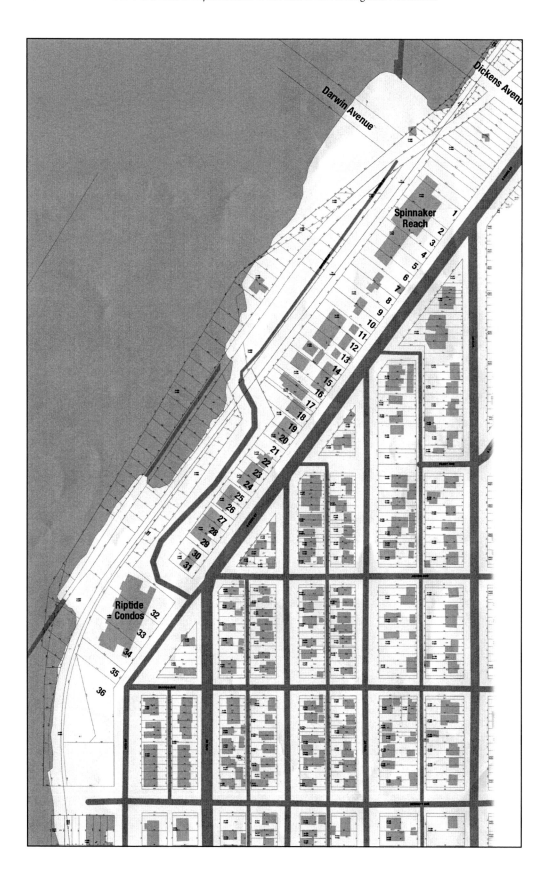

Chapter 14

E.K. Wood Industrial Sites

THIS CHAPTER of the Boulevard Park story examines that large piece of land that lies north of Easton Beach along the waterfront. The land, formerly the site of the E.K. Wood lumber mill, was platted in 1945 as the E.K. Wood Industrial sites. The creation of Boulevard Park depended upon securing the waterfront portions of that plat and its many ownerships. The story of the origins and final resolution of this important area makes a fascinating tale of settlement, development, division, and finally reunion. This is the broad waterfront section of the park that was first developed as the park and is most readily identified as Boulevard Park.

Its history takes us back again to the original 1853 donation land claims of Morrison and Pattle, when each man owned a portion of this part of the park. The dividing line between the two donation land claims runs directly through the center of the concrete pottery studio building at the tip of Pattle's Point. Pattle owned the land to the north; Morrison, the land to the south.

Pattle is said to have built a cabin on the point at the very edge of his claim on land that would come to be called Pattle's Point. Looking at the area now it is difficult to see it as a point, because of all of the land filling that has taken place over the years since 1853, but in those early days it was distinctly the point of land that protruded the farthest into the bay from the eastern shoreline.

The rocky point extended to just beyond the concrete pottery studio building, and then it curved in rapidly to the bluff that rises inland from the railroad tracks. All of the extensive lawn and playground area that exists there now is filled land created during the industrial era, and later by dumping construction debris between the piling of the lumber mill that once occupied the site.

To illustrate the extent and depth of the landfill it is helpful to read the report of the core drilling done in 2007 to test the ground under a proposed bandstand pavilion planned for the extreme north end of the large grass area. The hollow-core auger used in the test bore found five feet of dirt and sand in the top layer. From five feet to 23 feet, the report reveals highly organic fill material, large amounts of wood debris (chips and bark in sandy matrix). At 23 to 25.5 feet the boring found fine to medium sand and gravel with shell fragments, apparently the original sea bottom. And finally, at 25.5 feet they found "refusal" at bed rock, which they guessed was Chuckanut sandstone. In Pattle's day, where we now consider putting a bandstand, there was 23 feet of water.

There is much less fill of the shoreline south of Pattle's point and so it is easier to see the jutting point from this side. Look at the photo taken from the south end of the foot bridge shown on page 25, and let your imagination see water where the railroad track is now. Suddenly Pattle's Point seems a rather prominent geographical feature. It is indeed the tip of land that protrudes most deeply into the bay from the eastern shore.

William Pattle dug vigorously for coal at Pattle's Point hoping that the seam he had found on the surface would become a major deposit. It is said that he dug holes and trenches all over his point, but with little success. The trenches were to give him solace a year later in 1854 when there was trouble with the northern Indians who were coming down to raid the Lummi Indians and whites alike. Pattle is reputed to have loaded some of his trenches with blasting powder and fuses as defenses against the marauders. In fact, at one point when marauders were in the area, five townspeople gathered at Pattle's cabin for mutual protection. Two white Englishmen, Belville and Brown, had been attacked in a boat just to the south, killed by the northern marauders and beheaded.

The nervous settlers waiting in 'Fort Pattle' were expecting a night attack. In the middle of the night, unseen by the settlers, a group of marauding Indians in canoes were silently approaching the point for a surprise attack. In Pattle's cabin one of the settlers, a man named Williams, was trying to clear his flintlock for firing and was not able to do so. In frustration he pointed his rifle out the open cabin door, took an ember from the fire and applied it to the touch-hole. The gun fired into the air with a loud retort. Out in the bay the startled attackers in the approaching canoes were heard to shout and turn rapidly away. What had been a stealthy night attack was now a full fledged retreat. Wags began to call Pattle's home 'Fort Pattle' or 'Fort Retreat'.

This traumatic Indian attack caused the U.S. Government to send George Pickett and his U.S. Army unit to build and garrison Fort Bellingham.

Eldridge & Bartlett Mill

In 1883 Eldridge & Bartlett must have decided that their recently platted metropolis of Bellingham needed an industrial base in order to spur population growth and economic stability, so they decided to build a lumber mill at Pattle's Point. The mill would be called variously, The Eldridge and Bartlett Mill, or The Bellingham Mill, or by its nickname, The Red Mill, because of the bright red paint that covered all of its buildings. Its legal business name was Bellingham Mill Company. The mill was built at the very tip of Pattle's Point with most of its structures on wooden piling out over the water.

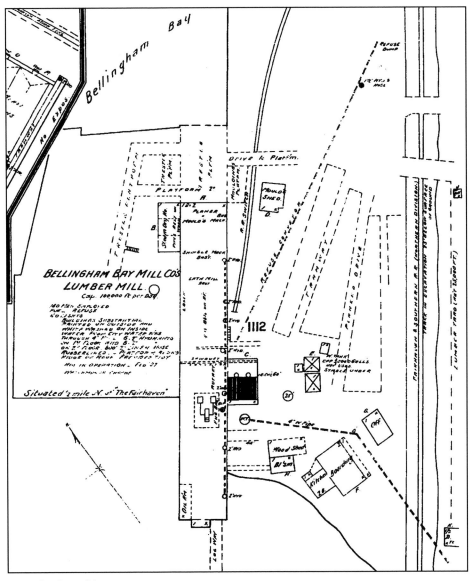

1890 Sanborn Map.

This copy of the 1890 Sanborn map of the mill shows the log chute by which logs were slid up to the saw as being just off-shore, and the long sawmill building extending north on piles over the water along the shoreline. Seaward of the mill building was a lumber storage and loading dock. This water orientation made sense when you realize that the logs were floated to the mill and stored in log booms until they were ready to be floated to the log chute and sawn; and that the finished product, the sawn lumber and lath, was transported to the eventual buyer by ship. This drawing clearly shows the mill, boarding house, and the Fairhaven and Northern track (now the Burlington Northern main line). The Northern Pacific trestle had not yet been built.

The Sanborn shows a boarding house with attached kitchen on the shoreline and a large woodshed and a small office. There are also two small dwellings, one with a stable under it. The Bellingham Bay Mill Company housed some of their workers.

Eldridge had no intention of running the mill himself; Bartlett, the money man, was living in Boston. Bartlett would own 75 percent of the mill and Eldridge 25 percent. In April of 1884 they signed a lease agreement with 64-year-old Converse J. Garland, who was married to a cousin of Bartlett. Garland was to lease the mill for a period of five years and the lease provided him an option to buy.

At the time the lease was signed the mill was not yet in operation, waiting for the installation of vital equipment. The mill and wharf had cost Eldridge and Bartlett the tidy sum of $62,000 to that point. Garland's lease empowered him to spend up to $12,000 more to get the mill operating. "Improvements to that amount may be paid for with the rents," implying that the owners would pay the additional costs by forgoing rent payments.

Unfortunately the troubles began even before the mill began operating. Cash was always short on the frontier in those days and the Bellingham Mill Company must

Gordon Tweit collection.

Photo of Bellingham Bay Mill engraving from the *Fairhaven Illustrated*, 1890.

Invoice header for Bellingham Mill Company.

have been under-capitalized from the beginning. It did not seem to have the cash to either pay the rent, nor the debts accrued in finishing construction, nor even to pay some of the wages of the employees. Evidence of pending trouble began as early as May 5th, 1884.

Here is a letter Eldridge wrote to a Seattle debtor on that date:

"Gentlemen; I was not here on Monday when your letter arrived and could not answer by return. I am sorry to say I am completely out of money at present. Mr. Garland is going to Seattle tonight to meet his family and he will call on you and pay you whatever he can spare. Had Mr. Cornwall not been taken sick we would have had quite a boom here by this time, as work would have been rushed on his road a month ago. People are doubtful about his road and hesitate to invest, but he is on the mend and as soon as he arrives work will be rushed on his road and also on bringing in water and pipes from Lake Whatcom and we will soon be in funds. As you have waited so obligingly on us, rest assured as soon as we can get in funds I will square your file."

Respectfully yours, Edward Eldridge

By 1885 the lawsuits began rolling in: Hawley vs. Garland, a suit over the lack of payment of $2000 for 32 live iron rollers attached to the mill; W.J. Martin & D.B. Edwards vs. Garland; $3300 debt for board and room for millworkers and money loaned; C.H. Shank vs. Garland; Alex Atkins vs. Garland; Gordon Hardware vs. Garland, Eldridge & Bartlett. It was obvious that the mill was failing and not paying its bills. In every case Garland admitted to the unpaid debt. The court declared liens against the mill and its equipment, and now Eldridge and Bartlett had to step in to defend their property against the threat of the sheriff's sale. Suit and countersuit ensued until 1885. It must have been a continual nightmare of courtrooms and legal fees for the beleaguered mill owners.

The troubles dragged on as the court ordered the mill sold to satisfy Garland's debts; the plaintiffs appealed, requesting injunctions to stop the sale of the mill and/ or valuable and essential equipment, claiming that it was their property and not

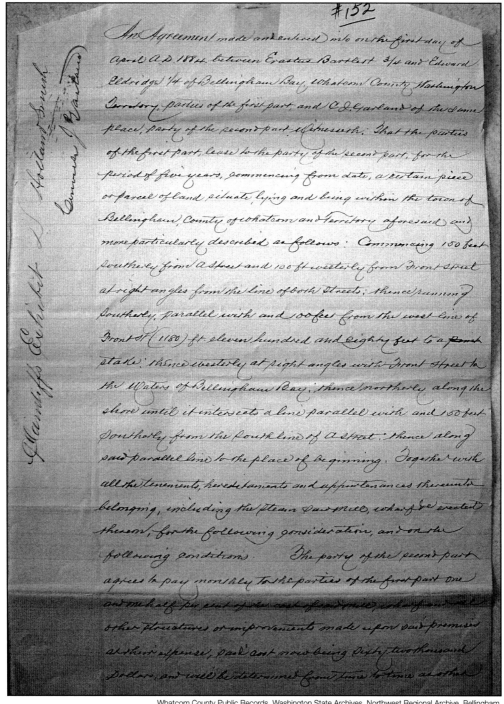

Photo of Garland lease, page 1.

Garland's. Finally, in 1888, an appeal was made to the State Supreme Court, and on July 5, 1890, Judge Irwin's decree came down. Garland, Eldridge and Bartlett owed Gordon Hardware $2528, and the mill and land must be sold to satisfy the debt.

Whatcom County Public Records, Washington State Archives, Northwest Regional Archive, Bellingham.

Photo of Garland lease, page 2.

It is interesting to note that in 1888 when the appeal was made to the Supreme Court, Eldridge and Bartlett had to post a $6000 appeal bond, pledging that amount to establish that they could indeed pay a judgement should their appeal fail. As was customary, then and now, a surety must add its guarantee to the pledged estates of the plaintiffs. In this case, the sureties for Eldridge and Bartlett were two men who were deeply involved with Nelson Bennett and the Fairhaven Land Company. They were E.L. Cowgill and E.M. Wilson.

The Fairhaven Land Company

In 1888 railroad tycoon Nelson Bennett concluded that the Northern Pacific railroad would select Fairhaven as the terminus of its transcontinental line. The railroad was at the time surveying the best route across the Cascades and the community that became its saltwater connection to the Orient was sure to reap huge economic benefits. Bennett was betting on Fairhaven. In 1888 he and C.X. Larrabee purchased what remained unsold of Dan Harris' original donation land claim for the princely sum of $75,000. Dirty Dan was now a wealthy man.

Requiring even more land for his great real estate speculation, Bennett opened negotiations with Eldridge and Bartlett for what remained of the 360 acres they had originally purchased from Pattle and Morrison and for several thousand additional acres that they had accumulated. In 1899 the deal was consummated. Together they formed the Bellingham Bay Land Company which bought the platted town of Bellingham and all the unplatted backlands of the original donation claims and merged those lands with Fairhaven. Fairhaven now stretched from Cowgill in the south to the border of Sehome (located approximately where State Street comes down the hill to meet the Boulevard at the "Welcome to Bellingham" sign). The exact location is indicated by the double granite centennial monument presently on the Bay Trail below the street level.

Considering the financial problems assailing the Bellingham Mill Company, it is surely no surprise that when Bennett, Wilson, Cowgill, and the Fairhaven Land Company came calling, Eldridge and Bartlett were more than ready to discuss a sale of their mill. They sold a 50 percent interest in 1890.

An article in the *Fairhaven Illustrated*, a Chamber of Commerce-type promotional magazine published just one time in 1890, describes the Bellingham Bay Mill Company this way.

> "This company is composed of the Fairhaven Land Company, and Eldridge & Bartlett, who are joint owners of this plant, known locally as the Bellingham Mill. It was erected some seven years ago by Eldridge & Bartlett, who oper-

Galen Biery Papers and Photographs #1734, Center for Pacific Northwest Studies, Western Washington University.

Nelson Bennett

The Fairhaven Illustrated, 1890. Gordon Tweit collection.

Edgar Lea Cowgill

ated it moderately for one year, when it was leased by certain parties for five years, who it was supposed would operate the property, but instead proved to be a virtual lease to the celebrated California Lumber Trust, who nailed the mill up and kept it idle during the term of the lease. The Fairhaven Land Company purchased a half interest in all the holdings of Eldridge & Bartlett late in 1889, and at the expiration of the lease the owners secured the services of Mr. J.S. Mundy, an old Pennsylvania lumberman, who took hold of the mill plant in April last; of necessity much overhauling was necessary to put it in order, and new and additional machinery was added. The mill began sawing about June 1st, and has pushed steadily forward with an aggressive business from that time to the present."

The article goes on to describe the mill and its products predicting a prosperous future for it.

It is also no surprise that the new co-owners of The Bellingham Mill Company, were eager to talk when Frederick J. Wood called on them in 1900 to discuss purchasing their newly re-organized lumber mill. Bennett and his friends were interested in the real estate boom, not a struggling lumber mill. Eldridge and Bartlett had probably suffered enough with the mill's financial problems. The deal was made in that year and the E.K. Wood era began.

E.K. Wood Company, Inc.

The new owners had adequate capital, experienced management, established markets, and perhaps times were becoming better on Bellingham Bay. The E.K. Wood Company seemed to prosper. The mill was immediately fitted with new and modern equipment, the size of the mill was increased and the wharf expanded. The company purchased large acreages of timberlands in the surrounding foothills. The mill employed many workers on steady shifts for many years.

Edwin Kleber Wood was born on February 17, 1840, in New York state. He answered Lincoln's call and enlisted in the Union Army in 1861, fighting in some of the bloodiest battles of the war—Bull Run, Antietam, Fredericksburg and Chancellorsville. He was wounded and discharged after the battle of Hanover Courthouse in 1863.

Looking for opportunities in the west he moved to the timber country of Michigan where, with his brother-in-law Clarence Thayer, he developed a lumber milling business. Eventually their operations moved to California where they incorporated the E.K. Wood Lumber Company on February 5, 1895. In 1888, as timber was becoming exhausted in Michigan, Wood had sent his 19-year-old son, Frederick J. Wood (1869-1937), west to reconnoiter lumbering opportunities on the west coast and to gain experience in the lumber business. Frederick first took a job as a bookkeeper at the S.E. Slade Lumber Company in San Francisco. A year later he moved to Hoquiam on Gray's Harbor, Washington Territory (Washington became a state November 11, 1889), where he managed a lumber mill, presumably a mill recently purchased by his

Whatcom Museum of History & Art

Frederick J. Wood

father's company. He remained there until 1900 when he found an opportunity to his liking at the troubled little mill at Pattle's Point. The Fairhaven Land Company and Eldridge and Bartlett were willing sellers. The purchase was completed in 1900.

Frederick Wood proved to be a capable manager. The E.K. Wood Mill Company in Fairhaven grew and grew until the Sanborn map of 1904 shows it extending for 1200 feet along the shoreline and 400 feet out into the waters of the bay. Its huge lumber wharf outlined in grey on the Sanborn map stretches 800 feet from north to south and extended on long wooden piles well out to deep water to accommodate the sailing ships that docked there to load lumber. The mill had the capacity to

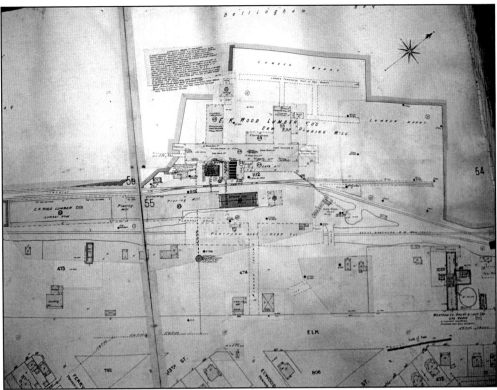

Sanborn Map, 1904.

cut 125,000 feet of lumber and 25,000 feet of lath every 10-hour shift, and employed 125 men.

The E.K. Wood Company became headquartered in San Francisco as its West Coast operations succeeded. Their largest mill was at Hoquiam on Grays Harbor. In 1923 they built an up-to-date lumber mill at Burroughs Bay near Anacortes. They also owned retail lumber yards in San Francisco, San Pedro, San Anselmo, and Los Angeles in California.

The Schooner Fleet

E.K. Wood not only owned timberlands, logged the trees, sawed the lumber and retailed it; they also transported it from their Pacific Northwest mills to their lumberyards in California and to overseas markets in China, Australia, Mexico, Hawaii and Fiji in their own fleet of three-, four-, and five-masted sailing ships. These beautiful and sturdy wooden ships joined a large number of lumber schooners plying northwest waters, delivering the product of its burgeoning lumber mills to ports all around the Pacific Rim.

The clipper *Glory of the Seas* moored among the lumber carriers at E.K. Wood Lumber Mill.

Most of the ships E.K. Wood Lumber Company built, owned and operated were built by the master builders at Hitchings & Joyce Shipyard in Hoquiam. This famous yard had been established by Peter Matthews in 1897. He operated it until his death, when his nephew George Hitchings took over. The yard was called Hitchings & Joyce until 1906, when it was bought and operated by the original founder's son Gordon F. Matthews. The shipbuilding skills and tradition ran deep in this notable family. The famed Grays Harbor yard built more lumber schooners than any other west coast shipyard, many of them for E.K. Wood Lumber Company.

Among the ships built for E.K. Wood were the following:

1888   *E.K. Wood*: Hall Brothers, Port Blakely, four-masted schooner. Went aground on Smith Island, November 1901, and was a total loss.

1895   *C.A. Thayer*: 219-ft., 453-ton, three-masted schooner, Hans Bendixsen, Humboldt Bay, CA. Still afloat at San Francisco Maritime National Museum.

1897   *Defiance*: Peter Matthews, Hoquiam, 604-ton four master, 179 feet long by 37.7 beam and 13.7 draft. The *Defiance* met her end in 1922 when she burned when loading copra in the Solomon Islands.

1898   *Dauntless*: Hitchings & Joyce, Hoquiam, 548 tons, four masts, blown up at Catalina Island in 1928 for the movie, "The Rescue," starring Ronald Coleman.

1899   *Fred J. Wood*: four-masted schooner, 681 tons, George Hitchings, Matthews Yard, Hoquiam. Scrapped in 1927.

1900   *Fearless*: Hitchings & Joyce, Hoquiam, four-masted schooner. Wrecked Nov. 25, 1927 at Tambores, Cuba.

1901   *Olympic*: Hitchings & Joyce, Hoquiam, steam schooner w/750 hp. triple expansion engine.

1902   *Resolute*: Hitching & Joyce, Hoquiam, 684 ton, four masts. Sold at New York in 1928 and reduced to a barge.

1902   *Alert*: Hitchings & Joyce,Hoquiam, 623 ton, four masts.

1902   *Shasta*: Hitchings & Joyce, Hoquiam, 722-ton steam schooner.

1919   *Vigilant*: George Matthews, Hoquiam, five-masted schooner, 244 feet, 22 ft. beam, sold in 1940, renamed *City of Alberni*. 1943, renamed *Condor*, burned in Bahia Blanca, Argentina, 1945.

The E.K. Wood fleet included a number of fabled schooners, none of them more celebrated than the *C.A. Thayer*, the last surviving ship of her kind. The *C.A. Thayer* has been preserved and restored and is a featured exhibit at the San Francisco Maritime National Museum. She was built by the famed lumber schooner builder Hans D. Bendixsen in his San Francisco yard and named after the Vice President of E.K. Wood Lumber Company and E.K. Wood's brother-in-law, Clarence A. Thayer. She was a three-masted schooner, 219 feet in length, with a cargo capacity of 575,000 board feet.

These classic ships were sailed with a small crew of eight or nine men. Small crews were made possible because the schooners' sails were largely handled from the decks, unlike square riggers which required large crews of men to climb into the rigging. When the era of the lumber schooners ended, the *C.A. Thayer* went on to have a long and storied history cod fishing in Alaskan waters that lasted until 1950.

The historic ship was saved from the ship breakers and now lives on as a tribute to and a reminder of the men and ships of a bygone period of marine history. A website describing the *C.A. Thayer*, her history and her restoration can be found on the internet.

Photo, Harriet Terry Delong, Reference Library, Center for Northwest Studies, Western Washington University.
The *Vigilant* at sea, taken from the Pacific schooner *Wawona*.

The *Vigilant*

Perhaps the favorite E.K. Wood Lumber Company schooner for Bellingham historians is the beautiful five-masted *Vigilant,* preserved in memory for hundreds of Bellingham families by the Helen Loggie engraving of the old ship moored at the

Photo of Helen Loggie's *Vigilant* engraving.

Bloedel Donovan Cargo Mill dock at the foot of Cornwall Avenue.

The *Vigilant* was built by Matthews in Hoquiam in 1919, and was christened by Marian Susan Wood, the young daughter of Frederick Wood. The *Vigilant* sailed the west coast lumber trade for many years, with Bellingham her home port. Her races to and from Hawaii with another great schooner, *Commodore*, became the stuff of legend. One voyage in 1932 saw her sail from Honolulu to Cape Flattery in only 13 days. Her first Captain, Matt Peasley, became a famous character immortalized in a series of books, the "Cappy Ricks" novels by Peter B. Kynes.

The *Vigilant* was 244 feet in length, 22 feet of beam and carried five towering 170-foot-tall masts. She was indeed a thing of beauty. The author remembers seeing her moored at the old pier at Bloedel Donovan at the foot of Cornwall Avenue in the late 1930s.

Helen Loggie, whose father was in the lumber mill business in Bellingham, was certainly Bellingham's best known artist of the 20th century. Her etchings brought her considerable regional, national and even international acclaim. She completed many sketches of the *Vigilant* and waterfront scenes; and finally in 1948, produced her rather famous etching of *Vigilant*. (She had drawn the ship many times in earlier years, as the *Vigilant* had burned in 1945.)

Bahia Blanco, Argentina, where the *Vigilant* ended her days.

The *Vigilant* had been sold to Canadian interests in 1940 and renamed the *City of Alberni*. The gallant ship experienced many voyages and adventures under the Canadian ensign. She frequently carried Canadian lumber to Australia, returning with sugar from Fiji, or copra from Samoa. She dodged the submarines and Japanese warships during the Second World War, sailing silently from the Northwest to the South Pacific and back.

In 1943 on a voyage to Durban, South Africa, *Vigilant* (*City of Alberni*) was damaged in a severe storm at latitude 41 degrees south. She had to make for Valparaiso leaking badly. Because there were no proper repair facilities in Chile, her Canadian owners chose to abandon her in Valparaiso. She was sold to Chilean interests and was renamed *Condor*. In 1945 *Condor* was damaged rounding Cape Horn; after repairs in Montevideo she was sent to Bahia Blanco, Argentina, to take on a load of wheat. Severe 40-degree rolls, due to ocean tides meeting the flow of the river, caused batteries lying on the radio shack to fall to the deck producing a short circuit and a fire that could not be controlled. She met her end in Bahia Blanca in 1945 after her storied career on the high seas. Perhaps Helen Loggie did her famous etching as a posthumous memorial to the grand old schooner.

The Clark/Wood/Sefrit Home

Marian Susan Wood, who had christened the *Vigilant*, grew up to marry Charles L. "Chic" Sefrit, the owner and publisher of *The Bellingham Herald*. After Frederick Wood's death in 1937, the Sefrits moved into her parents' large home at 703 14th Street and lived there for many years.

The house itself has an interesting story. It was designed and built for A.H. Clark in 1890. Clark followed Jim Wardner as president of the Fairhaven National Bank.

Clark/Wood/Sefrit home incarnations. Shown on next page in 2007.

Clark, a one time mayor of Fairhaven, left town under a cloud of criticism when the bank failed in 1896 as the Fairhaven boom died. His large Victorian house was purchased by Frederick Wood and his wife Anna who, tired of Victorian architecture, determined to modernize. In 1919 they called in the carpenters who tore off all of the Victorian towers, turrets and fancy work and converted it to the staid Tudor residence that it is today. It is hard to believe that the house you now see at the corner of 14th and Easton was once an ornate Victorian.

The Woods, and then the Sefrits, lived in the house until 1969. I attended the Campus School at what was then the Western Washington Normal School with the two Sefrit children, Anna Wood Sefrit, carrying the name of her paternal grandmother Anna Bale Wood, and her younger brother Frank. I remember both of them bearing a strong resemblance to the photo of their maternal grandfather Frederick J. Wood (see page 144).

The Clark/Wood/Sefrit home as it appears in 2007.

The Mill Site

The 1913 Sanborn Map shows in excellent detail the layout of the mill. Note the huge area of the 'lumber wharf'. It is helpful to locate the only remaining building, the 'steam turbine building', as a reference when trying to imagine the size of the mill. Sanborn shows it as the 30 foot by 40 foot dark building between the planing mill and the saw mill. It is labeled "Steam Turbine Generator 400 KW". The dark structure with the six black bars directly to its right depict the six boilers that supplied the steam to turn the turbine, which in turning created the electricity to power the circular saw and run the mill.

Measuring from the steam turbine building, the lumber wharf thrust 350 feet out into the bay and 800 feet from south to north.

Almost all of the two-story buildings shown on the Sanborn Map were erected on piling over the water. Many of the cut-off piles are still visible at low tide, and the pilings of the planing mill are especially visible at their full height along the shoreline close to the Burlington Northern track.

Above the bluff, facing on Front, or Elk (now State Street), was the concrete E.K. Wood office building. Its original address was 400 Elk Street. A 44-foot-wide wooden

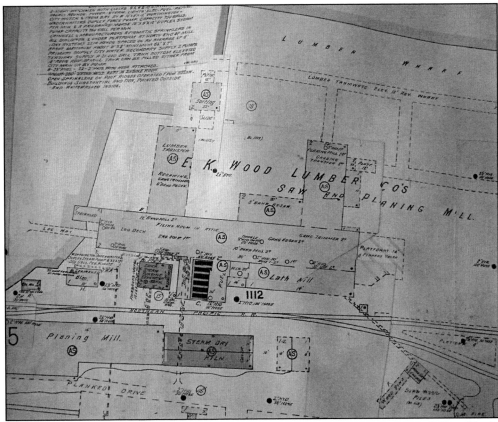

Sanborn Map, 1913.

plank incline reached down hill and across the railroad cut. A 400-foot-long platform covered the railroad cut and it was complete with an electric hoist or elevator to get people up from or down to the mill level. A condominium now stands where once stood the office building almost directly uphill from the steam turbine building.

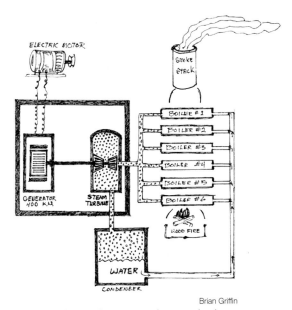

Brian Griffin

Drawing of how the steam plant worked.

Galen Biery Papers and Photographs #744, Center for Pacific Northwest Studies, Western Washington University.

A rare waterside view of the E.K. Wood Mill. The original Saint Joseph's Hospital is seen inside its large fenced enclosure on 17th Street (upper right). Starr Rock bouy is visible off the bow of the freighter.

The Padden house, 2007.

The Mill Fire

The E.K. Wood Mill was an industrial mainstay of the Bellingham economy for many years. At 5:05 PM on September 30, 1925, a fire broke out in the green planing mill. It had apparently begun in the hot box or gear box of a machine axle. Soon the entire building was engulfed in flames. David C. Morse, the future owner of Morse Hardware Company, when interviewed in 2006 at age 93, recalled as a boy running to the fire with some of his friends. The 13-year-old boys were ordered off the mill site by the firemen, but they sat on a lawn across State Street from the fire and watched the mill burn. The firemen were unable to extinguish the blaze and the mill was lost. The "Red Mill" was never to operate again.

E.K. Wood owned another saw mill in nearby Anacortes. That mill was completely electrified and apparently more modern and efficient than the Bellingham mill. The 'Red Mill' was finished. All operations were moved to Anacortes and in the ensuing years any surviving buildings at Pattle's Point were removed or demolished, the machinery sold or moved. The dock was eventually demolished leaving only a forest of piles on the waterfront. The final structural reminders of the mill were the concrete shell of the steam turbine building and the hulk of the old concrete office building standing above the bluff beside State Street. The remains of the now roofless concrete office building stood beside the busy street until after the Second World War.

E.K. Wood Mill, circa 1900. Note that State Street is built upon a wooden trestle. The trestle was eventually replaced by earth and stone fill. The John Padden house is prominent on 14th Street at extreme left of photo.

E.K. Wood Mill, circa 1903, Great Northern/Burlington Northern track at lower right, Northern Pacific trestle (now the wood walkway) was new. The steam turbine building (pottery studio, and now a coffee shop), is in front of the boiler building with twin smoke stacks.

Port of Bellingham Records, Washington State Archives;
Northwest Regional Archives, Bellingham.
In 1941 the author moved with his parents to their new home at 432 15th Street (indicated by arrow).

Childhood Memories

I was nine years old in 1941. Our new home was just two blocks up the hill from the abandoned mill site. One summer in the early 1940s my friends and I found great adventure in playing on the old mill land. I well remember the cement office building standing alone on the large empty site beside State Street. The derelict building was surrounded by grazing cattle owned by some urban farmer who must have rented the land from E.K. Wood Company. We explored the mystery of the concrete structure, climbing up into its windowless and roofless rooms. We wandered the piling-studded beach and examined the box cars that were frequently standing at a side track below the bluff, and sometimes we would risk trouble with the authorities because of our boyish behavior.

One hot summer day we came upon a single box car with its door locked in open position. The opening provided about two feet of open space which was no doubt intended to cool the cargo—room enough for small boys to peer inside and then to enter. We, of course, did both as our inspection found the car completely full of delicious ripe watermelons. How do I know they were delicious? Trusting that the statute of limitations has run its course after the ensuing 65 or 66 years, I will confess that we broke open several of those melons and had a marvelous afternoon of eatin' and spittin'.

The old mill site, by then a cow pasture, provides another childhood memory. The empty field atop the bluff was dotted with what in those days we called cow-pies. There were also occasional piles of old boards lying about. With the creativity of pre-teen kids we deduced that if we were to lay three or four partially dried cow-pies on the end of a board, we could swing that board and the pies would launch off of it and lay a salvo of smelly gunk on whatever target we might choose. About the time we came to that great conclusion the daily passenger train to Vancouver thundered by on the main line just below us. A great new scheme was born.

The next day, with loaded boards lined up on the edge of the bluff above the track, we waited like saboteurs for the afternoon passenger train. Right on schedule it rounded the curve and appeared below our waiting positions. As it passed our gunnery station we rose from the tall grass lining the cut and swept our laden boards toward the windows of the speeding train. With artillery-like precision the cow-pies stitched their pattern on the train, splatting with amazing accuracy along the windows of the passenger cars. I can only hope that none of the windows were open. The train sped on and we exulted in our great escapade. Soon we were searching the pasture for more ammunition, stockpiling for tomorrow's fusillade. Suddenly we heard the faint wailing of police sirens far to the north. Was it possible that our hilarious act of juvenile vandalism had been reported to the police? We didn't wait to find out. We boys fled for home, furtively crossing State Street and hurriedly melting into the alleys and byways of the residential blocks uphill that we knew so well. Chastened, we never did that again.

Not all of our boyish activities ended that well. One summer day in 1942 we got the horrible news that a boy named Donnie Paulsen, who was just a year younger than I and lived down the street, had been badly maimed as he tried to climb onto a moving freight car at the old mill site. He had reached for the steel ladder, lost his grip and his leg slipped under the wheel. The leg was pinched off above the knee. Donnie had been playing on the tracks alone. Without help he crawled up the steep embankment above the track, across the empty pasture, finally collapsing on the edge of State Street where he waved down a passing auto.

During that amazing and desperate crawl he was dragging his severed leg behind him. It was attached only by skin. The crushing effect of the wheel had apparently sealed the blood vessels in his leg so that he did not bleed to death. Amputation was completed at the hospital. After Donnie's tragedy the entire area below State Street was declared off limits by our parents. I don't recall that we objected.

Financial Woes

The fortunes of Frederick J. Wood—the president of a once huge lumbering, milling, shipping and retailing empire—were not invulnerable to the perils of business. In addition to a large share of E.K. Wood Company, Frederick Wood owned a major share of the Redwood Highlands Company, Limited; and in 1924 Wood, with Edward G. English, another lumberman with extensive interests, organized a new British Columbia corporation known as Wood & English, Limited. Each of the men owned half of the company. In 1924 they issued seven percent corporate bonds to raise one million dollars, secured by a mortgage on its assets to the Yorkshire & Canadian Trust. By 1930 they had accumulated other sizable bank debt. Wood and English pledged large amounts of stock that they owned in their other corporations to secure those debts. Wood had pledged 750,000 shares of E.K. Wood stock to secure his share of debt.

Wood & English Ltd. sustained heavy losses, and in his income tax return for the year 1930, Wood declared that the company was insolvent, its stock written off as a total loss. The company had offered its property for sale for the amount of its debts, exclusive of the debts owing to Wood and English, but had not found a buyer. Wood was to die in 1937, having committed all of his E.K. Wood stock to the indebtedness of Wood & English. His estate was declared insolvent. E.K. Wood Company soldiered on.

E.K. Wood Industrial Sites Plat

The abandoned mill site sat vacant and unused, except for the grazing cattle, from 1925 until after the Second World War. In 1945 the E.K. Wood Company apparently decided to convert some of its assets to cash. They platted the old mill site into 36 lots called the E.K. Wood Industrial Sites. The plat was filed in 1946 and sales began in 1947.

The lots were long and narrow, each lot extending from State Street, down over the bluff and across the tracks to the water's edge, and in some cases beyond and into the tide lands. The lots were put on the market and promptly began to sell.

Because of the natural break of the bluff some of the lots were broken up and sold as fractional lots, one part above the bluff, the remainder below. Others were sold in their entirety and broken up by later owners. In example, lots 1, 2, 3, 4, 5, & 6 were split. The Bellingham Boom Company bought the lower lots from which they operated a log dumping operation. The upland parts of those same six lots above the railroad tracks were bought by Martin L. Burgess in 1973 and eventually Spinnaker Reach was built on them.

It may be of interest to follow the sale transactions on these various lots. Refer to the map at chapter opening on page 134.

Lots 1, 2, 3, 4, 5 & 6: lower sections, Oct. 9, 1950, Bellingham Boom Company, $6,000. Upper sections, Mar. 12, 1973, Martin L. Burgess, $90,000 (Spinnaker Reach Condominium).

Lots 7 & 8: upper & lower sections, Nov. 9, 1947, George O. Falk, $2,653. Falk built his home on them. Lower sections, Falk sold to Bellingham Boom Company, Jan. 25, 1960.

Lots 9 & 10: upper & lower sections, Nov. 19, 1947, S.J. & Merle Mills, resold to

Edward M. & Dora Haan on Oct. 7, 1954. Lower sections, Haan sold to Edwin Goodridge, Jan. 29, 1966; and Goodridge sold to Bellingham Boom Company, Mar. 19, 1969.

Lots 11, 12 & 13: upper & lower sections, Oct. 9, 1947, Russell Melhart; resold the upper sections to Billie Johnson in 1952. Johnson sold to Gladys V. Van Moorhem on June 9, 1955. Lower sections, Melhart sold to George Falk on Feb. 15, 1954; Falk resold to Joe Means on Nov. 5, 1964; Means sold to Whatcom County Parks April 10, 1968.

Lots 14, 15 & 16: upper & lower sections, April 2, 1953, Wood to Frank and Billie Bostrom. July 1955 divorce settlement to Billie Johnson. 1956, Billie Johnson sold upper sections to Paul Johanson; 1964, Johanson to Ruby Cruikshank; 1973, Cruikshank to Lee Trott; Trott to Ron Benson; Benson to McKeown; McKeown to Monrab; Monrab to Frank Brooks.

Lower sections, July 1955, Billie Johnson sold to Bellingham Boom Company.

Lots 17 & 18: upper sections, March 19, 1953, E.K. Wood sold to L.F. & Grace Larson.

Lots 19 & 20: June 23, 1953, to Harold & Nellie J. Anderson - Monahan Garage.

Lots 21 & 22: October 22, 1956, E.K. Wood to B.W. & Doris Sutter.

Lots 23, 24, 25 & 26: May 29, 1956, Paul & Bertha Millard.

Lots 27, 28 & 29: May 1, 1953. Fred & Effie Jacobson.

Lots 17 through 29: Lower sections, June 4, 1956, E.K. Wood sold directly to Bellingham Boom Company.

Lots 30 & 31: upper & lower sections, Feb. 4, 1948, E.K. Wood sold to Allez; Allez to Herb Trunkey, Oct. 10, 1951; Trunkey to Marriott, Sept. 28, 1951; Lower section. Marriottt to City of Bellingham, March 25, 1992.

Lots 32 to 36: upper section & lower section. June 7, 1948. E.K.Wood to Provine; Provine to Harry Selene, Oct. 2, 1961; Selene to Port of Bellingham, Sept. 9, 1964; Port sold upper section of 32, 33, & 34 to Riptide Condominium. Lower section. Port to City of Bellingham, June 7, 1979; Lots 35 & 36 sold to City of Bellingham, April 22, 1979.

The fate of the upland parts of the E.K. Wood Industrial sites was not hard to predict. The excellent marine views and State Street vehicular access made them ideal locations for condominiums and apartments. While many of the lots made an intermediary stop as private dwelling locations, the development of multiple residence construction in the form of condominiums and apartments was inevitable and is now almost complete. The unbroken marine views and the convenient location is commanding top prices for the once cheap lots. As an example, in 2007 a condominium will be completed on the E.K. Wood plat that is rumored to be offering units for a price in excess of $1,700,000 each. Pattle and Morrison must be uneasy in their graves.

If the residential use of the upper sections of the lots was predictable, the ultimate use of the waterfront sections of the lots was not as easy to foresee. The old belief that we should save the waterfront for industry was still being voiced from time to time. Joe Means' small ship-building operation at Pattle's Point had sputtered and died. Log dumping and booming was coming to an end for ecological and economic reasons. The City was not excited about funding a park on the location. There was a fortunate hiatus in which the fate of the land was stalled, awaiting someone, or some event to push the balance in one direction or another.

Ken Hertz's Acquisitions

Fortunately for the citizens of Bellingham some solid work was being done to tip the scales toward the direction of a public use. The visionary and aggressive Whatcom County Park Director Ken Hertz had made deals that his park board could not refuse. Local architect Jim Zervas was chair of the County Park Board in the late 1960s. He recalls fondly that Hertz was constantly coming to the board with ideas and acquisition deals that they did indeed have a hard time turning down.

Former Director Hertz recalls that Whatcom County Treasurer Hugh Cory, a devoted salmon fisherman, was constantly pestering him about the lack of a small boat launch in Bellingham. Other salmon fishermen concurred. There was no place to put a trailered boat into Bellingham Bay. Hertz learned that Joe Means, who operated a small boat manufacturing operation at Pattle's Point, might be willing to sell. Means had built a marine railway for launching his ferro-cement boats and Hertz thought this launch site could be the answer to the fishermen's problem.

Means was indeed ready to sell and Hertz recalls that he was able to buy the water side sections of lot 11, 12 & 13 for what he called 'a very reasonable price'. The County Park Board completed the sale on April 10, 1968. The purchase included the old E.K. Wood concrete building, the marine railway, and 150 frontage feet of this historic site, Pattle's Point. Unfortunately the boat launch was not successful. You could launch your boat there in good weather, but if a storm came up while you were fishing you probably could not get the boat out again.

While negotiating for the Means property, Hertz realized that acquiring waterfront for public use should be an important goal for the County Park Department. He looked for other opportunities and his next negotiation, also in 1968, resulted in a stunning victory for Hertz and for the future Boulevard Park. He was able to convince the Northern Pacific Railroad to deed its entire right-of-way to County Parks for five dollars. This generous gift to the community included the old wooden trestle leading north from the Taylor Avenue dock, the level trail along the water north of Easton Beach, the wooden trestle to Pattle's Point and the long strip of former railroad land that bisected what is now the wide lawn of Boulevard Park. Nothing could have been more important to the future park.

The next year, 1969, Hertz was able to convince the Port of Bellingham to transfer to County Parks all of their waterfront west of the Burlington Northern Mainline on lots 32 thru 36. This additional acquisition put Easton Beach and most of the stone knoll behind it in County Park's hands.

Hertz did not have a specific park plan in mind as he picked up these scattered, but available pieces of land; he simply knew that one day they would be important to the community. It is interesting to recall that there was no help forthcoming from the City of Bellingham at this time.

Piecing together the lower section of the park became vastly easier because of Hertz's early purchases. In 1973 when the park project began, Rotary chairman Jim Fickel had only to get the agreement of the three public entities and two private owners, Dillingham Corporation and the Marriott family. Whatcom County Parks owned three crucial pieces, the City of Bellingham owned large amounts of street right-of-ways, and the State of Washington Department of Natural Resources owned a large section of what had once been water. Refer to map in Chapter 2, page 12.

The Marriott ownership of lots 30 and 31 was not a crucial matter, as the old railroad right-of-way now owned by County Parks guaranteed passage through those lots. The Marriotts did not want to sell and the park plans went forward without their piece. It was not until 1992 that Parks Director Byron Elmendorf was able to negotiate a purchase using Greenways funds.

The Bellingham Bay Boom Company

The Dillingham Corporation of Hawaii owned key sections of the land destined to be included in Boulevard Park. The story of how a Hawaiian corporation should come to own this land is an interesting tale illustrating the workings of the corporate food chain, of the big fish eating the little fish.

The story might have begun as far back as January of 1891 when many of Fairhaven's high rollers invested in a new company and a new scheme to build a large log boom sealing off the mouth of the Nooksack River where it emptied into Bellingham Bay. But let the words of the *Fairhaven Illustrated* tell the story as an echo from the nineteenth century. The article in its entirety follows.

The Bellingham Bay Boom Company

"In view of the vast timber interests centering on Bellingham Bay, and the known quantity of timber standing upon the Nooksack River and its tributaries, it was decided a few months ago by a party of gentlemen conversant with and experienced in the booming of logs to erect in the bay, at the mouth of the Nooksack River, a large and expensive receiving holding and sorting boom. A company was organized, consisting of E.L. Cowgill, general manager of the Fairhaven Land Co.; E.M. Wilson, treasurer of same company, and general manager of Fairhaven & Southern R.R. Co.; Gov. Geo. A. Black, land agent of Fairhaven Land Co.; Hon. H.Y. Thompson, vice-president of same company and attorney of F. & S.R.R. Co.; J.S. Mundy, general manager of the Bellingham Bay Mill Co.; W.S. Holcomb of Portland, Or.; Thomas J. Newman, attorney; W.D. Gilbert and S.P. Gilbert, capitalists and lumbermen of Burlington, Iowa.

"These gentlemen, who are all broad gauge in their views, and experienced in their business, possessed of large financial ability, and with an abiding faith in the great future of the city and bay, have proceeded with their task until the work is now drawing near completion, and in a very few days from this writing, and before it is in print, will be ready to receive and hold logs. The present holding capacity of the boom is 200,000,000 feet, but is so constructed that it can be increased to any amount. The capital stock of this company is one million dollars."

By way of background, the reader must understand that in the very early days of the white settlement of Whatcom County, the Nooksack River flowed not into Bellingham Bay, but down the Lummi River, or what is now called the Red River, into Lummi Bay behind Sandy Point. The river was influenced in that direction by a huge log jam just below Ferndale, called the "Portage Jam". This jam was so large and so old that the early settlers reported large trees growing in it.

The geography of the area indicated that the river could flow either into Lummi Bay or into Bellingham Bay and, in fact, had alternated in its destination many times in pre-history. Early day settlers, interested in freeing up river navigation to Ferndale and Lynden, determined to remove the log jam; and in 1877

Galen Biery Papers and Photographs #1746, Center for Pacific Northwest Studies, Western Washington University.

Thomas J. Newman

Newman was the attorney, or at least one of the attorneys, for the Fairhaven Land Company. In 1969 my wife and I purchased his old home at 1027 16th Street and found Thomas Newman's stock certificate among a great number of old papers the family left behind.

they succeeded in doing so by using repeated dynamite blasts. Now the river flow was split just below Ferndale with a substantial channel flowing down each branch to saltwater. Navigation as far as Lynden was possible and small steamers were engaged in that trade.

In 1886 the snag-removal boat of the U.S. Corps of Engineers visited the Nooksack. The snag-boat record reports, "filled up the outlet of Lummi Slough and now no water enters the slough". The improvement to river navigation must have been immediate. Now the Nooksack, with increased flow, emptied only into Bellingham Bay.

I would guess that the Corps diversion of the river was probably influenced by some political lobbying by those loggers, boat operators, and Bellingham Bay business people who would surely benefit from a larger and open river access to the interior of the county. The outlet into Bellingham Bay presented the additional benefit of being much closer to the communities that lined the shores of the bay.

By the late 1880s much of the timber close to the shores of Bellingham Bay had been logged. The vast timber resources of the Nooksack watershed beckoned and what better way to get the logs to the large mills around the bay than by floating them

Misc. Map Collection, Center for Pacific Northwest Studies, Western Washington University.

You can just make out faint white pencil marks in upper left hand corner of this old map found in Newman's home. The pencil marks trace the location of the log boom. The map must have been used to plan or illustrate the placement of the boom.

down the river, collecting them at the river mouth, and towing them across the bay to the mills when the weather allowed.

The Bellingham Bay Boom Company was formed to facilitate that process and to take advantage of the now-open river. They did build their boom across the mouth of the Nooksack as the state law at the time allowed. Its installation, however, was not without problems. The floating boom of chained logs completely sealed off the river exit, but it contained a 'trip' designed to allow the boom to be opened for the passage of watercraft. Apparently the 'trip' was frequently jammed with logs and river debris—so as not to be readily opened—much to the concern and frustration of those operating steamboats on the river. Little is known of the success or lack thereof of the booming operation, but we do know that the operators of the paddle-wheel steamers which traded on the Nooksack strongly objected to the blockage of navigation, as did the federal government.

The government, citing the Federal Rivers and Harbors Act of 1880, sued the company seeking an injunction which would cease the booming activity and cause the removal of the boom. The resulting legal battle was finally resolved in the U.S. Supreme Court in the case of U.S. vs. Bellingham Bay Boom Co., 176 U.S. 211 (1900). The Supreme Court reversed the decisions of two lower courts and ordered the boom to be in violation of federal law. The boom had to be removed.

If you will drive out Marine Drive and look across the river mouth you can still see piles driven into the mud. Those are the surviving piles that were driven in 1891 to hold the great log boom of the Bellingham Bay Boom Company.

The similarity in name and business activity between the Bellingham Bay Boom Company of the 1890s and the Bellingham Boom Company of the 1940s leads to a presumption that they are the same company. I have been unable to find proof of this connection and leave it to some future historian to establish the merit of my presumption. It is known that the modern Bellingham Boom Company became a subsidiary of Bellingham Tug and Barge.

In October of 1949 Bellingham Tug and Barge, its fleet of tugboats, and its subsidiary corporation were bought by Foss Tug and Barge, an almost legendary Seattle company because of its pioneer roots and the romantic appeal of the *Tug Boat Annie* fictional books and movie. Foss was itself swallowed by the Dillingham Corporation

Surviving piling from 1890 log boom shown in this 2007 photo. The boom is depicted in the *Fairhaven Birdseye* of 1891 (see page 32).

in 1969. Thus, as a result of this chain of corporate appetite for growth, the land that Rotary coveted as part of a new waterfront park came to be in the hands of a giant Hawaii-based corporation.

The Dillingham Deal

When E.K. Wood platted the old mill site and began selling land, the Bellingham Boom Company aggressively bought as much of the land west of the railroad track as it could. Their purchases were made in the late 1940s and 1950s while log booming was still a viable activity. Soon economic and environmental issues would change that prospect.

As timber became more and more valuable the traditional losses of logs by sinking, from storm, and during towing began to make water storage of logs un-economic. Government environmental issues with log booming also began to press for the end of the practice. By the time Rotary was putting together the pieces of what would become Boulevard Park, the Dillingham Corporation owned key pieces of the land needed for the park, and the land was not needed for log booming. Now fate and good fortune would play a hand.

Roy Jurgensen

Roy and Beth Jurgensen were sent to Bellingham in 1958 by Kaiser Permanente. Kaiser had recently purchased the Olympic Cement Plant in Bellingham and Jurgensen was sent to manage it. The Jurgensens were young and personable and they very quickly fit into the social scene of their new home. Jurgensen became a member of the Rotary Club of Bellingham and their circle of friends and acquaintances grew rapidly. The natural wonders of the area thrilled these two mid-westerners. They both entered community activities enthusiastically and made Bellingham their home.

The Jurgensens lived in Bellingham for only six years, but they sunk down deep roots in the community and the Pacific Northwest. In 1964, to their great disappointment, Kaiser transferred them to a plant in Los Angeles. Shortly after the move Roy began to look for a way to get back to the Pacific Northwest. In July of 1971 he was hired as the vice president of Foss Tug & Barge. Within a year he was made its president. He had found the perfect job. When Foss was sold to Dillingham Corporation fate was at work.

Rotary park chairman Fickel knew of Roy's position with Dillingham, and he knew that one of Roy's good friends in Bellingham was Fickel's brother-in-law Larry Johanson. When Fickel learned that the Johansons were to be guests on the Jurgensen yacht for an upcoming cruise into Canadian waters, he asked that Jurgensen be encouraged to influence Dillingham to sell their waterfront land.

Jurgensen related in a 2006 phone interview that Johanson made the pitch during the cocktail hour and that he had been an easy sell. His fond memories of Bellingham, his host of friends there, and the appeal of a waterfront park in a community that had no waterfront access convinced him. He knew that Dillingham had no use for the land and so he promised to see what he could do.

He went on to say that he had developed an excellent relationship with Dillingham's vice president in charge of real estate. Shortly after the Dillingham takeover, Jurgensen had negotiated the sale of some unneeded, but valuable land that Foss had owned at the Port of Everett. The Port was wanting to consolidate its holdings and wanted to buy the parcel. It had been appraised at $1,900,000, but Jurgensen had succeeded in selling it to the Port for $4,100,000. He indicated that the success of that negotiation had helped when he proposed to that same vice president that Dillingham simply give the land to the Bellingham Park Department.

The gift of the waterfront land was agreed to by the Honolulu headquarters and Jurgensen was of the belief that Dillingham did transfer the deed to Bellingham for the consideration of five dollars. In fact, he related that whenever he comes to Bellingham to visit he drives down to Boulevard Park and walks around considering it in some ways his park.

Unfortunately for the park project, the talented executive was hired away from the Foss presidency in August of 1974 to become the senior vice president of the huge ocean-going towboat company, Crowley Maritime. Without Jurgensen's persuasive influence, the Dillingham home office backed out of the agreement to give the land to Bellingham. Dillingham wanted money. The park land acquisition was placed in jeopardy. Rotary records indicate a difficult negotiation with Dillingham for a time, and the public record indicates that Dillingham finally sold to the City on March 31, 1976, for the sum of $55,000. Jurgensen did not learn of Dillingham's backing out of the gift until my phone conversation with him in June of 2007.

Roy Jurgensen's initial influence with the Dillingham Corporation got the transaction in motion. Without the Dillingham purchase the park could not have been built. Roy Jurgensen's pride in his role in the creation of Boulevard Park remains justified.

The purchase of the Dillingham property completed the Boulevard Park land assembly. Jim Fickel, acting for the Rotary Club, in partnership with the City of Bellingham, had seen to the purchase of the scattered pieces of waterfront land formerly in private ownership. The public agencies were to cooperate via interlocal agreements in which Whatcom County Parks, the State Department of Natural Resources, and the City of Bellingham dedicated their property and street right-of-ways to the community need for a waterfront park. The gas works land and the Burlington Northern land above the bluff had been purchased in 1975. Boulevard Park only awaited construction funding.

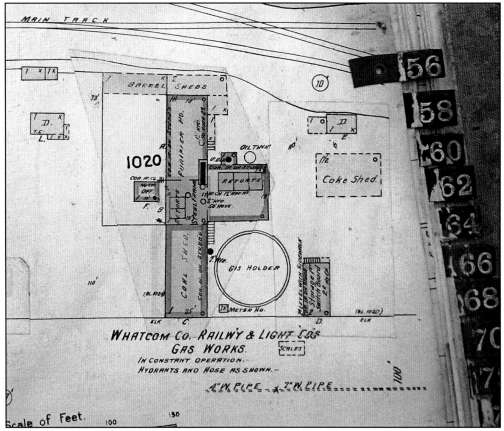

Sanborn Map, 1904.

Chapter 15

The Gas Works Site

THIS IMPORTANT PIECE OF THE PARK sits atop the bluff over the waterfront providing choice views across the bay. It adjoins at its southern border, the Spinnaker Reach Condominiums and extends for 300 feet along South State Street. The site can be easily identified as you drive along State Street by the small red brick building left as a historic relic during park construction.

This land was included in the William Pattle Donation Land Claim of 1853 that was eventually sold to Edward Eldridge and Erastus Bartlett. Presumably it was logged and then sat in its denuded state until June 10, 1890, when the Bellingham Bay Gas Company was organized.

The gas company was formed with capital of $200,000. Its president was H.Y. Thompson, its Vice President, Edward Eldridge, E.M. Wilson was the treasurer, and G.E. Brand, the secretary. Behind the scene was that master entrepreneur Nelson Bennett, who was the chief promoter behind almost everything happening in Fairhaven. The construction engineer was N.G. Olnore.

Since the plant was built on Eldridge and Bartlett land on the bluff above the waterfront sites, one can conjecture that Eldridge's ownership position and his vice presidency might be attributed to his trading land for ownership. However, it must also be recorded that Eldridge was a very astute businessman and a respected citizen with impressive political and social connections—always good qualities on the board of a private company requiring a franchise to sell its product. He served as a judge and speaker of the House of the Washington Territorial Legislature. At one time or another he was the president of the Bellingham Bay National Bank, Bellingham Bay Land Co., Bellingham Bay Water Co., and Bellingham Bay & Eastern Railway. He was a director of the Fairhaven & New Whatcom Street Railway Company, and Puget Sound

The gas works, circa 1930.

Loan, Trust & Banking Company, a Whatcom County Commissioner, the County Auditor, County Treasurer, Deputy Collector of Customs, and a believer in women's suffrage. In the year of his death, 1892, he was a delegate to the Republican National Convention. He no doubt contributed greatly to the company's founding.

The gas works plant cost $100,000 to construct. It was designed to create burnable gas from the abundant supply of local coal. The company owned franchises to sell gas in all three of the towns around the bay.

M.K. Elmon, the construction contractor, reported to the stockholders with the following message, "Gentlemen, your gas works was lighted on the night of December 18, 1890."

Initially the plant boasted just one storage tank for gas as shown on the Sanborn Map of 1904. Some years later, as demand grew, a larger storage tank was added. As a youth the author lived just a few blocks above the gas works. I remember well watching that big tank from my bedroom window. I was always intrigued by the way it changed its height from day to day. The huge steel tank would rise or sink in its steel containment structure, depending on the amount of lighter-than-air coal gas stored within it. Some days it would be almost to the top, and then several days later the great black steel circular tank might be ten or fifteen feet lower. It was years later that I was to learn that the weight of that steel tank was what provided the pressure to push the gas through the miles of pipe that had been installed to the homes and neighborhoods and businesses around the bay.

The gas left the plant through ten-inch mains which reduced in size as they got

farther and farther from the plant. By the time the gas reached its residential destination it was coursing through a pipe with only a half-inch hole. Gas was sold at the
price of $2.50 per 1000 cubic feet. With the help of Lynn Bell and Ray Trynzka of
Puget Sound Energy (PSE), I was able to determine that the price of gas today is approximately ten times less expensive than it was in 1890. Today gas is charged for by
an efficiency measurement of therms rather than cubic feet. Today's natural gas burns
about twice as hot as synthetic gas made from coal. The 1890's gas equates to a price
of 0.556 cents per 1000 therms. Converting 0.556 cents (55.6¢) of 1890's money to
2006 dollars results in an 1890 price of $12.71 per 1000 therms. PSE charges $1.243
per 1000 therms or about one tenth of the equivalent 1890 price. No wonder only the
rich plumbed their homes for gas and most folks cooked with wood in the 1890s.

The coal to manufacture the gas must have come from a number of local sources
over the years, but old records indicate that the gas works purchased its raw material from the Fairhaven Mine near Sedro-Woolley and from the Lake Samish Mine.
The coal would have been brought in over Nelson Bennett's Fairhaven & Southern
railway.

Coal gas became the modern fuel, replacing kerosene for lighting and in some in-
stances, wood for cooking. It was used for lighting and cooking at the Gamwell House
at 16th and Douglas. The classic old Victorian still has the original gas light fixtures in
place that were installed in 1892 when the house was built. Roland Gamwell bought
the very best for his magnificent mansion. Apparently anticipating the future his ornate light fixtures were equipped for both sorts of energy, either gas or electricity.

The author once bought and demolished a very old house on 16th Street just a
few doors south of Gamwell's mansion. I was surprised to find the old gas piping and
fixtures still in the house. I was even more surprised when disassembling the fixtures
that the lighter-than-air gas was still trapped in the lines and still gave off its charac-
teristic odor when I freed it from its pipe prison of untold years.

Ownership of the gas works changed a number of times during its business life.
Starting out as the Bellingham Bay Gas Company, it was quickly changed to the
Whatcom Fairhaven Gas Company, and then in 1912 the Whatcom County Railway
and Light Company Gas Works owned by Stone & Webster. Next the Puget Sound
Traction & Light & Power Company. Then Puget Sound Power & Light, and finally
the 1913 Sanborn Map, corrected to 1963, shows the site as belonging to Cascade
Natural Gas Company. All of these transitions of name and ownership are no doubt
worthy of a separate book, but for our purposes we are content to just know the succession of names and ownerships.

The gas works operated until 1956 when it fell victim to cheaper natural gas
which had reached Bellingham via the Cascade Natural Gas pipeline. It was cheaper

to transport natural gas through long pipelines from its underground source than to haul coal to Bellingham's shoreline and convert it to gas.

The now obsolete and shut down old plant was sold to a Gunnar Carlson. The site consisted of the entire block 83, the property north of Darwin Street, and included the tidal west end of the platted lots 1 through 12 lying west of the Burlington Northern track below the bluff and beside the water. The next owner was to buy the property from the widow of Gunnar Carlson by contract of sale on March 30th, 1967. The price was $50,000.

Lafayette Rogan Jones

That new owner was the legendary and visionary Bellingham business man Rogan Jones and his wife Catherine. A man before his time, Rogan Jones arranged to buy the land from Gunnar Carlson's widow for $50,000 on a contract of sale. This time his prescience was neither rewarded nor appreciated in many quarters. Jones' building request, relative to a nine-story residential tower, was turned down by a conservative city government process and the gas works property continued to lie unused.

Rogan Jones died in 1972 and his widow Catherine managed the property as executrix of his estate. Title company records show that the Gunnar Carlson contract was paid off in 1972 and Mrs. Jones owned the site without debt.

Rogan Jones had long been a member of the Rotary Club of Bellingham. It was to his widow, Catherine Jones, that members of the Rotary Club appealed. Mrs. Jones, also a civic-minded person, was asked by Rotary friends to option the property to the Club, with the understanding that the option would be transferred to the City to be included in the park. She optioned the site to the Club and some time later, on December 26, 1975, she completed the sale to the City. The negotiated price was $95,000.

Small brick building is a gas works survivor.

Several old structures remained on the land. They dated back to the gas works original construction in 1890. The park designers were wise enough to appreciate the historic value of these 115-year-old relics and chose to leave them for their historic interest. The small brick building, highly visible from the roadway, clearly marks the gas works site for all that pass by. The Sanborn Map identifies that building as "storage on the first floor" and "switch-board on 2nd level". There are large glass insulators protruding from the south wall indicating some sort of electrical use.

The second structure is a large circular concrete base which once served as the foundation for one of the two gas tanks. On top of this was once a tall steel framework that guided the great round steel tank, which I could watch from my boyhood bedroom window. The tank base now holds a picnic and observation shelter on its top. That shelter was built with

Rotary picnic shelter built on tank base.

a $17,000 contribution from the Rotary Club, which wanted to leave some tangible evidence of its role in the parks creation. A bronze plaque placed at its entrance commemorates the club's involvement.

The round tank base can best be seen by walking down the path toward the wooden bridge that crosses high above the Burlington Northern track and brings the walker to a set of stairs leading you down to the waterfront level. This wooden hog-wire-clad structure effectively gets people safely, if somewhat breathlessly, from one level of the park to the other.

The old gas works site serves as a visible introduction to Boulevard Park, a lofty view site, and a reminder of the beginnings of our municipal services, gas for light and cooking.

The bridge stairway over the railroad tracks.

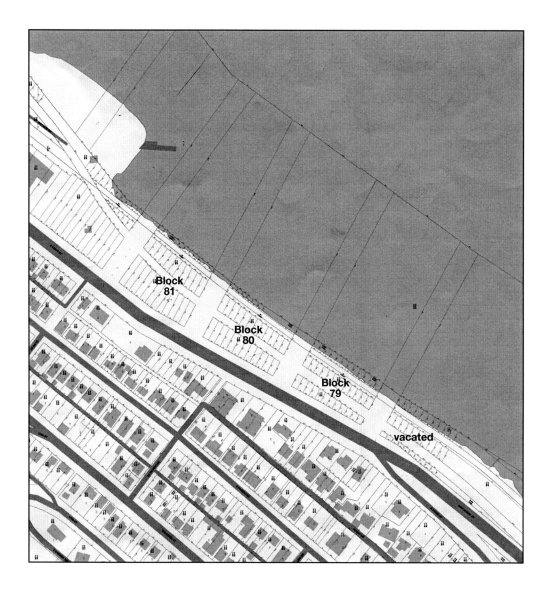

Chapter 16

The Burlington Northern Blocks

THE FOUR PLATTED BLOCKS north of the gas works block were owned by the Burlington Northern Railroad. It was three of those blocks (numbers 81, 80 and 79) running along the Boulevard that prompted the public concern that led to the creation of Boulevard Park, as reported in chapter one. Pete Zuanich, Malcom 'Dutch' McBeath, and George Livesey Jr. were able to buy a 40-year lease on this property; and it was here that they wanted to build a row of multi-family apartments.

It would be the challenge of Jim Fickel and his Rotary committee to persuade Zuanich and company to cease their development plans and indeed to give up their long-term lease on this property. All the participants to this persuasion are now deceased. We can only imagine the appeals to community welfare, the pleas for the common good, and the anguished considerations of the would-be developers.

Robert Gibb, M.D., a past president and long-time Rotarian, recalled that Zuanich, McBeath and Livesey were put under a great deal of pressure to give up their lease by their Rotarian friends. I believe that Rotary convinced the three men that it was in the community interest to not develop the land. In a 2006 conversation with Port of Bellingham Commissioner Scott Walker, Walker relayed that Pete Zuanich had once remarked that the partners had given up millions of dollars of profits by voluntarily giving up that lease. Actually they did get paid a modicum price by the City, which eventually bought out their lease for $16,000.

What is known is that they did give up their lease and Burlington Northern was persuaded by the crusading Rotarians to option the property to the City. Zuanich may have been right, A huge condominium or apartment project along that strip might have been extremely profitable, but Pete Zuanich and Dutch McBeath, and George Livesey Jr. had proven over many years, and in many ways, that they were good community members and had the welfare of their city in mind. All of them had long records of community activism and support. They were leaders in the Bellingham Junior Chamber of Commerce, which for many years was a strong force in advancing the community. McBeath might have been under a little greater pressure as he was a long-standing member of the Rotary Club of Bellingham, the very organization that was trying to assemble the land for the park.

The railroad right-of-way that slices through this land has now been converted to the South Bay Trail, a hiking-biking path that leads from Boulevard Park to the alley between Railroad Avenue and State Street behind Depot Market Square. The trail is built on the former Northern Pacific track. In 1903 Northern Pacific had purchased the Bellingham Bay and Eastern Railroad that had serviced the north shore of Lake Whatcom and the Blue Canyon mine bringing coal and timber to the salt water at Bellingham. The Northern Pacific extended that line across the trestles southward to service the industries at Fairhaven.

Burlington Northern had acquired the land astride this right-of-way along with the main line track on the waterside below. The City was to purchase all of blocks 81, 80, 79, and an additional block to the north, block 78, in December of 1975 for $60,000.

With the purchase of these four blocks and the gas works site the view from the Boulevard was secured. These two acquisitions meant that 1820 continuous feet of precious view frontage was in City hands. The initial goal of the YWCA Eco-Action group had been achieved. The views from the Boulevard were saved. Geography, the layout of the streets, and the City ownership of the railroad right-of-way all combined to improve on that excellent result.

A look at a map will show that the railroad right-of-way and the Boulevard converge into such a narrow strip north of the now City-owned blocks as to make any use of the narrowing strip of land virtually impossible. While those blocks are not owned by the City it would appear that all the view north to Wharf Street is preserved as well. If that be true, the length of continuous land from Spinnaker Reach Condominium all the way to Wharf Street with views interrupted only by trees is more than a mile long.

Chapter 17

Art in the Park

THE CITY WISELY APPLIED FOR A Washington State Art Grant
shortly after the Park was committed to. They invested those funds into two pieces of
art for their new park. Their foresight and their choices have stood the test of time.
Both works have endured 26 years of use by a not-always-gentle public and they give
every indication of serving for many years more. Perhaps the secret to their longevity
is the extremely tough and enduring materials they were constructed with; heavy steel
plate and huge granite boulders.

Western Stone Garden

This work is by Michael Jacobsen, a sculptor of stone who worked in Bellingham for
many years. In addition to his stone work, Jacobsen was an installation specialist for
the Whatcom Museum of History and Art, where he designed and installed art ex-
hibits for at least a decade.

Western Stone Garden is a collection of five huge granite glacial *erratics*, cut and
polished and set on the grass by the water's edge in a grouping. The massive stones
were torn from the Cascade mountain-tops during the last ice age, rolled and ground
under the advancing sheet of ice and carried along with it as it advanced over Puget
Sound country. When the earth warmed, the smoothed granite boulders were left behind as the glacier melted and lost its icy grip on the huge stones. Whatcom and San
Juan County are virtually littered with the erratic glacial cast-offs. The enduring hard-
ness of granite is evident if you consider that the polished surfaces of Western Stone
Garden were polished in 1978.

Western Stone Garden

The Conference Table

This interesting piece sits on the upper part of Boulevard Park beside South State Street on the old gas works site. It is a huge long bench (or table) made of laminated pieces of Douglas Fir, supported and contained by three plates of 3/4-inch-thick steel cut to create both table legs and people seated at the table. Each person portrayed is different. Some look like they are dealing cards, some just conversing. I think one of them is a dead ringer for the famous Bolshevik Nicholai Lenin.

These two art works have graced Boulevard Park since its inception and have demonstrated the wisdom of the City's investment in municipal art. I hope that additional pieces of enduring art will be placed in the park in future years. There are many excellent locations for public art within the one-mile length of Boulevard Park. Perhaps some generous donor will contribute the funds for a bronze at the Taylor Avenue Dock entrance, or a stone sculpture along the trail just north of Easton Beach. Public art in our parks and by-ways enhances the quality of our lives and the beauty of our parks.

Conference Table, created by Tom McClelland, is worthy of close examination. Stop some day as you drive by and take a look.

Does this fellow look like Lenin?

Chapter 18

The Boulevard

BOULEVARD PARK IS A NICE enough name for our park. It has certainly stood the test of time these 27 years and is universally accepted by our citizens. Therefore it pains me to tell you that the park is badly misnamed. The alarming reality is that whoever chose the name Boulevard Park was playing fast and loose with the facts.

The truth is that no part of the Park is adjacent to the Boulevard. It should not have been named Boulevard Park. Every inch of the park fronts either on South State Street, or 10th Street. I am sorry to tell you this, but perhaps we should be calling our beloved waterfront park by some other name.

Now I realize that among my readers are those of you that would call me a nit-picker and a wool gatherer. If you are so inclined I would only say that facts are facts. You may be comfortable calling the entire road along the bay from Wharf Street to Fairhaven, 'The Boulevard' (it is after all the community habit), but I am not. It is just such lazy colloquial habits that caused the park to be misnamed in the first place.

Better that we had listened to the advice of one of our now-deceased old timers, George Hunsby, who wrote to the Parks Board in 1979 suggesting that the new park be named 'Red Mill Park'. Now that has a nice romantic ring to it, and it is based on the true history of the site. That makes his suggestion most appropriate and valid.

Hunsby was an engaging and outspoken old guy who had lived his entire life in Fairhaven. I came across his letter in the Washington State Archives where the Park Department keeps its historical remains. He wrote to the Parks Board when in his nineties and reported that he had worked at the E.K. Wood Mill as a youngster, stamping lumber for shipment. He recalled stamping lumber to be loaded on the famous lumber schooners *Vigilant* and *Commodore* that regularly loaded Bellingham

Intersection of Boulevard and South State Street.

lumber bound for the Hawaiian Islands. Hunsby suggested naming the park 'Red Mill Park' in recognition of the nickname the E.K. Wood Mill had earned. It seems that all of its buildings were painted a vivid bright red. It was colloquially known as 'The Red Mill'.

Here is the truth of the situation. The Boulevard is the proper name of only that piece of roadway that leaves State Street at the Wharf Street intersection and follows to the right (Bay side) around the steep hill that the Armory, the old St. Joseph's Hospital, and the popular Cliff House Restaurant sit on. It joins State Street again just a dozen feet north of the Boulevard Park border, about where the large painted 'Welcome To Bellingham' sign is on the concrete retaining wall. That is 'The Boulevard'! All of the road south of that point is South State Street.

When streets were first laid out joining Sehome with Fairhaven through old Bellingham, State Street was laid out straight as a die. When the surveyors got to the steep 'Armory' hill they just kept going straight, right up and over.

The problems associated with driving a horse-drawn wagon over that steep hill soon became apparent. When it snowed the problem became even more apparent. Irritated folks began to suggest a new road that would be level and follow around the hill on the bay side. That road, to be called 'The Boulevard', would be level and enjoy a view of the bay and the mills for its entire length.

About that time the Interurban Electric Railway was being organized to connect Bellingham with Everett and beyond. The Interurban was essentially a railroad, and a railroad could not negotiate the steep hill presented by Elk Street (now State Street). They had no choice but to cut around the hill and create the virtually level Boulevard route. Their franchise agreement with the rather new City of Bellingham dictated that the right-of-way they excavated would be wide enough for both a railroad track and a public street. The Boulevard was built in 1910. It was a very popular and welcome addition and soon became much busier than the State Street hill. Before long folks were calling the entire road to Fairhaven, 'The Boulevard'.

I guess we will just have to live with the error, Boulevard Park has become a part of the Bellingham vocabulary and that will always be the Park's name. Even I must confess to liking the sound of it better than South State Street Park. At least now you know the truth. You know where the Boulevard truly is. And I have the satisfaction of having told you so. But, hmmm… Red Mill Park? Red Mill Park? It really has a nice ring to it.

Chapter 19

The Railroads

THE STORY OF BOULEVARD PARK cannot be completely understood without knowing the story of the various railroads that have run over the two tracks that have bisected the park land through the years. While the tracks remained the same for many years, the names of the railroads operating on them changed many times as the original small lines were purchased and merged into larger and larger lines, until the only surviving railroad became the present survivor—the Burlington Northern Railroad.

For many years competing railroads ran along our waterfront, one on the shoreline track that is now the Burlington Northern main line from Burlington to Blaine.

A second railroad left Fairhaven and ran out over a deep-water trestle, touching the end of the Taylor Avenue dock and continuing over what is now the Boardwalk pedestrian trestle, thru present day Boulevard Park and up the grade to cut through Bellingham in the alley behind the old Morse Hardware store building and the Masonic Temple. It then crossed Holly Street to deliver to Clark's and Hohl Feed & Seed. It then proceeded across the bridge over Whatcom Creek and up the steep Alabama Hill to Lake Whatcom. Then it ran along the north shore of Lake Whatcom on the old track bed (now the Ken Hertz Trail), to Blue Canyon (the site of the Blue Canyon Mine that operated there until 1920). It finally connected to the line running down the valley to Sedro-Woolley and on to Seattle.

A third railroad line that never crossed Boulevard Park land began at the Sehome Dock at the foot of Cornwall Avenue. It climbed the grade to Railroad Avenue and went through downtown and the north county to Sumas, with later branches to Lynden and Glacier.

The first railroads came to Bellingham Bay in the 1880s and the communities that they served were changed forever. The hope and expectation that a transcontinental railroad would make its Pacific terminus on Bellingham Bay was to fuel investment and keep the fires of speculation burning on the bay. The great Fairhaven Boom was fueled by the hope that Jim Hill would bring his Northern Pacific line over the Cascades and make Fairhaven its terminus. Even though that did not come to pass, in a very real sense, the expectation of that coming built Fairhaven and focused great attention on the Bellingham Bay towns.

The first railroads were small, specific-purpose operations that had their beginnings locally. Eventually they connected with larger lines expanding their operations up and down the coast. In their brief lives these tiny railroads enhanced the economies of the towns they served and induced the large railroads to connect to the fledgling towns of Fairhaven, Whatcom and Sehome.

This county's first railroad, The Bellingham Bay & British Columbia (BB & BC), was started in 1883 by the San Francisco owners of the recently closed Sehome Coal Mine, who owned thousands of acres north and east of Whatcom Creek. These wealthy investors (represented in Whatcom County by Pierre Cornwall) saw an opportunity to connect the soon-to-be transcontinental Canadian Pacific Railroad with the Pacific Ocean at their coal mine dock on Bellingham Bay. They foresaw a burgeoning community where they could sell their large land holdings at a profit. They started their rail line at their own Sehome Wharf (the namesake of Wharf Street), which was located at the foot of Dock Street (now called Cornwall Avenue). They drove a track through the forests of Whatcom County to Sumas at the Canadian border. The Canadian Pacific was finishing its transcontinental line down the Fraser River Canyon and had committed to a connection with the fledgling American line at Sumas.

The BB & BC began in 1883 and finally made the Canadian connection in 1892, after years of delays and the huge effort of cutting their line through the immense stands of timber of Whatcom County. The BB & BC began at the foot of (now) Cornwall Avenue, climbed the grade up the embankment to Railroad Avenue and went north. Its old grade can still be walked through the trees below the Bay Trail. You can enter the grade at Railroad and Laurel in front of the Housing Authority habitation. The old grade angles down the side of the embankment and meets the Burlington Northern track at Wharf Street. The BB & BC did not touch the Boulevard Park area, but no history of local railroading would be proper without mentioning it. The pioneer railroad was eventually purchased by the Milwaukee & St. Paul Railroad, which operated on Railroad Avenue until 1980.

In December 1888, that millionaire railroad-builder and land developer, Nelson Bennett and his partners (in the Fairhaven Land Company) formed the Fairhaven

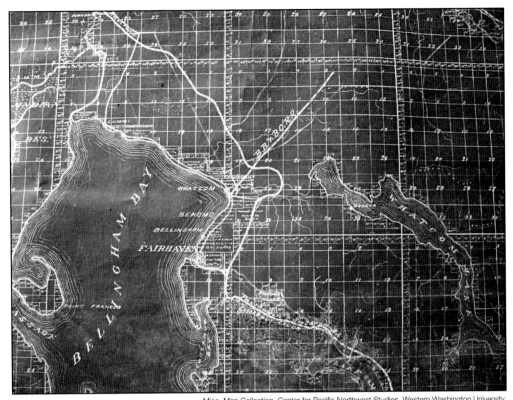

Photo depicts an 1890 map produced by the Fairhaven Civil Engineering firm of Allerton & McFarland. It shows the first plan to take the railroad around Sehome Hill.

and Southern Railway with the specific purpose of bringing coal from the Cokedale mine near Sedro-Woolley to Fairhaven. The track ran from the mine (located not far from the former Northern State Hospital), along Friday Creek, up the Fish Hatchery Hill grade, along Lake Samish, and down into Fairhaven along what is now the southbound lane of Interstate 5. Running through Happy Valley it terminated at the waterfront at 9th Street and Harris Avenue.

This old map was found by the author amongst a number of papers left in the house that he and his wife purchased at 1027 16th Street in 1969. The house was built in the 1880s by Thomas J. Newman, a Fairhaven attorney who worked closely with the Fairhaven Land Company. The map no doubt was used in the planning of various business activities of the time. It clearly shows the railroads of that day.

In 1890, the year the map was published, Bennett and his partners extended their Fairhaven and Southern line to the north seeking to connect to the Canadian market at Blaine. This extension (which began at 9th Street and Harris Avenue) was to be called the Fairhaven and Northern. This map calls it "the Northern Division of the Fairhaven & Southern". The track was to branch from the Southern in Happy Valley and head north behind Sehome Hill taking an inland route toward Blaine. That route is shown by the heavy white line. It proved to be more practical to build the track along the waterfront almost to the Nooksack River before turning inward. The Fairhaven and Northern track was built along the shoreline on the very same right-of-way used by the Burlington Northern to this day. The track was laid on a great trestle that crossed Bellingham Bay, well out from the New Whatcom shoreline.

A June 1, 1890, newspaper article reports, "the piles are driven on the Fairhaven & Northern nearly across the New Whatcom Waterfront". The depicted route was originally proposed and abandoned as impractical because of land acquisition and topographical problems. This map perhaps was used by Newman, as lawyer for the Fairhaven Land Company, to permit or at least promote the northern route through the city. The Fairhaven & Northern reached the border at Blaine on December 1, 1890.

In an interesting side note, Newman, who was a stockholder and officer of the Bellingham Bay Boom Company, must also have used this map in planning the installation of that ill-fated log boom at the mouth of the Nooksack River. Notice the penciled lines detailing the shape of the log boom (shown larger on page 164), no doubt placed there by Newman himself in contemplating the log boom. The imagination readily conjures up the picture of this very map surrounded by the Boom Company founders—Nelson Bennett, E.M. Wilson, Cowgill, Newman, Black, Thompson and the other incorporators—as they smoked their cigars and hatched their scheme to seal off the river.

The map also shows that at this date, 1890, the Bellingham Bay and British Columbia Railway had penetrated only a few miles into the deep woods of the county. We know that they were still two years from their goal, Sumas and the Canadian border.

Soon after arriving in Blaine, Bennett and his Fairhaven & Southern backers cast their eyes to the south with the goal of connecting their line with the Great Northern at Burlington. Bennett's people built their line along the Chuckanut shore, pioneering the route which is still in use to this day. The Chuckanut track was no doubt built to attract freight business, but it must also have been motivated by Bennett's sure knowledge that a right of way from Burlington to the Canadian border would stimulate great interest for the owners of the Great Northern in buying his tiny Fairhaven & Southern. If that was his thinking it proved to be sound. The Great Northern did acquire the Fairhaven & Southern Railroad in 1902, presumably at a nice profit for Bennett and his friends.

As if to confuse railroad historians, the Great Northern operated its Fairhaven acquisition as a subsidiary for a number of years. They first called it the Seattle & Montana Railway before finally using the Great Northern name a decade later. Just

The Pacific American Fisheries Company started up in 1899. By 1910 the P. A. F. most of the waterfront along the south... the 1920s, The P. A...

Gordon Tweit collection.

The Northern Pacific freight station can be seen on trestle at far right of photo.

one more name in the long list of railroad companies of Whatcom County history.

In 1891 another local railroad was formed
by Bennett and prominent engineer J.J. Donovan
(Fairhaven City Councilman and Bellingham business icon), to tap the riches of the Blue Canyon
Mine and the timber country surrounding Lake
Whatcom. The Bellingham Bay and Eastern ran
up Alabama Hill to the lake, then out along the
north shore to Blue Canyon. This line and its flat
roadway along the lake has become the popular
Ken Hertz Trail. The Bellingham Bay and Eastern
was sold to the Northern Pacific in 1903. Northern
Pacific extended the line south down the alley be-

1890 *Fairhaven Illustrated*,
Whatcom Museum of History & Art

J.J. Donovan

tween Railroad Avenue and State Street, cutting the grade which is now the popular
South Bay Trail below the Boulevard. The tracks crossed the Fairhaven & Southern
line just below the gas works plant on the waterfront, and cut through what is now
Boulevard Park, to break out on the long trestle across Harris Bay that touched the
tip of the Taylor Avenue dock and served the lumber mill, flour mill, and warehouses

at Taylor Avenue, and then continued via a trestle across Harris Bay to the canneries at the south end of the Bay. The Northern Pacific built its freight station on the trestle just few dozen feet south of the Taylor Avenue dock.

The new Park Department's boardwalk across the water is built on that old right-of-way.

At some point after the consolidation of Fairhaven and Whatcom into Bellingham, the Northern Pacific relocated its the freight and passenger station to Bellingham, where it was housed in a brick and frame building on the site of the present Whatcom Transit Authority bus station at Railroad and Magnolia. Part of the original brick station is still to be seen at the recently remodeled bus facility.

Consolidation of the railroads has proven a boon for the City of Bellingham. The demise of the Milwaukee St. Paul Railroad allowed the City to purchase Railroad Avenue and the Depot Market site. The popular La Fiamma Pizza building was formerly the Milwaukee St. Paul Railway Express shipping office. The Northern Pacific right-of-way provided room for the downtown bus terminal and the Ken Hertz Trail. Boulevard Park was made possible by Hertz's prescient deal on the South Bay Trail and the Northern Pacific land through the Park and over the trestle. And finally, the views from the Boulevard were preserved by the purchase of those four important blocks north of the gas works from Burlington Northern.

March of 1970 saw consolidation of the Northern Pacific, the Great Northern, and the Burlington lines—merged into the ultimate entity the present Burlington Northern Railway.

For the purposes of our Boulevard Park history it suffices to remember that the Bellingham Bay and Eastern (later the Northern Pacific) ran across the southside trestle; the Fairhaven and Southern and its Northern division (later the Great Northern and finally the Burlington Northern) have occupied the shoreline track which is now the Burlington Northern Main line.

First train of the Fairhaven & Southern (northern division) at Harris & 9th. J.J. Donovan, wearing his bowler hat, stands proudly with his son in the foreground.

1904 Sanborn Map, a leather and canvas bound book.

Appendix 1

The Sanborn Map

FIFTY YEARS AGO, I returned home from Army duty in Korea and joined my father's insurance firm, Northwestern Insurance Agency. I was intrigued to find on a large table in the mail room, a huge cloth- and leather-covered book filled with heavy cloth and paper pages containing a graphic and printed description of every residential and commercial building in Bellingham. This massive tome measured 23 inches by 26 inches, and was easily five or six inches thick.

My father explained that the well-worn old book was a Sanborn Map, prepared and maintained by the Sanborn Map Company of Pelham, New York. It was published as a service to the fire insurance industry, which for almost 200 years had subscribed to mapping services like Sanborn to assist them in making risk selections and establishing prices for the insurance that they sold on the mapped properties.

The ability to make underwriting decisions by consulting a detailed map was far more cost efficient than sending an inspector to look at each risk. The underwriter could learn vast amounts of information from just perusing a good fire insurance map. Location, address, available fire protection, construction materials, type of roof, location of boilers or machinery, size of buildings, distance from other flammable structures—all information that helped the insurance underwriter decide if he wanted to insure a given building, and what price to charge for the risk.

Sanborn Map Company surveyors would scour the country keeping the maps up to date by gleaning information from county courthouses, real estate agents, and most often by on-the-site measuring, and examining structures themselves. Prior to 1929, Sanborn would publish new pages or entire new books from time to time. After 1929 they handled updates by printing them on small patches which they periodically mailed out to subscribers to be pasted into the large books over the previous image of the building. I remember using the sticky white paste myself a few times. Several of the rapidly changing industrial buildings in my father's Sanborn had three or four layers of pasted patches.

Somehow, the Sanborn people kept up with each and every change made to a building. At the employment peak just before the Second World War, there were 700 surveyors keeping track of the building changes in 12,000 cities and towns in the United States, Canada, and Mexico.

A new book cost from $12 to $200, depending on the size and complexity of the community covered. I have not been able to learn the annual cost of their update service.

Each map was drawn on a scale of fifty feet to one inch, and was printed on sheets 21 by 25 inches. These map sheets were originally sold individually as a bundle of paper sheets, but eventually they were attached to long-wearing cloth pages and bound into the huge and heavy cloth and leather books. These massive tomes each measured a standard 23 by 26 inches, and were up to eight inches thick.

The 1904 Bellingham Washington Sanborn, in the possession of the Washington State Archive at Western Washington University, weighs in at a full 24.5 pounds; while its successor, the 1916 version, at least one third thicker, overcame my scale which had a 30-pound maximum capability; mute evidence of Bellingham's rapid growth during that period.

Insurance mapping began in London toward the end of the 18th century. Maps of London, commissioned by the Phoenix Assurance Company Ltd., have been found dated 1785. In the 1790s Phoenix expanded their area of operation to the Indies, Canada, and the United States. The first map made for them in America was made shortly after the turn of the 18th century and was of the town of Charleston, South Carolina.

The war of 1812 disrupted commercial relationships with English companies and insurance companies began shortly thereafter to be formed in the United States, the first in Philadelphia. As the need for insurance mapping grew with the domestic industry, various map-making companies came into being. The industrial revolution and economic growth spurred by the end of the American Civil War spawned an ever-increasing number of American insurance companies.

In 1867, J.B. Bennett, manager of Aetna Fire Insurance Company, hired Daniel Alfred Sanborn to do fire maps of several towns in Tennessee. The Sanborn Map Company, as it would eventually come to be called, was born. In the same year Sanborn did a map of Boston for Aetna, the scale of 50 feet to one inch, printed on 21- by 25-inch sheets was established as the standard. Over the years Sanborn's company grew

1904 Sanborn Map title page.

by merger and purchase of competing firms, until by 1902 it had established itself as the major insurance map maker.

The company's instruction and training manual for surveyors stated their credo, "Our maps are made for the purpose of showing at a glance the character of the fire insurance risks of all buildings." Insurance companies owned libraries of the huge books,

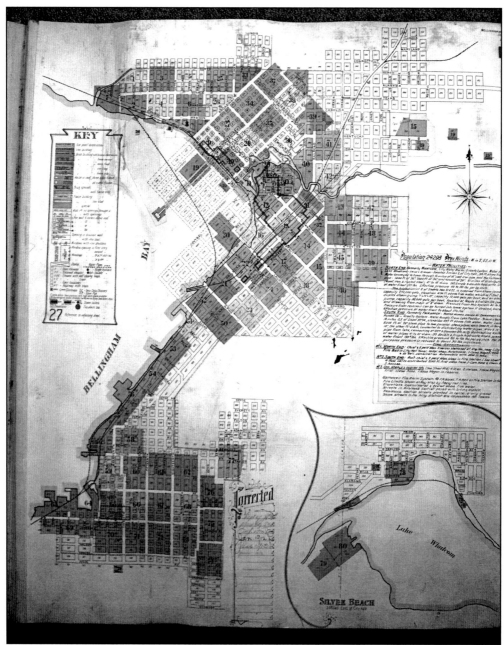

Reference Library, Center for Northwest Studies, Western Washington University.

Color-coded index page for the Sanborn Map.

and up-to-date insurance agents had to own the Sanborn for the community or communities in which they sold insurance.

In the 1960s changes in insurance underwriting practices began to make the old maps obsolete and they rapidly fell into disuse. Fortunately, many of them were given to museums and libraries and state archives where they now serve as priceless records of the growth and change of cities and industries, and as research records of what used to be. The largest collection of Sanborns is owned by the Library of Congress. The author has found the Sanborns in the collections of the Whatcom Museum of History and Art, and the Washington State Regional Archive at Western Washington University to be invaluable tools of research.

The Sanborn Map Company still exists, providing modern mapping and survey services to a variety of industries using the latest digital and electronic methods.

Appendix 2

The Pattle Lease

Pattle, Thomas & Morrison to F. R. Loomis: Lease

Territory of Oregon
County of Thurston S.S.

This indenture of lease made this eleventh (11th) day of April in the year of our lord one thousand, eight hundred and fifty three (1853) between William R. Pattle, John Thomas, and James Morrison of Island County, Territory of Oregon, of the first part, and F. Rogers Loomis, Agent, of the city of San Francisco, State of California, of the second part.

Witnesseth; That whereas the said parties of the first part have (pursuant to the provisions of the act of congress approved Sept. 27th, A.D. 1850, with an act to create the office of surveyor general of public lands in Oregon, and to provide for the survey, and to make donation to settlers of the said public lands) settled upon the following described pieces, or parcels of land situated, lying and being in the east side of Bellingham Bay, Island County, Territory of Washington.

To Wit; that certain piece or parcel of land fronting on said bay, and bounded on the south by a blazed cedar tree on "Mineral Point" and running thence in a northern direction one half mile and in an eastern direction one half mile from the shores of said bay, said piece or parcel of land is known as the claim of William R. Pattle and is designed to embrace one quarter of a section, or one hundred and sixty acres.

Also, that other certain piece or parcel of land fronting on said bay and bounded on the north by the said blazed cedar tree, and running south one half mile, and east from the shore of said bay one half mile, said piece or parcel of land is known as the claim of James Morrison and is designed to embrace one quarter of a section or one hundred and sixty acres.

Also, that certain other piece or parcel of land fronting on said bay, and bounded on the north by James Morrison's southern boundary, and running south one half mile, and east from the shore of said bay one half mile, said piece or parcel of land is known as the claim of John Thomas, and is designed to embrace one quarter section or one hundred and sixty acres, which three said claims are held in common by the parties of the first part, for agricultural purposes, and said pieces or parcels are now in the actual occupation of the said parties of the first part, under the provisions of said act.

And whereas there have been discovered veins, beds, or mines of coal on said land, which are supposed to run through said land, and which said parties of the first part are unable to develop and work. Now therefore it is agreed and understood by the parties of the first part, their heirs, administrators and assigns forever, that for and in consideration of the rents, covenants, and agreements on the part of the said F. Rogers Loomis, the party of the second part, his heirs, executors, and assigns to be paid, done, and performed, the said parties of the first part have demised and leased, and do herby demise and lease unto the said party of the second part, his heirs, executors, administrators and assigns, all the said pieces and parcels of land herein before described for the full term and period of ninety and nine years from the date hereof, for the purpose of opening, exploring, and working said coal mines, beds, or veins, or any other mines that may be found or discovered thereon, and for making, and constructing roads, railways, bridges, canals or other ways for transportation of coals, and such other matter as the party of the second part or his assigns may elect to transport over, through and across said lands.

And the said parties of the first part, their heirs, executors, administrators, and assigns do for the hereby covenant and agree that for the purposes of opening, working and exploring any such coal or other mines, or minerals on said lands, and for the construction of all the necessary fixtures, machinery, roads, canals and other improvements the said party of the second part or his assigned may enter upon and take possession of any parts or portions of said lands so described. Said party or his assigns may elect so to do, and to build there on without lets or hindrance, all such houses, towns, and villages, and may make and construct all roads, railways, plank road, bridges, canals, wharves and piers as may be necessary to enable said party of the second part or his assigns to successfully prosecute the business of coal or other mining, it being the object and intention of the said parties of the first part, hereby to clothe the said party of the second part, his successors and assigns with full, absolute, complete, and perfect power under this lease to take and use at any and all times, any and all portions of said lands as may be needed in the working and management of said coal or other mines, and in the making of all roads, railways, canals, wharves and piers for transportation or other purposes connected therewith.

And we the said parties of the first part do further covenant and agree for ourselves, and our heirs, executors, administrators and assigns, that we will truly, under said act of congress do and perform every act necessary to secure and perfect or title to such lands, and that this lease shall continue whenever the patents may issue, it being hereby expressly understood, that the said pieces of parcels of land are to remain for agriculture purposes, but that the said party of the second part or his assigns have the sole, exclusive and absolute control over any and all parts of the same for mining purposes and for opening and making roads and other means of communication with the mines, and for such other purposes connected therewith, as said party or his assigns may require.

And it is hereby further covenanted and agreed by the party of the second part, and his assigns, that the agreed consideration to be paid to the said parties of the first or their assigns shall be the sum of seventy five dollars per month until the full term of four years from the date of settlement on said lands to each and every one of the said parties of the first part, which said monthly sum of seventy five dollars, shall be, and is hereby made payable at the end of every quarter at the office of the Oregon Coal Mining Association in Oregon, but it is hereby distinctly understood and agreed by and between the parties hereto that no payment shall be made nor come due to the parties of the first part until a test of the coal on said lands shall have been made by the party of the second part, or his assigns in San Francisco, and the same shall have proved satisfactory, then and not until then shall the parties hereto of the first part become entitled to the monthly consideration herein expressed.

And it is hereby understood that whenever patents shall issue to the said parties of the first part, for the land herein before described, then the party of the second part or his assigns, shall pay to each and every one of the parties of the first part; that is to say, to William R. Pattle, John Thomas, and James Morrison, or their assigns the sum of two thousand five hundred dollars, in consideration of all rents or profits thereafter to the parties of the first part, their executors, administrators or assigns, and said parties of the first part hereby covenant and agree for themselves and their heirs, executors, administrators and assigns, that the said sum of two thousand five hundred dollars so to be paid shall constitute the full and entire and only consideration to be paid by the said party of the second part, or his assigns, during the continuance of this lease, except the said monthly sum as herein provided.

And it is further hereby covenanted and agreed by the parties of the first part, their heirs, executors, administrators and assigns that this said lease shall be renewed for the term of fifty years from the expiration hereof for the purposes herein specified for an annual rental of one dollar payable annually.

And it is further hereby covenanted and agreed by the said party of the second part and his assigns, that he will not use any portion of said lands herein referred to, except for the purposes specified, it being the positive and express understanding of all parties hereto that this instrument is to be deemed a lease to enable the party of the second part or his assigns, to open and work any coal or other mineral in or upon said lands, to transport the produce of the same, and such other matter as may be required over and across said lands and that all the profits, benefits and advantages arising or accruing therefrom shall belong exclusively and solely to the said party of the second part and his assigns.

And it is further hereby covenanted and agreed by the parties of the first part, that whenever the party of the second part or his assigns shall signify his readiness in writing to enter into the enjoyments of the privileges hereby demised, the said parties of the first part will place said party of the second part or his assigns in peaceable possession thereof.

And it is further hereby agreed that at the end and termination of this lease all improvements therein made by the party of the second part or his assigns and the fee for the land on which they may stand shall become the absolute property of the said party of the second part or his assigns. And it is further hereby distinctly understood and agreed by and between the parties hereto, that in event of the tests of coal from said lands, which is to be made in San Francisco, proving unsatisfactory to said party of the second part or his assigns, then this lease shall be of no effect and all the covenants and agreements herein contained shall be null and void.

And finally, we the said parties of the first part, do hereby acknowledge and declare, that, this instrument is freely and unconstrainedly made and executed by us, for the uses and purposes herein specified, and in consideration of the covenants herein contained on the parts of the said party of the second part, together with a further consideration of one dollar, current money of the United States of America, in hand paid, the receipt thereof is hereby acknowledged.

And the said parties of the first part agree that they will forward one hundred sacks of coal from said lands without unnecessary delay, to the address of the said party of the second part, in the city of San Francisco for the purpose of enabling the said party to make the tests thereof as aforesaid. It is understood that the cost of transportation, shall be sustained by the party of the second part.

In witness whereof, we have hereunto affixed our hands and seals, in the town of Olympia, Territory aforesaid in the day and date first above written. James Morrison signing by attorney, William R. Pattle, and the other parties signing for themselves.

Signed, Sealed and delivered in presence of W.A. Howard & A.M. Poe
        F. ROGERS LOOMIS, Agent
        WILLIAM R. PATTLE,
        JOHN THOMAS,
        JAMES MORRISON, by Attorney William R. Pattle,

I, Alonzo M. Poe, a notary public duly commissioned and sworn for the county of Thurston, Oregon Territory, hereby certify that William R. Pattle, John Thomas, James Morrison by Wm. R. Pattle, his attorney duly empowered, and F. Rogers Loomis, all of whom are known to me, appeared before me this day and acknowledged the above to be their free act and deed for the purposes specified. Witness my hand and official seal on this eleventh day of April, A.D. 1853, in this town of Olympia, and territory aforesaid.

Recorded Aug. 1 & 2, 1883.
    R.H. Lausdale, recorder, Island Co., W.T., tres. $6.00

Appendix 3

Pattle/Doyle Bond

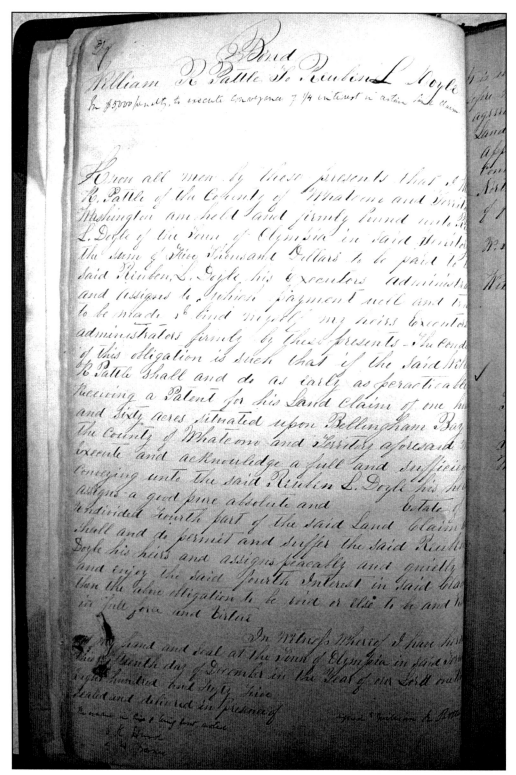

Old record book showing the Pattle/Doyle bond. It's just two pages and is a credible demonstration of what the old documents look like.

21

It is understood and agreed between the parties herein before mentioned that the undivided one fourth Interest agreed to be conveyed shall apply to the Coal in said Land Claim and at any time the said Doyle makes application for a division of the Land the portion conveyed for his use shall be sett off to him on the North side of said Claim having an equal proportion of front and back

Signed in Duplicate at Olympia W.T. this fifteenth day of December A.D. 1855

Witness
J.E. Hurd
S.H. Brown

Sgnd. William K. Pottle.
Kintzen L. Doyle

Deed

Frank Mahoney to Thomas Jones

This Indenture made this ninth day of March in the year of our Lord one thousand eight hundred and fifty seven between Frank Mahoney of Whatcom Whatcom County Territory of Washington of the first part and Thomas Jones of the same County & Territory above mentioned of the second part witnesseth that the said party of the first part for and in consideration of the sum of three hundred and fifty dollars to him paid in hand by the said party of the second part the receipt whereof is hereby acknowledged hath bargained and sold and by these Presents doth bargain and sell unto the said party of the second part and to his heirs

Research: Deeds, Leases, Patents, Titles

Notes made by the author from reading Books of Deeds of Whatcom County, archived at the Washington Regional Archive at Western Washington University.

Books A through D

Page 1: December 8, 1853; A recording of the sale of all of the Proprietor's stock in the Puget Sound Coal Mining Association owned by John A. Peck of San Francisco to James H. Ray for the amount of $7,000. The stock amounted to 2/15th of the corporate stock.

Page 2; February 17, 1854; A recording of the sale by James H. Ray to O.B. Merrill, both of San Francisco, all of Ray's stock in the Puget Sound Coal Mining Association for the sum of $3,000.

Page 3; The Amendment of the 1853 lease between Thomas, Pattle and Morrison and F. Rogers Loomis. The amendments indicate that Loomis had assigned the lease to the Puget Sound Coal Mining Association. It further clarifies that the lease is only for the mining of coal and other minerals and is not a sale of land, also that the lessee has the right at cessation of the lease to remove buildings, equip. etc., if done in six months from cessation. The third provision calls for the payment of the monthly lease amounts either from the date of settlement of the lands by the lessors, or the testing of the coal as required by the lease depending on the decision of Judge Hoffman. Apparently Judge Hoffman was decided upon as an arbitrator. Fourth, the lessors agree to survey and map the lands involved in the lease, and fifth the lessors agree to pay all the back rents upon the judge reaching the decision. Agreement signed by Morrison, Thomas and Pattle by their attorneys-in-fact, and by Robert Rogers, president of the PSCMA, by George Bates, James Ray, L.H. Thomas, F. Rogers Loomis, Horatio N. Squire, Charles Minturn and William S. Howard.

Page 5; May 26, 1854, in the San Francisco court of Judge Ogden Hoffman Jr., the judge heard the case and made the following finding:

"I decide that the terms of this agreement require that the payment of rent to be from the date of settlement and not from the date of the testing of the coal."

Page 13; December 15, 1855. A Bond wherein Pattle binds himself in the amount of $5,000 to deliver, as soon as he gets his Patent to the land, an undivided 1/4 of the coal mining rights to his donation land claim on the north 1/4 with an equal frontage on east and west sides to Reuben L. Doyle.

"The condition of this obligation is such that if the said William Pattle shall and do as early as practicable receiving a patent for his land claim of one hundred and sixty acres (etc) he will execute and acknowledge Doyle's rights to the coal."

Photo taken

Page 74; Promissory note from Edward Eldridge to Richards and Hyatt;

Promise to pay the sum of $62.00 in six months at 2-1/2% per month interest. As security he assigns his rights and title to two cows to apply to the payment of the said note, "the surplus of any cow sale to apply to include any goods my family may realize during my absence."

Book of Records of Deeds, 1861

Book G, Page 108

PATENT — James Morrison Land Claim

The United States of America; To all to whom these presents shall come, Greetings. Whereas there has been a deposit in the General Land Office of the United States, a certificate numbered three hundred and fifty seven of the register and received at Olympia, Washington Territory, whereby it appears under the Act of Congress, approved the 21st day of September 1850, entitled an Act to create the office of surveyor general of the public lands in Oregon and to provide for the survey and to make donations to settlers of the said public lands and the legislation supplemental thereto, the claim of James Morrison of Whatcom County, Washington Territory, notification number 645 has been established to the donation of one quarter section or one hundred and sixty acres of land and that the same has been surveyed and designated as claim number 37, being part of section one in the township 37 north of range two east, according to the official plat survey of returned to the general land office by the surveyor general being bounded and described as follows. To Wit; beginning at a point 77 chains and 79 links west, and five chains and 20 links south of the northeast corner of section one, and running west thence 34 chains and 66 links, thence south seven chains, hence south 54 degrees west 11 chains, thence south 10 degrees west, three chains and 50 links, thence south 14 degrees and 45 minutes east six chains and 50 links, and thence south nine degrees east and 11 chains and 50 links, thence south eight degrees and 45 minutes west two chains and 75 links, thence east 43 chains and 32 links, and thence north 39 chains and 95 links to the place of beginning in the district of lands subject to sale at Olympia, Washington Territory, containing one hundred and sixty five acres and eighteen-hundreds of an acre.

Now Know Ye; That the United States of America, in consideration of the premises, and in consideration of the Act aforesaid, have given and granted, and of three presents do give and grant unto the said James Morrison and to his heirs the tract of land above described, to have and to hold the said tract with its appurtenances unto the said James Morrison and to his heirs and assigns forever.

In testimony thereof, I Andrew Johnson, President of the United States, have caused these letters to be made Patent, and the seal of the general land office to be hereunto affixed.

Given under my hand and seal at the city of Washington the sixteenth day of June, in the year of our lord, one thousand eight hundred and sixty six, and of the independence of the United States, the ninetieth.

By the president   ANDREW JOHNSON

Recorded vol. 2, page 447 in the General Land office.

Recorded in Whatcom County, Sept. 7, 1867 by Edward Eldridge, recorder

------

BOOK A. OF DEEDS, Page 170

A deed dated June 12, 1861, between Seth Doty of Unionville, and David Leach of Unionville. In consideration of three thousand dollars Doty sells to Leach "all of my rights to title, and interest whatsoever in the Union Coal Company and works and real estate thereunto. It being an equal undivided one-eighth interest in the whole of the claim."

BOOK D. OF DEEDS, Page 249

A certificate signed by W.R. Pattle on June 15, 1855, wherein he says, "at the request of Reuben L. Doyle I have examined all the records in my office consisting of books A,

B, C, D, & E, there being all the books in which a recorded deed or other instruments of conveyance, and find no record of any conveyance from Pattle of his land claim except a bond for a deed to Reuben Doyle on Dec. 15, 1855 for one-fourth of said claim. This is to certify that I, Wm. R. Pattle on this day make over to James Houstin one-sixteenth interest in the coals that may be found on my claim in return for labor done by him for me."

(His date of June 15 is before the "except Dec. 15")

BOOK D. OF DEEDS, WHATCOM COUNTY

Page 298 is a clear and simple deed from James Morrison to Seth N. Doty. Morrison sells his donation land claim for the sum of three thousand (3,000) dollars on March 1, 1861.

Photos taken

BOOK D. OF DEEDS, Page 311

A deed dated April 13, 1861, wherein Seth N. Doty sells to David Leach, both of Whatcom County, for two thousand dollars, an undivided one-third of all of his undivided one-fourth interest in the Morrison Donation claim.

BOOK D. OF DEEDS, Page 313

A deed dated June 5, 1861, wherein Seth Doty sells to David Leach for one thousand dollars an undivided one fourth of Doty's undivided one sixth in the Morrison donation land claim.

Page 391 is a deed dated March 2, 1861, wherein Doty sells to Charles E. Richards for the sum of $3,750 three-quarter undivided interest in the Morrison donation land claim. This description also commences at a point in the rock on the beach designated by a bar of iron embedded in the rock.

Photos taken

Page 394 is a clear and simple deed dated March 3, 1861, two days after Morrison sold his land claim. In this deed Doty sells back to Morrison one square acre for one dollar. It is the acre that lies in the "extreme S.W. corner" of the Morrison land claim.

Photos taken

BOOK A. OF RECORDINGS, Page 27

CONVEYANCE of one sixteenth interest in the land claim of William R. Pattle to James Houston.

"This is to certify that at I, Wm. R. Pattle, do this day make over to James Houston one sixteenth interest in the coals that may be found on my claim situated in Bellingham Bay, Washington Territory for labour done by him for me."
10th day of June 1855.

BOOK E. OF DEEDS, Page 1

A deed dated March 13, 1861, wherein Charles E. Richards sells to Alexander H. Bailey of San Francisco, an undivided 1/4 interest in the 160 acre Morrison claim. Selling price, $1,000, described as beginning on a point on the rock on the beach designated by a bar of iron, the same being situated 6.87 chains west and 5.24 chains south of the corner to fractional section one and thirty-six in township 37 thirty-eight north, range two east, thence with the meanderings of the beach half a mile south to a point on the beach 92 links west of a post, the southwest corner of claim. Said post marked with the letters W.P & W.M. thence east 42.50 chains to another market post as above thence west to the place of beginning. Being part of fractional section one of the said two thirty seven north range 2 east, containing one hundred sixty acres more or less and being known as the Morrison Donation Claim.
Photo taken

BOOK F. OF DEEDS. Pages 26 & 27

A contract between C.E. Richards and Seth N. Doty regarding the Morrison coal claim. In consideration of an undivided 3/4s of the premises known as the Morrison coal claim, by Seth Doty. Mr. Doty is to assume 3/4 of the indebtedness of the claim to Morrison and 3/4s of the moneys expended by Doty from the time he took possession of the claim until the time "righters" bought in. Richards agrees to provide Doty his pro-rata share of the capital required to open the mine and getting it in a shape ready to ship coal. Doty is to pay to Richards interest on the money at 14 percent per annum until paid, and Richards is allowed to hold the receipts until all the money advanced had been returned at interest.

BOOK F. OF DEEDS. Page 29

A mortgage dated June 12, 1861, wherein David Leach of Unionville and Seth Doty agree that David Leach buys from Doty for three thousand dollars, the Union Coal Company Claim and works, being the undivided one-fourth of said claim described in a deed from James Morrison to Seth Doty dated March 1, 1861. This is the mortgage promising to pay.

BOOK G. OF DEEDS, Page 1.

A deed dated August 20, 1861, wherein Charles E. Richards sells to James R. Doyle of San Francisco, all of the undivided one fourth part of the Morrison Donation Claim for the price of one thousand dollars.

BOOK G. OF DEEDS, Page 86

A deed dated Feb. 4, 1862, wherein Alexander H. Bailey of San Francisco sells all of the undivided one fourth of the Morrison land claim to Charles E. Richards for the amount of ten thousand dollars.

BOOK G. OF DEEDS, Page 89

A deed dated December 11, 1865, wherein Seth Doty, now of Solano, California, sells to Charles E. Richards, now of San Francisco for five hundred dollars, his undivided one fourth interest in the Morrison Donation Claim.

BOOK G. OF DEEDS, Page 110

A deed dated December 16, 1865, wherein James R. Doyle, of San Francisco, and Charles E. Richards of Bellingham Bay, "now of the City of New York", sell to Robert Vance of the City of New York, for ten thousand dollars, the Morrison Donation claim, with no exceptions as to percentage, coal etc. Looks like Vance owns the whole thing.

BOOK G. OF DEEDS, Pages 118 & 119

A deed dated August 7, 1866, wherein Robert H. Vance of the state of New York, sells to Erastus Bartlett, of Augusta, Maine, one half of nine-tenths parts of the Morrison donation land claim for the price of five thousand dollars ($5,000). Property description is identical to that above.

BOOK G. OF DEEDS, Page 215.

A deed dated April 4, 1870, wherein Reuben L. Doyle sells to Erastus Bartlett, of the city of Boston, Mass., the Pattle donation claim for two thousand dollars, gold coin. It describes the property and mentions one hundred sixty acres more or less EXCEPT one sixteenth of the coal within said premises to have and to hold all and singular the above mentioned premises and the appurtenances with the exception mentioned above.

BOOK K. OF DEEDS, Page 35

A deed dated August, 29 1871, wherein Erastus and Helen Bartlett sell to Edward Eldridge for the sum of three thousand dollars, one fourth of the land known as the Pattle donation claim; and in addition, one quarter of the O'Conner land claim, less four acres that O'Conner has retained; and other lands as well. This looked to be some sort of a partnership adjustment perhaps prior to their platting of Bellingham.

BOOK K. OF DEEDS, Page 37

A deed dated August 28, 1871, wherein Bartlett deeds to Eldridge for six hundred dollars, half of 960 acres.

BOOK K. OF DEEDS, Page 70

A deed dated Oct. 25, 1871, wherein Robert H. Vance of Nevada sells to Erastus Bartlett for one thousand dollars, an undivided one half of the Morrison donation claim

BOOK K. OF DEEDS , Page 72

A deed dated October 25, 1871, wherein Robert H. Vance of California, sells to Erastus Bartlett of Massachusetts, one undivided twentieth of a parcel of land for a price of $50.00. It is described as the Morrison donation claim.

BOOK K. OF DEEDS. Page 72

An appointment by James R. Doyle of Charles E. Richards as his attorney-in-fact to deal in real estate matters. Dated Oct. 25, 1871. Specifically to give him authority to sell his one quarter interest in the Morrison Donation Claim.

POWERS OF ATTORNEY, ETC: BOOK 5, Page 555

William Reed Pattle is giving power of attorney to Kenneth McLea of San Francisco to do all matters for him in regard to his 160 acres on Bellingham Bay, and the coal that may be on the land. It is dated 18 July, 1857.

BOOK OF DEEDS. #7, Page 113;

A notice of Sheriffs Tax sale of the 1 acre belonging to James Morrison at the S.W. corner of his claim to Erastus Bartlett. The 1875 taxes were delinquent and so on 18 April, 1888, the acre was sold to Bartlett for three dollars, that being enough to pay the back taxes and whatever charges there might been.

BOOK OF DEEDS. #5, Page 90

A patent #287 dated August 7, 1871, to Maurice O'Conner for one hundred sixty acres of land in sections 12 and one, Twp 37N, Rge 2E. Signed by Ulysses Grant.

BOOK OF DEEDS. # 5, Page 91

A patent #288 dated 11 March, 1867, to Edward and Teresa Eldridge, three hundred and twenty acres in sections 23, 24, & 25, Twp 38N, Rge 2E.

BOOK OF DEEDS. #14, Pages 246, 247

A deed from Erastus Bartlett and Edward and Teresa Eldridge to The Fairhaven Land Company dated the 5th of April 1890 wherein, in consideration of forty thousand dollars, Eldridge and Bartlett sell:

"...being an undivided one half that certain tract of land in the town of Bellingham and being between front street and the line of ordinary low water on Bellingham Bay, the same being marked 'Reserved for mill purposes' on a plat of the town of Bellingham filed for record in said county on the 24th day of April 1883 and recorded in book B page 1 of the records of town plats, excepting a strip of land one hundred feet wide along front street the entire length of said mill reserve, and a strip of land one hundred and fifty feet wide off of the north end of said reserve, provided that there shall be left in said reserve two acres of land. Also that certain mill wharf machinery fixtures, tools and implements, waterfront and privileges now situated on said mill reserve being a one half of said lands mill wharf all appurtenances and thereto belonging."

BOOK OF DEEDS. #11, Page 83

U.S. Patent to Edward Eldridge dated 10 October 1871, for eighty acres of land in section 3, Twp 38N, Rge 2E. It does not say what they paid but it is given under the authority of an Act of Congress of the 24th of April 1820 providing for the sale of the public lands.

Page 84, Another U.S. Patent dated 10 October 1872, to Eldridge and Bartlett under the same act, for 640 acres in section 23, Twp 39N, Rge 1E. Again price is not mentioned.

Page 85, another U.S. Patent dated 10 October 1871, to Erastus Bartlett for the S.E. quarter of section 5 and the N.E. quarter of section 8 in Twp 38N Rge 2E. 320 acres.

Page 86, another U.S. Patent dated 10 October 1872, to Eldridge and Bartlett for the N.E. quarter of section 22, Twp 39N, Rge 1E. 160 acres.

Page 87, another U.S. Patent dated to Edward Eldridge for the S.E. quarter of Section 12 in Twp. 38N, Rge 2E. 160 acres.

Page 88, another U.S. Patent dated 10 October 1872, to Edward Eldridge for the north half of section 24,Twp 39N, Rge 1E. 320 acres.

Page 89, another U.S. Patent dated 10 October 1871, to Edward Eldridge for the SW quarter of the NW quarter of section 21, and the NE quarter of the SE quarter of Section 32, Twp 38N Rge 3E. Containing 80 acres.

BOOK OF DEEDS. #15, Pages 71, 72

A deed from Erastus Bartlett, Edward and Teresa Eldridge dated 16 May 1890, wherein they sell all of their land platted and unplatted to the Bellingham Bay Land Company for $1,000,000. One million dollars. The deed describes lot by lot the platted lots of Bellingham on both the Morrison and Pattle claims. Second, all of the Morrison claim lying east of 5th Street, and all of the rest of the Pattle claim that is not shown as lots. Excepting the Mill Reserve. Also the whole of the Thomas Jones donation land claim of 321 acres.

BOOK OF DEEDS. #15, Page 73

A deed from Erastus Bartlett, Edward and Teresa Eldridge, dated 16 May 1890, wherein they sell to the Fairhaven Land Company for one dollar the land described in the Bellingham plat as the "Railroad Reserve".

======

BOOK OF DEEDS. #32, Pages 158, 158, 160

1. A decree from the Superior Court, Judge Winn, dated Aug. 1, 1891. The Bellingham Bay Land Co. vs. Robert Vance, Erastus Bartlett, James Morrison, Seth N. Doty.

This was apparently a lawsuit to clarify title to the land that comprised the original Morrison Donation Claim. None of the defendants appeared. The judge heard the plaintiff's case and found that each of the defendants had been at one time an owner of the described real estate, but that the Bellingham Bay Land Company holds title to the property through a chain of conveyances from James Morrison, who got the land from the U.S.

2. The mortgage between Seth Doty and James Morrison dated March 1, 1861, for $2,800 payable in five years was paid off.

3. The mortgage dated June 12, 1861, for $3,000 executed by David Leach was paid off.

4. The plaintiff and defendants have been in the open, notorious, peaceable, quiet and adverse possession of the said premises and he finds for the plaintiff who owns the land in fee.

BOOK OF DEEDS. #33, Pages 2, 3

A deed dated June 21, 1856, between William Reed Pattle, master mariner, of Whatcom County in the Territory of Washington, party of the first part, and Kenneth MacLea, merchant of the city of San Francisco, state of California, party of the second part, Whereas the said party of the first part heretofore, to-wit, previous to the eleventh day of April 1853, did locate and settle upon and ever since has actually occupied and held possession and now occupies and holds possession of a certain piece or parcel of land situated in said county and territory containing one hundred and sixty acres, to-wit, fronting on Bellingham Bay in said territory, beginning at a blazed cedar tree on Mineral Point, on said bay being also the North West corner of the claim of James Morrison, thence in a northeasterly direction along the shore of said bay one half mile to a blazed fir tree standing on the bank of said bay, forming the north easterly corner of the tract of land hereby described and being also the southwest corner of the claim of Mrs. Ann Pattle, the wife of the said party of the first part, thence at

right angles east to a blazed cedar tree with a pile of stones around it, thence south to a blazed fir tree standing on a knoll, thence west to the place of beginning being the certain one quarter section of land numbered and designated number six hundred and sixty five, for which the said party of the first part has heretofore, to wit, on the fifth day of December 1855 deposited and paid into the proper U.S. Land Office in said territory, the full price at the rate of one dollar and 25 cents per acre, to wit, the sum of two hundred (200) dollars, according to the law of congress in such case made and provided. Now therefore this indenture witnesseth, that the said party of the first part, for and in consideration of the sum of Two Thousand dollars in cash, and also of other good and valuable consideration, heretofore paid by the said party of the second part to the said party of the first part, the receipt whereof is hereby acknowledged, has granted bargained, sold and conveyed and by these presents does grant, bargain, Sell and convey unto the said party of the second part, the undivided one half part and interest of and in the said described premise together with all and singular the tenement and hereditaments, timber, coal and coal mines, minerals, and appurtenances thereunto belonging or in any way appertaining, situated or existing within the boundaries of the same, so that the same and all the rights and privileges of the said party of the first part in to and concerning the said described tract of land and premises under the United State Laws are one and hereafter shall be owned, held and enjoyed by the said parties hereto equally as equal co-owners thereof.
(This was signed in San Francisco.)

BOOK OF DEEDS. #33, Page 3
A deed dated May first, 1860, wherein Kenneth MacLea and Wm. R. Pattle and Robert Simson of San Francisco sign an indenture made at Saint Johns, Newfoundland, selling their entire interest to Simson for ten thousand dollars ($10,000).
BOOK OF DEEDS. # 33, Pages 429 to 443
Numerous U.S. Patents (fourteen) selling to Eldridge or Bartlett, or both, in the year 1889 a total of 4,798 acres in Whatcom County.

ARTICLES OF INCORPORATION of the Bellingham Bay Land Company
KNOW ALL MEN BY THESE PRESENTS; That the undersigned, Edward Eldridge, Erastus Bartlett and Nelson Bennett hereby form themselves into a body corporate under the name and with the powers for the purposes hereinafter set forth. Name, Bellingham Bay Land Co., Principal office Fairhaven. Capital stock, $1,000,000 dollars divided into ten thousand shares at $100 per share.
The objects for which this company are organized are: for the purchase and sale of lands, the leasing or mortgaging of the same, the acquisition of lands from the Govt.

of the United States and from private individuals, the laying out of town sites, with powers to plat the same and to dedicate streets, alleys and public property therein, etc. etc.

Trustees are Nelson Bennett, E.L. Cowgill, E.M. Wilson, Edward Eldridge and Erastus Bartlett, and C.X. Larrabee

Date of incorporation, 12 May 1890

BOOK OF DEEDS. #35, Page 573

A deed dated August 3rd, 1893, wherein Robert Simson and Jeanette Simson of the state of Cal., sell to The Bellingham Bay Land Company for $3,500 the land described as follows. "Beginning at a point five chains and 88 links west, and five chains and 20 links south of the southeast corner of section thirty six, in Twp 38 North of Range 2 East and running thence west 56 links thence north 49 degrees and 30 minutes east 20 chains, thence north 12 degrees and 30 minutes, east 3 chains and 82 links, thence north 31 degrees and 30 minutes east 10 chains and 69 links thence north 36 degrees and 30 minutes east 9 chains and 15 links thence north 45 degrees east 3 chains and 50 links thence north 36 degrees east 3 chains thence east 25 chains and thence south 39 chains and 60 links to the place of beginning.

Afterword

Bellingham's south-side waterfront continues to evolve. Since the arrival of the white man in 1852 the scene has constantly changed, influenced by the community's needs, opportunities and calamities. The land which held Dan Harris' ocean dock and hotel morphed into the buildings and shipyard of Pacific American Fisheries and Bellingham Canning Company and eventually became the southerly terminus of the Alaska Ferry system. The great lumber mills of the late 1800s and early 1900s gave way through storm, fire or economic evolution to the Fairhaven Boat Haven, then the Uniflite boat building plant, and currently the Port of Bellingham's multi-use light industrial park. The industrial complex around the Taylor Street dock has been supplanted by a luxury hotel and spa and a well-used public park. The area that held William Pattle's cabin fortress eventually welcomed a great lumbermill, and a coal gasification plant, both of which were to be reclaimed by the public in the form of Boulevard Park.

While much has changed, much has remained the same. A shipyard still operates at the foot of Harris Avenue, a direct descendent of Pacific American Fisheries. Arrowac Seafoods still processes fish where the great salmon canneries once stood. The railroad still runs along the shoreline where Nelson Bennett and his Fairhaven & Southern first built the track in 1890, and high on the bluff overlooking it all stands the venerable 1912 industrial building of The Reid Brothers Boiler Works, still making and repairing pressure vessels for industry.

Who can predict what the future holds for this historic land along the water, but if I were a betting man, I would place my money on the community holding on to the public use of that waterfront so long denied it. I would predict that Boulevard Park has become the final use of this land and will serve the citizens of Bellingham for untold generations.

I earnestly hope that this book will serve to increase the reader's understanding and appreciation for what has gone on before, as well as to record in history the true facts of how a community reclaimed a significant portion of its waterfront.

Brian L. Griffin, 2007
Knox Cellars Publishing Company

Information Sources

INSTITUTIONS

Bellingham Public Library: *Bellingham Herald* clippings file, Fairhaven newspaper
   micro-film collection, various publications.
Center for Pacific Northwest Studies; Western Washington University, Ruth Steele,
   Archie Shiels Collection, Howard Buswell Collection, P.R. Jeffcott Collection,
   Pacific American Fisheries Collection, Port of Bellingham Collection, Galen
   Biery Collection, Bellingham Parks & Recreation papers.
Chicago Title Company, Bellingham, WA. Eric Cuello, John Holzheimer, Addie
   Brown.
Gordon Tweit collection. Bellingham, WA.
Washington State Regional Archives: James Copher; various regional archives.
Whatcom Museum of History & Art, Jeff Jewell, Archivist.

PUBLICATIONS

Edson, Lelah Jackson, *The Fourth Corner*. 1960
Hutchings, Clark & Hudson, *Lummi Island History*
Jeffcott, Percival R., *Blanket Bill Jarman*. 1958
Jeffcott, Percival R., *Nooksack Tales and Trails*. 1949
Joy, Aaron M., *History of Bellingham Parks*
Koert, Dorothey & Galen Biery, *Looking Back*, Vol. 2. 1982
Koert, Dorothey & Galen Biery, *Looking Back*, the Collectors' Edition. 2003
McCurdy, H.W., *Marine History of The Pacific Northwest*
Radke, August C., *Pacific American Fisheries, Inc.* 2002
Rotary Club of Bellingham, *Tattler*
Rotary Club of Bellingham, Board of Directors Minutes
Roth, Lottie Roeder. *History of Whatcom County*, 2 volumes. 1926
San Anselmo Historical Museum, www.SanAnselmohist.org/robson
Sanborn Maps
Sleasman, Margaret Radisich, *Pacific Northwest Croatian*, various volumes
Smith, Curtis F., *The Brothels of Bellingham*. 2004
United States Census records
Google Search

ORAL INTERVIEWS

Arvin, Jeff: President, Cascade Joinery

Bornstein, Jay: President, Bornstein Seafood Inc.

Bryson, Leslie: Bellingham Parks & Recreation Dept.

Douglas, Joel: former lessee, Taylor Ave. Dock

Dubigk, Gay L.: Exec. Dir. Northwest Work Force Development Council

Ebenal Construction Co.: unknown worker. Waldron Building.

Elmendorf, Byron: former director, Bellingham Parks & Recreation Dept.

Geyer, William: former Community Development Director, City of Bellingham

Glenn, Thomas: retired manager, Port of Bellingham

Green, Delight: member YWCA Eco-Action

Harmony, Molly: Lummi Island historian

Hertz, Ken: former director, Whatcom Co. Parks; former Mayor, City of Bellingham

Hofeditz, Jack: retired manager, Hohl Feed & Seed

Ivary, John: Retired, Bellingham Parks & Recreation Dept.

Jeffers, Garreth: daughter of George Jeffers, Edmonds, Washington

Jewell, Jeff: Archivist, Whatcom Museum of History & Art

Johanson, Larry: Rotary Club of Bellingham

Jones, Dale: Historian & volunteer, Bellingham Railroad Museum

Jones, Shirley: member YWCA Eco-Action

Jurgensen, Roy: former president, Foss Tug & Barge; Sr. V.P. Crowley Maritime

Knowles, George: Helen Loggie expert, former owner of the Leopold Hotel

Kuljis, Martin: retired fisherman

McCollum, Barbara Welsh: scion, Welsh family, Bellingham Canning Co.

McEvoy, Patrick: McEvoy Oil Co.

Moles, Robert Sr.: Rotary Club of Bellingham, Moles Funeral Home

Morse, Sr., David: retired, Morse Hardware Co.

Nordvedt, Art: former president, Uniflite Boat Co.

Roberts, Kip & Kitty: Friday Harbor, Wa.

Reid, Robert: Reid Bros. Boiler Works

Rose, Ann: president, YWCA Eco-Action, former Bellingham City Council member

Trzynka, Ray: Puget Sound Energy

Tweit, Gordon: Fairhaven Historian, former Fairhaven Pharmacy owner

Wahl, Tim: Bellingham Parks & Recreation Dept., historian

Walker, Scott: Port of Bellingham Commissioner

About the Author

Brian Griffin was born and raised on Bellingham's South Hill above the waterfront that was to become Boulevard Park. He first saw the light of day on November 1, 1932, at St. Joseph's Hospital (when the hospital was still located on State Street above the Boulevard). He lived with his parents and sister in homes at 16th and Garden Streets, then at 17th and Bennett, and finally from the age of nine, at the long-time family home at 432 15th Street, just two blocks above the old gas works. Still a southsider, Griffin and his wife have lived for more than 40 years at their home on Knox Avenue above Fairhaven.

He has enjoyed a long career in business and civic affairs in Bellingham. For 35 years he was an insurance broker and was one of the founders of The Unity Group. He was a founder and president of The Children's Company. Upon retirement from the insurance industry he parlayed his interest in native bees into a unique business, Knox Cellars Native Bees, propagating and selling Orchard Mason Bees on a nationwide basis. During his 14 years in the bee business he wrote and self-published two very successful books, *The Orchard Mason Bee* and *Humblebee Bumblebee*, and developed more than 30 products supporting the propagation of native bees.

Griffin attended the Campus School, Bellingham High School, and Whitman College, graduating with a degree in English Literature. He was a Special Agent in the U.S. Army Counter-intelligence Corps serving in Inchon, Korea.

Always a devoted civic activist, he initiated and led the effort that resulted in construction of the Bellingham Parkade in 1970. He was a leader in the unsuccessful effort to build a shopping mall in Bellingham's downtown rather than allow Bellis Fair Mall to decimate the city center. He successfully promoted the local improvement district which funded the bollards and street trees downtown during a critical period in community history. His interest in the Boulevard Park story stems in part from his role in encouraging the Rotary Club of Bellingham to take on the project and to expand its vision to include the waterfront as part of the park.

In 2001 Griffin organized the public/private effort which resulted in construction of Fairhaven Village Green and most recently he chaired the Depot Market Square Committee which envisioned, planned and executed, with the City of Bellingham, Depot Market Square, a community center and market venue in Bellingham's downtown, and the home of the Bellingham Farmers' Market.

Brian Griffin researching the Books of Deeds, Washington Regional Archives, WWU.

Continuing his interest in his community, and a resolute believer in the power and potential of public/private partnerships, Griffin is now researching and writing about how such partnerships have changed Bellingham over the years. This book is the first result of that effort.

He and his wife Marya have two daughters and six grandchildren. His life is filled with civic and family activities, painting, wood-working, writing and many other interests.

Index